Microsoft® Office Excel® 2010: Part 1 (Second Edition)

Microsoft® Office Excel® 2010: Part 1 (Second Edition)

Part Number: 091018
Course Edition: 1.01

Acknowledgements

PROJECT TEAM

Author	Media Designer	Content Editor
Tim Barnosky	Alex Tong	Catherine M. Albano

Notices

DISCLAIMER

While Logical Operations, Inc. takes care to ensure the accuracy and quality of these materials, we cannot guarantee their accuracy, and all materials are provided without any warranty whatsoever, including, but not limited to, the implied warranties of merchantability or fitness for a particular purpose. The name used in the data files for this course is that of a fictitious company. Any resemblance to current or future companies is purely coincidental. We do not believe we have used anyone's name in creating this course, but if we have, please notify us and we will change the name in the next revision of the course. Logical Operations is an independent provider of integrated training solutions for individuals, businesses, educational institutions, and government agencies. Use of screenshots, photographs of another entity's products, or another entity's product name or service in this book is for editorial purposes only. No such use should be construed to imply sponsorship or endorsement of the book by, nor any affiliation of such entity with Logical Operations. This courseware may contain links to sites on the internet that are owned and operated by third parties (the "External Sites"). Logical Operations is not responsible for the availability of, or the content located on or through, any External Site. Please contact Logical Operations if you have any concerns regarding such links or External Sites.

TRADEMARK NOTICES

Microsoft® Office Excel® 2010: Part 1 (Second Edition)

About This Course

The breadth of business, educational, and organizational information in existence today is absolutely staggering. Organizations the world over rely on this information to make sound decisions regarding all manner of affairs. But, with the amount of available data growing on a daily basis, the ability to make sense of all of that data is becoming more and more challenging. Fortunately, the days of performing calculations and analyzing data on paper are pretty much gone. Imagine having to calculate what percentage of your organization's sales occurred in one small town in Brazil. If your organization operates in multiple countries and generates billions of dollars in revenue annually, it could take a lifetime to isolate the exact figures you need and then compare those to the rest of your revenues. But, who has that kind of time? This is exactly where the power of Excel can help.

By applying the robust functionality that's built into Excel to your organization's raw data, you will be able to gain of level of insight into that data that would have been nearly impossible just a couple of decades ago. Excel can help you organize, calculate, analyze, revise, update, and present your data in ways that will help the decision makers in your organization steer you in the right direction. Of course, knowing exactly how to ask Excel the questions that you need answered, which questions you can even ask, and how to interpret the answers Excel gives is necessary before you can even begin to embark on the journey ahead. This course aims to provide you with the foundational Excel knowledge and skills necessary to begin that journey.

This course covers Microsoft Office Specialist exam objectives to help students prepare for the Excel 2010 Exam and the Excel 2010 Expert Exam.

Course Description

Target Student

This course is intended for students who wish to gain the foundational understanding of Microsoft Office Excel 2010 that is necessary to create and work with electronic spreadsheets.

Course Prerequisites

To ensure success, students will need to be familiar with using personal computers, and should have experience using a keyboard and mouse. Students should also be comfortable working in the Windows 7 environment, and be able to use Windows 7 to manage information on their computers. Specific tasks the students should be able to perform include: opening and closing applications, navigating basic file structures, and managing files and folders. To obtain this level of skill and knowledge, you can take any of the following Logical Operations courses:

- *Microsoft® Windows® 7: Level 1*

- *Introduction to Personal Computers Using Windows® 7*

Course Objectives

Upon successful completion of this course, you will be able to create and develop Excel worksheets and workbooks in order to work with and analyze the data that is critical to the success of your organization.

You will:

- Get started with Microsoft Office Excel 2010.
- Perform calculations.
- Modify a worksheet.
- Format a worksheet.
- Print workbooks.
- Manage workbooks.

The LogicalCHOICE Home Screen

The LogicalCHOICE Home screen is your entry point to the LogicalCHOICE learning experience, of which this course manual is only one part. Visit the LogicalCHOICE Course screen both during and after class to make use of the world of support and instructional resources that make up the LogicalCHOICE experience.

Log-on and access information for your LogicalCHOICE environment will be provided with your class experience. On the LogicalCHOICE Home screen, you can access the LogicalCHOICE Course screens for your specific courses.

Each LogicalCHOICE Course screen will give you access to the following resources:

- eBook: an interactive electronic version of the printed book for your course.
- LearnTOs: brief animated components that enhance and extend the classroom learning experience.

Depending on the nature of your course and the choices of your learning provider, the LogicalCHOICE Course screen may also include access to elements such as:

- The interactive eBook.
- Social media resources that enable you to collaborate with others in the learning community using professional communications sites such as LinkedIn or microblogging tools such as Twitter.
- Checklists with useful post-class reference information.
- Any course files you will download.
- The course assessment.
- Notices from the LogicalCHOICE administrator.
- Virtual labs, for remote access to the technical environment for your course.
- Your personal whiteboard for sketches and notes.
- Newsletters and other communications from your learning provider.
- Mentoring services.
- A link to the website of your training provider.
- The LogicalCHOICE store.

Visit your LogicalCHOICE Home screen often to connect, communicate, and extend your learning experience!

How to Use This Book

As You Learn

This book is divided into lessons and topics, covering a subject or a set of related subjects. In most cases, lessons are arranged in order of increasing proficiency.

The results-oriented topics include relevant and supporting information you need to master the content. Each topic has various types of activities designed to enable you to practice the guidelines and procedures as well as to solidify your understanding of the informational material presented in the course. Procedures and guidelines are presented in a concise fashion along with activities and discussions. Information is provided for reference and reflection in such a way as to facilitate understanding and practice.

Data files for various activities as well as other supporting files for the course are available by download from the LogicalCHOICE Course screen. In addition to sample data for the course exercises, the course files may contain media components to enhance your learning and additional reference materials for use both during and after the course.

At the back of the book, you will find a glossary of the definitions of the terms and concepts used throughout the course. You will also find an index to assist in locating information within the instructional components of the book.

As You Review

Any method of instruction is only as effective as the time and effort you, the student, are willing to invest in it. In addition, some of the information that you learn in class may not be important to you immediately, but it may become important later. For this reason, we encourage you to spend some time reviewing the content of the course after your time in the classroom.

As a Reference

The organization and layout of this book make it an easy-to-use resource for future reference. Taking advantage of the glossary, index, and table of contents, you can use this book as a first source of definitions, background information, and summaries.

Course Icons

Watch throughout the material for these visual cues:

Icon	Description
	A **Note** provides additional information, guidance, or hints about a topic or task.
	A **Caution** helps make you aware of places where you need to be particularly careful with your actions, settings, or decisions so that you can be sure to get the desired results of an activity or task.
	LearnTO notes show you where an associated LearnTO is particularly relevant to the content. Access LearnTOs from your LogicalCHOICE Course screen.
	Checklists provide job aids you can use after class as a reference to performing skills back on the job. Access checklists from your LogicalCHOICE Course screen.
	Social notes remind you to check your LogicalCHOICE Course screen for opportunities to interact with the LogicalCHOICE community using social media.
	Notes Pages are intentionally left blank for you to write on.

1 | Getting Started with Microsoft Office Excel 2010

Lesson Time: 1 hour, 30 minutes

Lesson Objectives

In this lesson, you will get started with Microsoft Office Excel 2010. You will:

- Navigate the Excel user interface.

- Use Excel commands.

- Create and save a basic workbook.

- Enter cell data.

- Use Excel Help.

Lesson Introduction

You want to use Microsoft Office Excel 2010 to store and analyze data for your organization. But you're new to Excel and it's hard to know where to begin. In order to take advantage of everything Excel has to offer, you must first understand the lay of the land. How do you interact with Excel? What, precisely, can it do? How do you get Excel to do these things for you? These are questions you likely have in mind. It is precisely these types of questions this lesson aims to answer.

Like many Microsoft Office applications, Excel has a standard layout that provides you with access to all of the commands, work areas, options, and settings you will need to begin developing and using electronic worksheets in your day-to-day life. Taking the time to become familiar with Excel's layout, its various parts, its commands, and its terminology is a critical first step toward your goal of storing and analyzing organizational data.

TOPIC A

Navigate the Excel User Interface

Imagine you've just moved to a new city, a city to which you've never been. It's easy to see how difficult it may be at first to find the nearest grocery store, gas station, restaurant, or department store. And, with a number of each of these types of establishments available, it may be even more challenging to find your favorite grocery store or the best restaurant right away. Beginning to use a new computer application can be much like moving to a new city. There is plenty of available functionality, and there are often a number of different ways to perform the same tasks. But, you may not know where to find what you need. Basically, you need a map.

Finding your way around this new city, Excel, is your first step toward leveraging its powerful, robust functionality. By taking the time to locate and identify the various components of the Excel user interface, you will familiarize yourself with the landscape that will become critical to your eventual mastery of Excel.

Microsoft Office Excel 2010

Microsoft Office Excel 2010 is an application that is part of the Microsoft Office 2010 suite of user-productivity software. Excel is a powerful electronic spreadsheet program that allows you to store, present, manipulate, and analyze a number of different types of data. Excel's functionality enables you to work with and analyze massive amounts of raw data in order to obtain actionable organizational intelligence. This intelligence will help you make sound business and organizational decisions on a number of fronts with the aim of achieving increasing levels of success.

Figure 1-1: Microsoft Office Excel 2010.

Spreadsheets, Worksheets, and Workbooks

A *spreadsheet* is simply a paper or an electronic document, arranged in tabular form, that is used to store, manipulate, and analyze data. A *worksheet* is an electronic spreadsheet that is used for entering, storing, and analyzing data in Excel. Think of worksheets as individual pages within Excel that display and allow you to work with your data.

A *workbook* is an Excel file that serves as a container to store related Excel worksheets. If you apply the individual page analogy to the workbook as well, the worksheets are the individual pages, whereas the workbook is the binding that holds the pages together. The default number of worksheets in a new Excel 2010 workbook is three. But you can add or remove worksheets to suit your needs and you can name, rename, and rearrange the order of worksheets in a workbook. The number of worksheets that a workbook can contain is limited by your computer system's available memory.

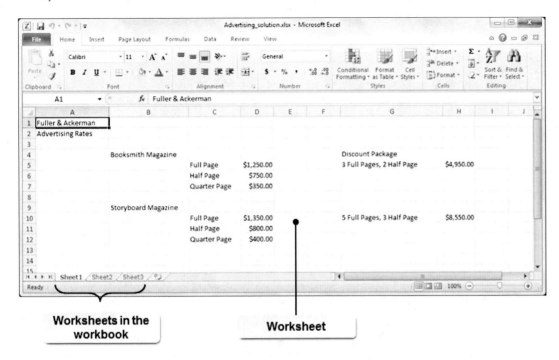

Figure 1-2: Excel workbooks act like binders for related worksheets.

Cells and Ranges

An Excel worksheet is arranged in a tabular format, meaning it consists of a series of columns and rows that intersect to form cells. A *cell* is a singular object that you can use to input and store data. Each individual rectangle that you see on an Excel worksheet is a separate cell.

In Excel, a *range* is a group of cells that typically contains related data. A range can consist of an entire row or column, a group of cells in a row or column, or a group of cells that covers multiple rows and columns. You can use ranges to organize your worksheets by related sets of data.

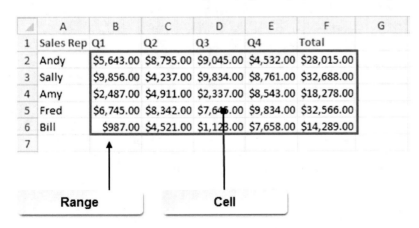

Figure 1-3: Cells and a range on an Excel worksheet.

Cell Regions

You may also come across the term *region* in reference to worksheet cells. A region is simply a group of contiguous, populated cells. A region is different from a range because a range can, technically, contain blank cells, rows, or columns; a region does not.

Cell and Range References

In Excel, cells are identified by using *cell references*. Think of a cell reference as the name of a cell, used to differentiate it from among the other cells on a worksheet. A cell reference consists of a letter and a number. The letter refers to the *column headers* in Excel, whereas the number refers to the *row headers*. So, the cell on a worksheet that is located at the intersection of column C and row 5 has the cell reference C5.

Column headers are displayed along the top of an Excel worksheet and are used to differentiate individual columns. Column headers begin with the letter A for the first column and run through the course of the entire alphabet. But, Excel supports far more columns in a single worksheet than the 26 letters of the alphabet. In fact, a worksheet can contain up to 16,384 columns. So after Z, column headers continue with AA through AZ. After AZ comes BA through BZ, and so on. Once the column headers have exhausted all of the possible combinations through ZZ, they continue with AAA, AAB, AAC, and so on.

Row headers are displayed along the left side of an Excel worksheet and are used to differentiate individual rows. Row headers begin at 1 and increase sequentially through row 1,048,576. The last possible cell reference in an Excel worksheet is XFD1048576.

You will use *range references* to identify particular ranges of data in your worksheets. A range reference consists of two cell references separated by a colon. The first cell reference identifies the top-leftmost cell in a range; the second cell reference identifies the bottom-rightmost cell in a range. So, for example, the range of cells that includes the first five rows in columns A through D is A1:D5.

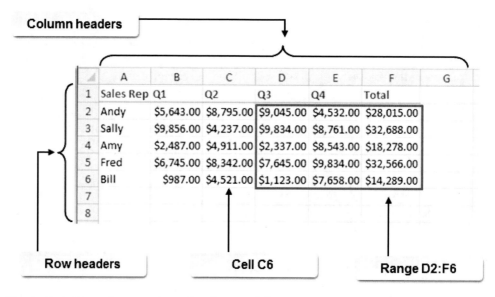

Figure 1–4: Use column and row headers to define cell and range references.

The Excel User Interface

The Excel user interface contains all of the workspaces and commands that you will use to create and work with workbooks and worksheets. The default view of the Excel user interface (UI) that appears when you first open Excel actually consists of two separate windows, one inside the other. The outer window is the application window, which contains the various Excel commands and displays pertinent information about the current workbook. The inner window displays the currently active workbook, which contains the column and row headers, the tabs that represent the worksheets within the workbook, and any data entered in the currently selected worksheet.

Figure 1-5: The application and workbook windows in Excel 2010.

The Application Window

As previously mentioned, Excel's *application window* contains the commands you will use to work with your Excel workbooks along with particular information about the currently active workbook. It consists of seven main elements, each of which you will use for particular purposes.

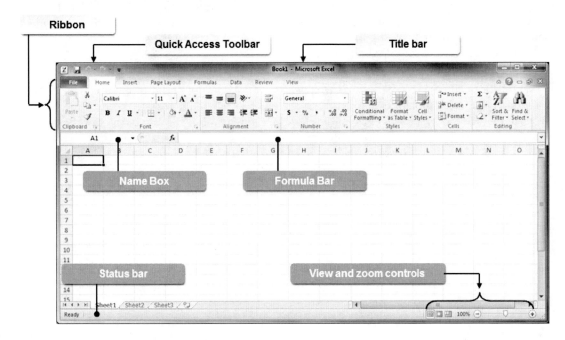

Figure 1-6: The Excel application window.

The following table details the functions of the various application window elements.

Application Window Element	Description
Title bar	Displays the file name of the currently selected workbook if the workbook is maximized within the application window.
Quick Access Toolbar	Provides you with easy access to commonly used Excel commands, such as **Save**, **Undo**, and **Redo**. You can customize the **Quick Access Toolbar** to suit your needs.
Ribbon	Provides you with access to the most commonly used commands for working with Excel workbooks and worksheets. The ribbon is organized into a series of tabs, each containing groups of related commands. You can customize the ribbon to suit your needs.
Formula Bar	Displays the contents of the currently selected cell in a worksheet. You can also use the **Formula Bar** to edit cell contents.
Name Box	Displays the cell reference for the currently selected cell, or the cell reference of the active cell in the currently selected range. The **Name Box** can also display custom range names and can be used to navigate to a particular cell.
Status bar	Displays the status of various conditions pertinent to Excel, such as the mode of the active cell, and whether or not **Caps Lock** or **Number Lock** are enabled. You can customize what information displays on the status bar.
View and zoom controls	Provides you with quick access to commands that change the current workbook view and change the magnification level of the displayed worksheet.

The Workbook Window

The *workbook window* is displayed within the Excel application window. You can open multiple Excel workbooks simultaneously, but all workbooks will appear within a single instance of the application window. There are a couple of important items to point out about the relationship between the workbook window and the application window.

- There are two separate sets of **Minimize**, **Maximize/Restore**, and **Close** commands; one for each of the windows. The commands at the very top-right corner of the application window are for the entire application; the commands just below those along the top-right side of the ribbon (when the workbook is maximized within the application window) belong to the workbook. If you restore the workbook window down or minimize it within the application window, the **Minimize**, **Maximize/Restore**, and **Close** commands attach to the workbook window.

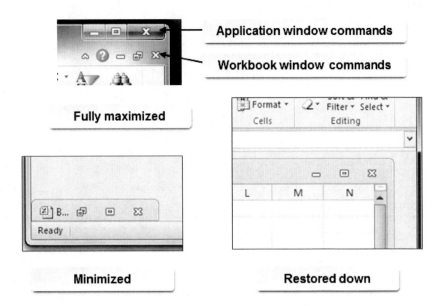

- The title bar in the application window displays the title of the currently selected workbook only if the workbook window is maximized within the application window. Otherwise, the title is displayed along the top-left corner of the workbook window.

The workbook window consists of seven main elements you will use to work within your workbooks.

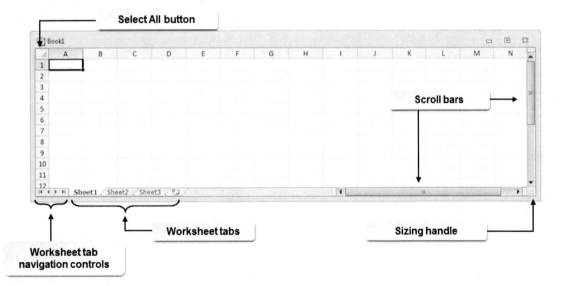

Figure 1-7: The workbook window.

The following table details the functions of the various workbook window elements.

Workbook Window Element	Description
Column headers	Identify each separate column with a unique letter or letter combination.
Row headers	Identify each separate row with a unique number.
Select All button	Enable you to select all cells in the worksheet.

Workbook Window Element	Description
Cells	Contain the data and formulas you enter into worksheets.
Scroll bars	Enable you to navigate vertically and horizontally across worksheets.
Worksheet tab navigation controls	Enable you to navigate among the various worksheets within a workbook.
Worksheet tabs	Enable you to select a particular worksheet within a workbook. You can use worksheet tabs to name, rename, and arrange worksheets, and you can apply certain formatting options to the tabs.
The sizing handle	Enables you to scale the view of a workbook up or down within the application window.

The Backstage View

The *Backstage view* is displayed when you select the **File** tab on the ribbon. At the top of the left pane in the Backstage view, Excel displays a series of commands you can use to save and access Excel workbook files. Below these commands are a set of vertically arranged tabs that provide you with access to commands and options for working with your Excel files, and for configuring Excel application settings and options. Common tasks you may perform in the Backstage view include previewing and printing workbooks, saving and accessing Excel files, applying security options, and sharing workbooks with colleagues. You can exit the Backstage view by selecting any of the ribbon tabs.From a high level, you can think of the Backstage view in these terms: the Backstage view is where you typically go to do things to your Excel files, whereas the other ribbon tabs are where you go to do things within your Excel files.

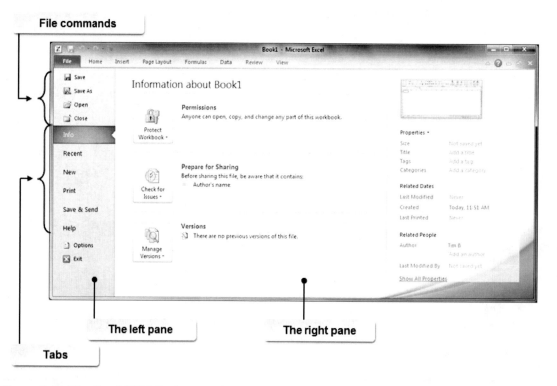

Figure 1-8: The Excel 2010 Backstage view.

The following table describes the various elements of the Excel Backstage view.

Backstage View Element	Description
Left pane	Displays the file commands and the various Backstage view tabs.
File commands	Enable you to open, close, and save your Excel workbook files.
Tabs	Provide you with access to commands for working with your Excel workbooks and various settings and options for configuring the Excel environment.
Right pane	Displays various commands and options for working with your Excel workbook files depending on the tab you select in the left pane.

 Access the Checklist tile on your LogicalCHOICE course screen for reference information and job aids on How to Open Workbooks.

Mouse Navigation

As with many Microsoft Office applications, Excel 2010 provides you with a number of options for performing the same task. This is no different from navigating your worksheets and workbooks. One of the most basic methods you will use to navigate your workbooks and worksheets is by using the mouse.

 Note: This course assumes the use of a desktop computer, or a laptop computer or a touch-screen device with a mouse attached. As touch-screen devices are becoming commonplace, you may find yourself using Excel 2010 on a touch-screen device without a mouse. Consult your device's operation manual for common equivalents to mouse-click commands.

 Note: For an animated guide on navigating the Excel user interface, view the LearnTO **Navigate the Microsoft Excel 2010 Interface** presentation from the **LearnTO** tile on the LogicalCHOICE Course screen.

The following table describes some of the most commonly used mouse navigation techniques within Excel 2010.

Navigation Option	Mouse Command
Select a particular cell.	Select the desired cell.
Select a range of cells.	Click and drag to select the desired range of cells.
Select an entire column or row.	Select the desired column or row header.
Move the worksheet display up or down by a single row.	Select one of the vertical scroll arrows.
Move the worksheet display left or right by a single column.	Select one of the horizontal scroll arrows.
Move the worksheet display by more than one row or column at a time.	Click and drag the vertical or horizontal scroll bars to the desired view.
Move the worksheet display one screen at a time.	On the vertical scroll bar, select the area between the scroll bar and the desired direction's scroll arrow.
Display a different worksheet.	Select the desired worksheet tab along the bottom of the workbook window.

Keyboard Navigation

Excel 2010 also provides you with a number of options for navigating your workbooks and worksheets using keyboard commands.

 Note: This knowledge block assumes the use of a desktop or a laptop computer, or the use of a touch-screen device with an attached keyboard. If you are using Excel 2010 on an exclusively touch-screen device, consult your device's operation manual or support material to determine if these keyboard shortcuts will work or if there are equivalent commands.

The following table describes some of the most commonly used keyboard navigation techniques in Excel 2010.

Navigation Option	Keyboard Command
Move one cell up, down, left, or right from the currently selected cell.	Press the **Up**, **Down**, **Left**, or **Right** arrow key.
Move to the cell in column A of the current row.	Press the **Home** key.
Move to the first or last column or row of data.	Press and hold **Ctrl**, and then press the **Up**, **Down**, **Left**, or **Right** arrow key.
Scroll up or down by one screen.	Press the **Page Up** or the **Page Down** key.
Scroll left or right by one screen.	Press **Alt+Page Up** or **Alt+Page Down**.
Move one cell to the right.	Press the **Tab** key. This will also enter any data you have typed into the cell.
Move one cell to the left.	Press **Shift+Tab**.
Move one cell down.	Press the **Enter** key. This will also enter any data you have typed into the cell. To enter data without navigating away from the cell, press **Ctrl+Enter**.
Move one cell up.	Press **Shift+Enter**.
Move to cell A1.	Press **Ctrl+Home**.
Navigate left or right through the worksheets in a workbook.	Press **Ctrl+Page Up** or **Ctrl+Page Down**.

Basic Data Entry

As cells act as individual storage objects for the data you will enter into Excel worksheets, it follows that you will need to be able to enter the necessary data into your worksheet cells. When you select a cell in Excel, it becomes the *active cell*, and it is only into the active cell that you can initially enter data. An active cell is displayed with a solid black border around it. When you select a range of cells, only one cell within the range is the active cell; that is the cell that is displayed without a blue background. You can use the **Tab** and the **Enter** keys to navigate among cells within a selected range while maintaining the range as your selection. In addition to dragging to select a range with your mouse, you can press and hold **Shift** to select a contiguous range of cells, or you can press and hold **Ctrl** to select a non-contiguous group of cells.

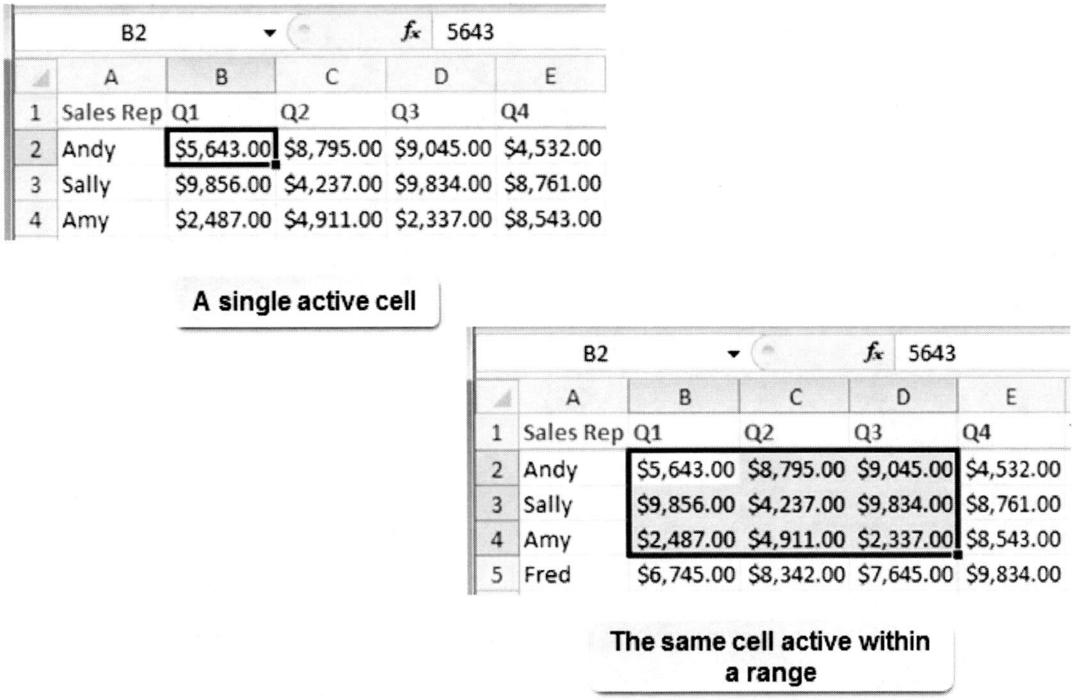

A single active cell

The same cell active within a range

Figure 1-9: Active cell contents appear in the Formula Bar and the Name Box displays the active cell reference.

As with the navigation options, there are several ways you can enter data into the cells in your worksheets. The following table describes the various methods for entering data into worksheet cells.

Data Entry Method	Description
Directly into the active cell	The most basic method of entering data into a cell is to select the cell, type the data, and then press either the **Tab** or the **Enter** key. Pressing **Tab** will enter the data and navigate one cell to the right. Pressing **Enter** will enter the data and navigate to the first open cell in the next row down.
	If there is already data in the cell, using this method will overwrite the previous data.
Using the **Formula Bar**	You can also enter data directly into the **Formula Bar**. Simply select the desired cell, select the **Formula Bar** to place the insertion point there, type the data, and then press either **Tab** or **Enter**.
Using Edit mode	You can use Edit mode to either enter new data in an empty cell or edit existing data. Using Edit mode is more useful for editing existing data; entering Edit mode is simply an extra step if you're just adding new data.
	To enter Edit mode, either double-click the desired cell, select the desired cell and then place the insertion point in the **Formula Bar**, or select the desired cell and then press **F2**. Once in Edit mode, you can place the insertion point wherever you like, in the cell or the **Formula Bar**, and edit the existing data as you normally would in a word-processing application. Once you've edited the data, regardless of where the insertion point is, you can press either **Tab** or **Enter** to enter the data and navigate to the desired next cell.

Note: To enter data in a cell and keep that cell as the active cell, press **Ctrl + Enter** to enter the data. Also, you can use the **Up**, **Down**, **Left**, or **Right** arrow keys to enter data and then navigate one cell in the desired direction.

Cell Modes

When interacting with the cells in your worksheets, an active cell can be in one of three modes: Ready, Enter, or Edit. Excel displays the status of the selected cell on the left side of the **Status bar**. These three modes allow you to interact with worksheet cells in different ways.

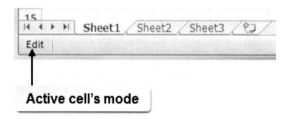

Active cell's mode

Cell Mode	Description
Ready mode	Ready mode tells you a cell is selected and that it is waiting for you to interact with it. Excel will not display a cursor in either the active cell or the Formula Bar when in Ready mode.
Enter mode	Excel puts the selected cell in Enter mode once you start typing data into it. Excel will enter Enter mode whether you are adding data to an empty cell or you are completely overwriting existing data in a cell. When the active cell is in Enter mode, there is an active insertion point (cursor) in the cell.
Edit mode	You can enter Edit mode in several different ways. Essentially, Edit mode is the same as Enter mode, except you are typically editing existing cell data instead of adding new data. To enter Edit mode, select the desired cell, and then do one of the following: select the **Formula Bar** to place the insertion point (cursor) there, press the **F2** key, or double-click the cell. When in Edit mode, there is an active insertion point (cursor) in either the active cell or the **Formula Bar**.
	Using the F2 key or selecting within the Formula Bar will always put the active cell in Edit mode, even if there is no existing content.

 Access the Checklist tile on your LogicalCHOICE course screen for reference information and job aids on How to Navigate the Excel Environment.

ACTIVITY 1-1
Navigating the Excel User Interface

Data File

C:\091018Data\Getting Started with Microsoft Office Excel
2010\footprint_sports_holiday_schedule.xlsx

Before You Begin

You are logged in to your computer and the desktop is displayed, but Excel 2010 is not open.

Windows 7 is set to display file extensions.

Scenario

My Footprint Sports started in Greene City in 1980 with one store and rapidly expanded throughout the state of Richland. Known for its superior customer service and wide range of products, My Footprint Sports has continued to grow and now has stores throughout the United States, as well as stores in select cities in Canada and Mexico. Recent industry rumors indicate that expansion into Europe is on the horizon.

You have recently joined My Footprint Sports as a sales manager. Your responsibilities include using Excel to analyze sales trends and other company data. You have used other spreadsheet applications to work with data in the past, but not Excel. So, you realize you'll need to get up to speed on how Excel works, and fast. You decide to start by locating the critical user interface elements you'll work with most often. Your HR representative provided you with the company paid holiday schedule for the current year as an Excel workbook file as part of the onboarding and orientation process. Because you need to plan your paid time off anyway, you decide to open that file in Excel to explore the user interface.

 Note: Activities may vary slightly if the software vendor has issued digital updates. Your instructor will notify you of any changes.

1. Open Excel 2010.
   a) From the desktop, select the **Start** button.
   b) In the **Start** menu, select **All Programs**.
   c) Select the **Microsoft Office** folder.
   d) Select **Microsoft Excel 2010**.

   e) If Excel does not appear full screen, select the application window's **Maximize** button.

2. Pin the Excel icon to the taskbar for easier access.
   a) Right-click the **Excel** icon on the taskbar.
   b) From the pop-up menu, select **Pin this program to taskbar**.

3. Open the **footprint_sports_holiday_schedule.xlsx** file.
   a) On the ribbon, select the **File** tab.
   b) In the left pane of the Backstage view, select **Open**.
   c) In the **Open** dialog box, navigate to the **C:\091018Data\Getting Started with Microsoft Office Excel 2010** folder.
   d) Select the **footprint_sports_holiday_schedule.xlsx** file and then select **Open**.

e) Verify that the file opened and that the file name appears on the **title bar**.

4. Navigate the ribbon.
   a) Select several of the ribbon tabs other than the **File** tab.
   b) Verify the displayed commands change for each tab.

5. Explore the Backstage view.
   a) Select the **File** tab.
   b) In the left pane, locate the **Save**, **Save As**, **Open**, and **Close** commands.
   c) Select the various tabs below the file commands.
   d) Verify that the commands and options in the right pane change for the various tabs.
   e) Select any ribbon tab to exit the Backstage view.

6. Navigate the worksheet with the mouse.
   a) Ensure cell **A1** is selected. Verify that it is displayed with a thick black border and that **A1** appears in the **Name Box**.
   b) Verify that **Day** appears in the **Formula Bar**.
   c) Select cell **C11**. Verify that it is now the active cell, that **C11** appears in the **Name Box**, and that **Christmas** appears in the **Formula Bar**.
   d) Click and drag from cell **A1** to cell **A11**. Confirm that the range **A1:A11** is selected and that cell **A1** is the active cell.
   e) Verify that **A1** appears in the **Name Box** and that **Day** appears in the **Formula Bar**.
   f) Press the **Enter** key.
   g) Verify cell **A2** is now the active cell, that **A2** appears in the **Name Box**, and that **Wed** appears in the **Formula Bar**.
   h) Press the **Enter** key until cell **A11** is the active cell.
   i) Select cell **A2**.
   j) Press and hold **Shift**, and then select cell **C2**.
   k) Verify that the range **A2:C2** is selected and that cell **A2** is the active cell within the range.
   l) Select cell **A3**, press and hold **Ctrl**, and then select the range **A11:C11**.
   m) Verify that cells **A3**, **A11**, **B11**, and **C11** are all selected.

7. Use the keyboard to navigate the worksheet.
   a) Select cell **A1**.
   b) Use the **Down** arrow and **Right** arrow keys to navigate to cell **C11**.
   c) Use the **Up** arrow and **Left** arrow keys to navigate back to cell **A1**.
   d) Press the **Enter** key to navigate to cell **A2**. Press and hold **Shift** and press the **Enter** key to navigate back to cell **A1**.
   e) Press the **Tab** key to navigate to cell **B1**. Press and hold **Shift** and press the **Tab** key to navigate back to cell **A1**.

8. Leave the workbook open.

TOPIC B

Use Excel Commands

You've navigated your way around the Excel environment and entered basic cell data. Having taken these few important first steps, you're ready to begin taking advantage of the wide array of functionality Excel 2010 has to offer. But, in order to do so, you'll need to be familiar with where to look to find the commands you need.

Knowing how to get to the data you want to work with is one thing; having the knowledge and the skills to manipulate and analyze that data is quite another. You'll need to know where the commands you want to execute are located and how to interact with the various elements of the Excel user interface in order to begin taking advantage of Excel's data analysis functionality.

The Ribbon

The *ribbon*, a common interface element shared by all Microsoft Office 2010 applications, is a component of the Excel 2010 user interface. The ribbon is a graphical user interface that contains all of the most commonly used commands you will need to create, modify, and work with your Excel workbooks. It was designed as a way to provide quick access to frequently used commands without the need to extensively navigate menus and sub-menus. The ribbon is displayed along the top of the Excel application window and is organized into a series of tabs that contain command groups. These ribbon groups contain sets of functionally related commands that you will use to enter, format, revise, and work with your workbook data.

 Note: This course uses a streamlined notation for ribbon commands. They'll appear as "[Ribbon Tab]→[Group]→[Button or Control]" as in "Select **Home→Clipboard→Paste**." If the group name isn't needed for navigation or there isn't a group, it's omitted, as in "Select **File→Open**." For selections that open menus and submenus, this notation convention will continue until you are directed to select the final command or option, as in "Select **Home→Cells→Format→Hide & Unhide→Hide Rows**."

 Note: Some Excel 2010 command buttons are split, meaning there are actually two separate buttons you can select independently. This is often the case with commands that have multiple options/variations accessible by selecting a down arrow. The **Paste** command button in the **Clipboard** group on the **Home** tab is an example of this. For these commands, you will be directed to either select just the button, as in "Select **Home→Clipboard→Paste**," or you will be directed to select the down arrow if necessary, as in "Select **Home→Clipboard→down arrow→Paste Special**."

Some ribbon groups also display a *dialog box launcher*. These downward-facing arrows in the bottom-right corner of some groups open dialog boxes that provide you with access to even more commands and options related to the functionality of the particular group's commands.

The ribbon is a customizable element of the Excel user interface. You can add tabs, groups, and individual commands to suit your particular needs and work habits. You can also hide the ribbon to create more workable space within the application window.

Tabs

Minimize/Expand the Ribbon button

Help button

Dialog box launcher

Commands

Groups

Figure 1-10: The Excel 2010 ribbon.

 Note: If you'd like a virtual tour of the ribbon, view the LearnTO **Navigate the Office 2010 Ribbon** presentation from the **LearnTO** tile on the LogicalCHOICE Course screen.

The following table provides a description of the various ribbon elements.

Ribbon Element	Description
Tabs	Organizes the ribbon at the highest level according to task functions such as inserting objects, working with formulas, and configuring the view of your worksheets.
Groups	Contain functionally related sets of commands that you will use to perform most Excel tasks.
Commands	Execute the desired action or configure the desired settings and options.
Dialog box launchers	Open dialog boxes containing further commands or options related to the functionality of the group's commands.
Minimize/Expand the Ribbon button	Hides or displays the ribbon depending on your particular needs.
Microsoft Excel Help	Opens the **Excel Help** window, which provides you with access to a number of support resources for Excel 2010.

The following table describes the types of commands each of the ribbon tabs displays.

Ribbon Tab	Contains Commands For
File	Working with your Excel files and configuring system-wide and application settings and options. Selecting the **File** tab accesses the Backstage view, providing you with access to these commands and settings.
Home	Some of the most common tasks you will perform. The **Home** tab displays commands for basic text formatting and editing; applying various styles and formatting to your data; and sorting, filtering, and searching your data.
Insert	Inserting a variety of objects, such as charts, tables, and graphics, into your workbooks; creating and editing hyperlinks; adding headers and footers to worksheets; and inserting equations and symbols.
Page Layout	Applying themes and effects to worksheets; configuring the overall layout of your worksheets; and arranging worksheet objects.

Ribbon Tab	Contains Commands For
Formulas	Inserting and working with formulas and functions; naming cells and ranges; troubleshooting workbook data, functions, and formulas; and setting calculation options.
Data	Importing data from other sources; performing various data analysis tasks; and organizing worksheet data into a hierarchical structure.
Review	Reviewing, proofing, adding comments to, and sharing your workbooks.
View	Configuring workbook views, arranging multiple workbook windows simultaneously, and setting the magnification level.

Screen Tips and Key Tips

Excel 2010 provides two features that can help you identify and access various elements of the user interface: screen tips and key tips. *Screen tips* appear when you place the mouse pointer over commands and some other elements of the user interface. Screen tips appear in a small pop-up window and provide information such as a command's name, a description of what the command or screen element does, and the keyboard shortcut that performs the same function.

Key tips differ from screen tips in that they allow you to actually interact with particular commands on screen. Key tips appear along the ribbon and the **Quick Access Toolbar** when you press the **Alt** key. Key tips appear as either a single alphanumeric character or a sequence of them. To access the particular tab or engage the particular command associated with a key tip, simply press the corresponding key or sequence of keys on the keyboard. It is important to note that key tips do not function the same as keyboard shortcuts. If a key tip is displayed as a sequence of characters, you press the corresponding keys one at a time, not at the same time as you would with a keyboard shortcut such as **Shift + Enter**. To turn off key tips, simply press the **Alt** key again or select any screen element with the mouse pointer.

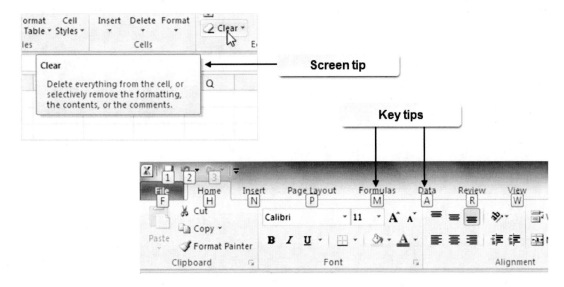

Figure 1-11: A screen tip and key tips in Excel 2010.

The Quick Access Toolbar

The *Quick Access Toolbar* is another element of the Excel user interface that provides you with easy access to commonly used commands. The **Quick Access Toolbar** appears above the ribbon in the top-left corner of the Excel application window. By default, the **Save**, **Undo**, and **Redo** commands are displayed on the **Quick Access Toolbar**. Like the ribbon, the **Quick Access Toolbar** can be customized. You can add or remove commands by using either the **Excel Options** dialog box or the **Customize Quick Access Toolbar** menu.

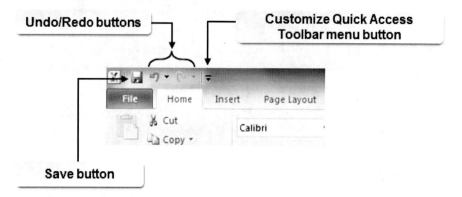

Figure 1-12: The Quick Access Toolbar.

The Mini Toolbar and Context Menus

Excel 2010 provides you with two other options for easily accessing certain commands: the *mini toolbar* and *context menus*. The **mini toolbar** is displayed when you right-click the active cell on a worksheet. It is a small, rectangular, pop-up window that contains a set of common text editing and formatting commands that you can use to work with the data in the active cell.

In Excel 2010, there are actually multiple versions of the **mini toolbar**, the main version that is displayed when you right-click an active cell, and variations of the main **mini toolbar** that are displayed when you right-click various other objects on worksheets, such as images and charts.

Context menus also appear when you select or right-click particular objects or data within worksheets. Context menus display a list of commands and options that pertain to working with the specific type of content you have selected, hence the name "context" menus.

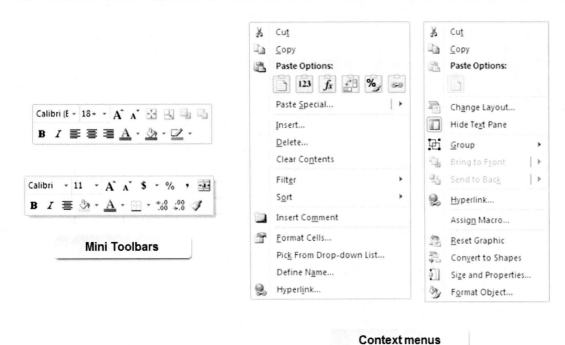

Mini Toolbars

Context menus

Figure 1-13: Variations on the mini toolbar and context menus in Excel 2010.

> Access the Checklist tile on your LogicalCHOICE course screen for reference information and job aids on **How to Use the Ribbon, the Quick Access Toolbar, and the Mini Toolbar.**

ACTIVITY 1-2
Using Excel Commands

Before You Begin

The footprint_sports_holiday_schedule.xlsx file is open.

Scenario

You are now familiar with the overall general layout of the Excel 2010 environment. You'd like to focus on discovering where some of the commonly used commands are. You decide to use screen tips to help you begin to identify some of the commands you've been wondering about. And, you want to look over one or two of the dialog boxes to see what commands are available there.

You have also just received an email message from the HR department informing you of an error on the holiday schedule, which you'll need to correct. You already have the holiday schedule workbook open, which works out well as you also want to add a few entries to the worksheet to help you plan your vacation time.

---

1. Use screen tips to identify common commands.
   a) Ensure the **Home** tab is selected.
   b) In the **Font** group, point the mouse pointer at several of the commands to view their screen tips.
   c) Do the same for several commands in each of the other groups.
   d) Select the **Insert** tab.
   e) View the screen tips for several commands in each of the command groups.

2. Examine the commands in a dialog box.
   a) Select the **Home** tab.
   b) In the **Font** group, select the **dialog box launcher**.
   c) Verify that the **Format Cells** dialog box opened.
   d) Select the various tabs and review some of the available commands.
   e) Select the **Close** button to close the **Format Cells** dialog box.

3. Add data to a cell.
   a) Select cell **C12**.
   b) Type *And day after* and press **Enter**.
   c) In cell **C13**, type *Consider NY's Eve* and press **Enter**.

4. Replace existing data in a cell.
   a) Select cell **A2**.
   b) Type *Tue* and press **Enter**.
   c) Verify that the cell content has changed.

5. Save and close the file.
   a) On the **Quick Access Toolbar**, select the **Save** button.
   b) Select **File→Close**.

TOPIC C

Create and Save a Basic Workbook

Although knowing how to open and work within existing workbooks is an important skill set, you will, undoubtedly, need to create your own Excel workbooks to suit your particular needs. It's likely you will be called upon to amass, analyze, and present data for a number of different purposes and regarding a number of different subjects. You are also likely to need to present similar information to multiple audiences. As such, you'll find yourself creating a variety of different workbooks that you will need to save as separate items and saving multiple versions of the same workbooks for various purposes.

Microsoft Excel 2010 provides you with a number of options for creating and saving new workbooks and for saving variations of the same workbooks with different names or in different locations. Becoming familiar with this basic functionality will provide you with the ability to keep track of and manage your Excel workbook files.

The New Tab

The Backstage view's **New** tab provides you with a variety of options for creating new Excel workbooks. You can create a new blank workbook to start from scratch, or you can decide to start with an existing Excel workbook or template, and then make changes to suit your needs.

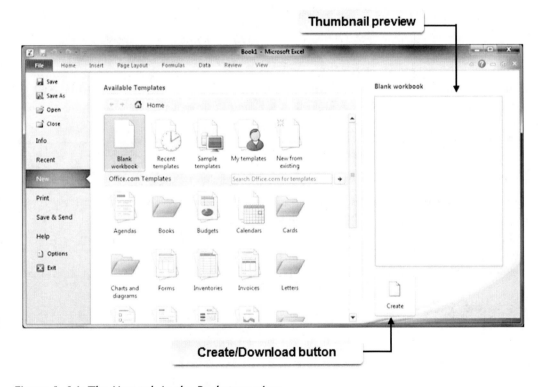

Figure 1-14: The New tab in the Backstage view.

You will use the options available on the **New** tab to create new Excel workbooks.

New Tab Element	Is Used To
Available Templates section	Create a new blank workbook, create a new workbook from an Excel template that is saved locally, or create a new workbook from an existing workbook file.
Office.com Templates section	Search for and create a new Excel workbook from one of the thousands of workbook templates available on Office.com.
Search Office.com for templates field	Enter specific search criteria to locate the desired Excel workbook template.
Thumbnail preview	View a preview image of the currently selected new workbook option.
Create/**Download** button	Create a new Excel workbook or to download the selected Excel workbook template file from Office.com.

 Note: For information on points to consider while developing a new workbook, view the LearnTO **Design Effective Workbooks** presentation from the **LearnTO** tile on the LogicalCHOICE Course screen.

Excel 2010 File Formats

The default file format for Excel 2010 workbook files is the XLSX format. This is an XML-based file format that allows Excel to compress files when you close them, making them up to 75 percent smaller than files saved in the previous Excel file format, XLS. When you open an XLSX workbook file, Excel automatically unzips it. The XLSX file format also provides other benefits over the previous file format, such as easier recovery of damaged files, increased security and protection functionality, and greater compatibility with other applications.

Microsoft Excel 2010 also supports a host of other file types that enable you to open workbook files from previous versions of Excel and share files in a variety of formats with other users. The following table provides a partial list of the file types available in Excel 2010.

File Type and Extension	Description
Excel Workbook (.xlsx)	The default file type in Excel 2010.
Excel Macro-Enabled Workbook (.xlsm)	Allows you to save workbook files containing Visual Basic for Applications macrocode.
Excel Binary Workbook (.xlsb)	Compressed, binary-based file format that reduces file size and improves performance in complex, calculation-dense workbooks. May not be compatible with some applications that work only with XML-based files.
Excel 97-2003 Workbook (.xls)	The previous default Excel file format. The XLS format is a binary file format, which isn't as compatible with other computer applications as the newer, XML-based file format.
Excel Template (.xltx)	The default file type for Excel templates. This format is used to save workbooks as templates so that you can create new workbooks based on the template contents, layout, and format.
Excel Macro-Enabled Template (.xltm)	The default file format for Excel macro-enabled templates.
Excel 97-2003 Template (.xlt)	The default template file format in previous versions of Excel.

File Type and Extension	Description
PDF (.pdf)	Allows you to save workbooks in the Adobe Portable Document Format (PDF).

Displaying File Name Extensions

By default, Windows 7 does not display file extensions for common file formats. To turn the display of file extensions on, select **Start→Control Panel→Appearance and Personalization→Folder Options**. Then, in the **Folder Options** dialog box, on the **View** tab, in the **Advanced settings** section, uncheck the **Hide extensions for known file types** check box, and select **OK**.

The Save and Save As Commands

Excel provides you with two options for saving your new and existing workbook files: the **Save** command and the **Save As** command. You use the **Save** command to save changes to an existing workbook without changing the file name or the file location. You use the **Save As** command to save new workbook files or to make changes to existing files, such as the file name and location. Both the **Save** and **Save As** commands are accessible at the top of the left pane in the Backstage view. The **Quick Access Toolbar** provides access to the **Save** command by default.

 Note: If you select **Save** to save a new workbook file, Excel 2010 automatically opens the **Save As** dialog box, as you must specify a location and a file type when saving new files.

Figure 1-15: The Save and Save As commands in the Backstage view.

The Save As Dialog Box

Selecting the **Save As** command, or the **Save** command for new files, opens the **Save As** dialog box. You will use this to name and select a location for your files and to select the file type in which to save your workbook files.

Compatibility Mode

When you open a workbook file in Excel 2010 that was created by using Excel 2003 (or an earlier version), Excel opens the file in *Compatibility mode* and the **Title bar** displays the file name with the text *[Compatibility Mode]* next to it. You can open and work with files in Compatibility mode to preserve the original file format, allowing you to subsequently open the file in previous versions of Excel. Keep in mind, some Excel features are not available in all versions of Excel.

Figure 1-16: The Title bar of a workbook file open in Compatibility mode.

The Convert Option

When you open a workbook in Excel 2010 that was created in a 97-2003 version of Excel, and you no longer need to keep the workbook in the previous file format, you can convert the workbook into the Excel 2010 file format, XLSX. Using the *Convert option* provides you with access to all of the features and functionality available in Excel 2010. Often, converting a file to the newer file format will also reduce the size of your workbook file.

When you convert a workbook, Excel replaces the old file with a copy of the workbook in the XLSX or the XLSM file formats. The previous version file is no longer available for you to work with. You can access the **Convert** option from the **Info** tab in the Backstage view of any workbook that is open in Compatibility mode. This option will not appear for workbooks open in the XLSX file format.

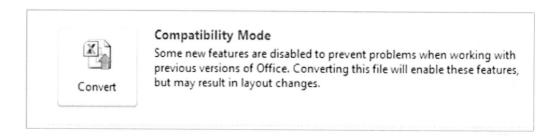

Figure 1-17: The Convert option.

The Compatibility Checker

The *Compatibility Checker* in Excel 2010 allows you to test the compatibility of objects and data in an Excel 2010 workbook when you intend to save it in an earlier Excel file format. This is typical when you need to share a file you created in a newer version of Excel with a user who has an older version of Excel installed on his or her machine. Selecting the **Check Compatibility** command opens the **Microsoft Excel - Compatibility Checker** dialog box, in which you can view a list of features in your Excel 2010 file that are not supported in earlier versions of Excel. You can access the **Check Compatibility** command by selecting **File→Info→Check for Issues**. Excel will also run the Compatibility Checker automatically when you attempt to save a current Excel workbook file in the previous file format.

Unchecking the **Check compatibility when saving this workbook** check box allows you to save in previous versions without the Compatibility Checker running automatically. However, be careful when you uncheck this feature; you will lose certain functionality when you save back to previous versions.

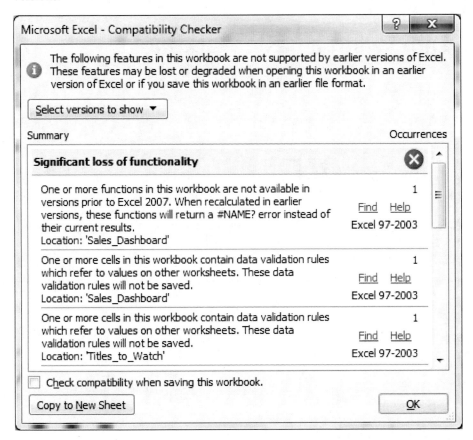

Figure 1–18: The Microsoft Excel – Compatibility Checker dialog box.

There are two levels of compatibility issues the Compatibility Checker can detect: minor loss of fidelity and significant loss of functionality. With minor compatibility issues, you can likely save the workbook in an earlier file format with limited loss of functionality. Common changes when saving back to an earlier file format include the removal of table and text formatting not supported in earlier versions.

When you encounter significant compatibility issues, it is recommended that you not save your file in the earlier file format. Doing so may cause you to lose data, to experience formula or calculation failures, or to experience other serious issues.

 Access the Checklist tile on your LogicalCHOICE course screen for reference information and job aids on How to Create and Save a Basic Workbook.

ACTIVITY 1–3
Creating and Saving a Basic Workbook

Before You Begin
Excel 2010 is open.

Scenario
Now that you're more familiar with the Excel user interface and some of its basic commands, you feel comfortable enough to create your first new workbook. A colleague has emailed you some basic sales data for two new products, and you expect more data soon. So, you decide to create a new workbook, enter the data, and then save the workbook so you can add more data to it as it comes in. Another colleague has asked for a copy of the file, but she works in Excel 2003. So, you'll also have to save a copy of the file in an earlier format.

1. Create a new blank workbook.
   a) Select **File→New**.
   b) In the right pane, in the **Available Templates** section, ensure **Blank workbook** is selected.
   c) Below the thumbnail preview, select **Create**.

2. Add column labels for the data.
   a) Ensure cell **A1** is selected, type *Product* and press **Tab**.
   b) Ensure cell **B1** is selected, type *Quantity* and press **Tab**.
   c) Ensure cell **C1** is selected, type *Price* and press **Enter**.

3. In the **Product** column, enter the product names.
   a) Ensure cell **A2** is selected, type *Bike* and press **Enter**.
   b) In cell **A3**, type *Golf Cart* and press **Enter**.

4. In the **Quantity** column, enter the quantity data.
   a) Select cell **B2**, type *550* and press **Enter**.
   b) In cell **B3**, type *820* and press **Enter**.

5. In the **Price** column, enter the price data.
   a) Select cell **C2**, type *685* and press **Enter**.
   b) In cell **C3**, type *259* and press **Enter**.

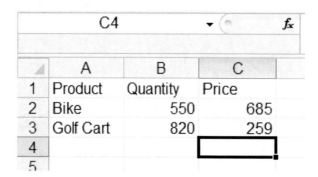

6. Save the workbook in the default Excel 2010 file format.

    a) Select **File→Save As**.

    b) In the **Save As** dialog box, ensure the **C:\091018Data\Getting Started with Microsoft Office Excel 2010** folder is still selected.

    c) In the **File name** field, type *my_new_products*

    d) In the **Save as type** drop-down menu, ensure **Excel Workbook (*.xlsx)** is selected.

    e) Select **Save**.

    f) Ensure the file name now appears in the **title bar** with the .xlsx file extension.

7. Save a copy of the workbook file in a previous file format.

    a) Select **File→Save As**.

    b) In the **Save As** dialog box, ensure the **C:\091018Data\Getting Started with Microsoft Office Excel 2010** folder is still selected.

    c) In the **Save as type** drop-down menu, select **Excel 97-2003 Workbook (*.xls)**.

    d) Select **Save**.

    e) Ensure the file name now appears in the **title bar** with the .xls file extension.

8. Close the workbook file but leave Excel 2010 open.

    a) In the top-right corner of the workbook window, select the **Close Window** button.

    b) Ensure the workbook closed but the application remains open.

TOPIC D

Enter Cell Data

People use Excel for an incredibly wide range of reasons and purposes. Some people use it simply as a way to organize and review information. Some may use it as a type of calendar or planner. And many people use it to analyze data and perform complex calculations. In fact, Excel is so versatile you'd be hard pressed to find someone who is familiar with all of Excel's capabilities. Given all of the possibilities of working with Excel, it should come as no surprise that Excel can recognize a wide variety of data types. You'll likely work with many, if not most, of these data types at some point.

With the incredible array of information types you can enter into and work with within your Excel workbooks, you'll need to be familiar with what these data types are and how Excel deals with them. Having a working knowledge of how Excel sees data is an important first step to developing the skills you'll need to crunch your numbers and keep track of your important information.

Data Types

One of the most fundamentally important things to understand about Excel is that it is not a "what you see is what you get" type of environment. Often, the value or text that appears within a cell is not what is actually stored in the cell. A simple example of this is the result of a calculation. If you have a formula entered in a cell, by default, the cell will display the result of the formula. For example, if the cell contains a formula that is the equivalent of "1 + 1," the cell will display the result of that formula: 2. But 2 is not the actual cell data; the formula is. Although this may, at first, not seem highly important, as you begin to work with the more complex functionality in Excel, this will become a critical concept to understand.

 Note: When you are actively editing a cell's content, the cell displays the content as it's entered, similar to the way the **Formula Bar** displays cell content. So if a cell contains a formula, while you edit the content, the cell displays the formula. When you enter the content, Excel switches back to displaying the formula result in the cell.

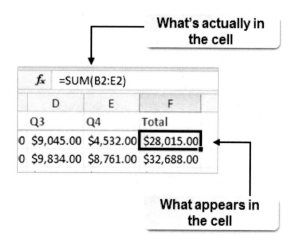

Figure 1-19: The difference between what you see in a cell and what's actually in the cell.

Although Excel cells can contain an incredible array of content, there are really only a few general categories of data that you'll work with. In essence, they boil down to values, labels/text, formulas, and dates and times.

Data Category	Description
Values	Numeric constants that do not change unless you edit the cell contents. Examples include 1, 345, 11.6, and .002.
Labels/Text	Alphanumeric text not used to perform calculations or store numeric values. These can largely be viewed as labels for related sets of data on a worksheet. Examples include "Sales," "Q1," and "Percent of the Whole."
Formulas	Mathematical equations used to perform calculations or data analysis. Formulas are dynamic, so the displayed value can change if you change the cell data feeding the formula.
Dates and times	Date and time values. These can be used both as simple labels or as part of certain mathematical or logical operations.

The Cut, Copy, and Paste Commands

While Excel is a different beast than other Office applications, such as Word and PowerPoint, you'll find some of the functionality is quite similar. The **Cut**, **Copy**, and **Paste** commands are a good example of this. You will use the **Cut**, **Copy**, and **Paste** commands to either make a copy of cell data and place it in another cell, or to remove data from one cell and put it in another. Copied data is temporarily stored on a Microsoft Office tool known as the clipboard. Data on the clipboard can be reused in other locations on the same worksheet, within the same workbook, and in other workbooks and applications. The **Cut**, **Copy**, and **Paste** commands are displayed in the **Clipboard** group on the **Home** tab.

Figure 1-20: The Clipboard group displays the Cut, Copy, and Paste commands.

To refresh your memory, or in case you are not familiar with the **Cut**, **Copy**, and **Paste** commands, the following table offers a description of each.

Command	Performs This Action
Cut	Removes data from the selected cell or removes the selected data, and places a copy of it on the clipboard.
Copy	Makes a copy of the data in the selected cell or a copy of the selected data, and places the copy on the clipboard.
Paste	Places the data most recently added to the clipboard in the destination cell or location.

One important distinction to make in Excel regarding the use of these commands is the difference between using **Cut**, **Copy**, and **Paste** on entire cells versus using them on selected data. If you select a cell, using the **Cut** or the **Copy** command will affect all of the data within the cell; remember what you see isn't necessarily the data in the cell. You can also select a portion of the cell data to cut or copy. You can do this within the cell if it's in Edit mode, or in the **Formula Bar** with the desired cell selected. The same is true of the **Paste** command. You can either paste the clipboard content into an entire cell or you can place it alongside other cell content in a cell in either Edit mode or in the **Formula Bar**.

In addition to the **Cut**, **Copy**, and **Paste** commands from the ribbon, Excel allows you to use keyboard shortcuts to perform these tasks.

Command	Keyboard Shortcut
Copy	Ctrl+C
Cut	Ctrl+X
Paste	Ctrl+V

When you use the **Cut** or the **Copy** command to copy content to the clipboard, Excel displays an animated, dashed-line box, often referred to as "dancing ants" or "marching ants," around your selection to help you verify that you have copied the correct content. After you paste the content and begin to perform another task, Excel stops displaying the dancing ants.

B	C	D
1	Q2	Q3
5,643.00	$8,795.00	$9,045.0
9,856.00	$4,237.00	$9,834.0
2,487.00	$4,911.00	$2,337.0
6,745.00	$8,342.00	$7,645.0
$987.00	$4,521.00	$1,123.0

The Undo and Redo Commands

Inevitably, as you work with Excel, you will make a mistake. After all, you're only human. Fortunately, Excel, like many other Office applications, provides you with the **Undo** and **Redo** commands to help you correct errors as you work. The **Undo** command will cancel out the last action you performed, or the last several actions you performed, so you can correct any mistakes you've made while working with your workbooks. The **Undo** command works on a wide variety of actions including entering data/typing text, performing calculations, adding objects to your worksheets, and formatting worksheets and worksheet objects. Once you've used the **Undo** command, Excel activates the **Redo** command, which will cancel out the last undo action or a series of undo actions.

By default, the **Undo** and **Redo** commands are available on the **Quick Access Toolbar**. You can also use the keyboard shortcuts **Ctrl+Z** and **Ctrl+Y** to use the **Undo** and **Redo** commands respectively.

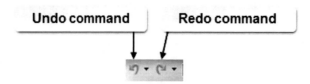

Figure 1–21: Use the Undo and Redo commands to cancel or repeat previous actions.

The AutoFill Feature

Excel 2010 includes a number of features meant to make your life a bit easier. One of these is the *AutoFill feature*. The AutoFill feature attempts to recognize an existing pattern in the data you have already entered, and then apply that pattern to filling in additional cells. Let's look at an example.

Say you enter the following values into the following cells in column A: A1: 1, A2: 2, A3: 3, and A4: 4. Clearly, you are attempting to create a sequential numbered list in the first column, or at least that's what Excel will assume. If you use the AutoFill feature to fill in the remaining cells in column A, Excel will follow the pattern and fill in the remaining cells with 5, 6, 7, 8, 9, 10, and so on. If you would like AutoFill to recognize a repeating pattern, say 1, 2, 3, 1, 2, 3, you would need to enter at least two cycles of the pattern to be sure Excel recognizes it as a pattern and not a sequence of numbers. If you start with only a single value, Excel will simply repeat it. AutoFill works for text as well as numeric values, so Excel would, for example, recognize a pattern such as lettering the first column instead of numbering it or entering the days of the week or the months of the year.

To use the AutoFill feature, you must first select the sequence of cells upon which you want the pattern based. When you select a cell or a range, Excel displays the cell or range within a solid black border. At the bottom-right corner of the border, Excel displays a **fill handle**. To use the AutoFill feature, you simply drag the **fill handle** until the border surrounds the desired range of cells, and then release it. When the mouse pointer is directly over the **fill handle**, it is displayed as a thin black plus symbol ✛ instead of the usual thick white plus symbol ✛.

The AutoFill feature can also assist you with entering duplicate text entries in the same column. If you begin to type something into a cell that matches the beginning of another cell's content, Excel will attempt to automatically complete the entry for you to match the existing content. If you intended to enter a duplicate entry, you can simply press the **Enter** key, and Excel will automatically complete the entry. However, as you type, if the sequence of characters deviates from the other cell's content, Excel will stop displaying the entry and will simply let you continue to type the desired cell content. This works only with entries that consist of just text or a combination of text and numbers. Excel will not automatically complete duplicate entries of numeric values.

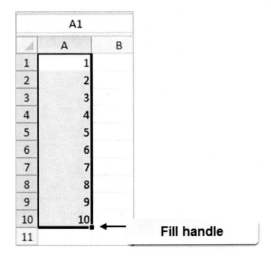

Figure 1-22: A column of cells populated by the AutoFill feature.

AutoFill Options

Excel 2010 also provides you with several options for deciding how to apply the AutoFill options when you use the feature. After you release the fill handle, Excel displays a small icon on the lower-right side of the range. Selecting that icon opens a menu, providing you with access to four options for choosing how to apply the AutoFill.

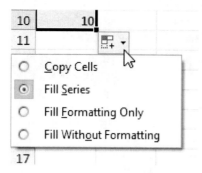

Figure 1-23: The AutoFill options in Excel 2010.

The following table describes the various AutoFill options.

AutoFill Option	Description
Copy Cells	Ignores any recognizable pattern and fills the remaining cells with the same data the originally selected cells contain.
Fill Series	The default AutoFill option. Excel applies the pattern it recognizes in filling the remaining cells.
Fill Formatting Only	Applies any formatting in the originally selected cells to the remaining cells without populating the cells with content.
Fill Without Formatting	Fills the remaining cells with data based on the recognized pattern while ignoring any formatting applied to the originally selected cells.

Excel Errors

As you begin to enter more and more data in your Excel worksheets, you'll be more likely to occasionally encounter an error. There are a number of common issues that can cause errors in Excel, each returning a unique error message. It is important to understand what causes these errors and how to resolve them, though you are unlikely to encounter many of them until you begin working with complex formulas and functions.

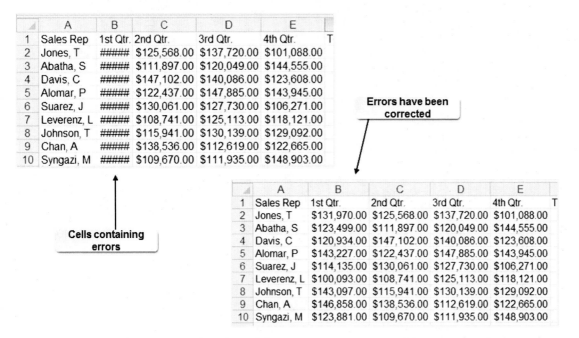

Figure 1-24: A common Excel error, a series of pound signs, or hashtags, indicates a column is too narrow to display all cell content.

The following table lists some of the common Excel error messages, what they mean, and possible solutions.

Error Message	What It Means	What to Do
#####	The most common cause of this error, which is often referred to as "railroad tracks," is that a column is too narrow to display all cell content. You may also see this error if dates or times in your worksheets contain negative values.	Either adjust the column width to accommodate cell content or correct your date or time entries.
#VALUE!	An Excel formula has encountered an unexpected value. For example, text where it thinks numeric values should be.	Correct the data entry or the cell reference in the formula. Or, enter a different formula.
#DIV/0!	A formula you have entered is forcing Excel to divide a value by zero. This can happen either when zero is the value in the cell or a cell contains no value at all.	Correct the data entry or the cell reference in the formula. Or, enter a different formula.
#REF!	This error indicates an invalid reference. One common cause is deleting a cell that a formula references.	Update the formula or restore the deleted cell.
#NULL!	You have tried to reference the intersection of two ranges that do not actually intersect.	Correct the intersection reference.

One other common error indicator you'll encounter occasionally is a green triangle icon in the top-left corner of a cell. This indicates some other type of error involving formulas that still returns a valid value. Most commonly, users encounter this error indicator when they enter a formula in a cell that doesn't match other formulas entered into adjacent cells. So, while the formula itself is valid and returns a valid value, Excel recognizes it doesn't seem to match surrounding formulas and flags it as a possible mistake.

When you select a cell containing an error indicator, Excel displays a drop-down menu. This menu indicates the type of error Excel flagged and provides you with access to options for correcting or ignoring the error and access to Help resources about the particular error.

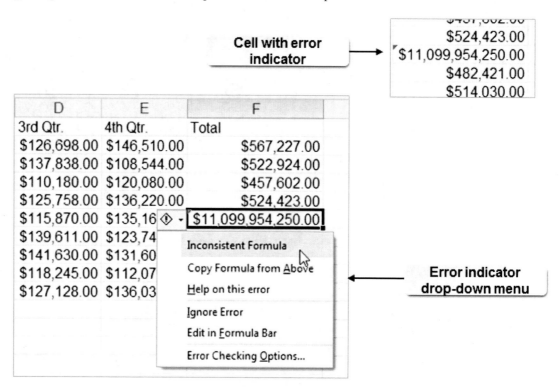

Figure 1-25: Green triangle indicators flag valid formulas that don't seem to fit with surrounding formulas. Here, the user mistakenly multiplied a set of values instead of adding them, which doesn't match the surrounding data.

The Clear Command

As you need to enter data into worksheet cells, it stands to reason that you will also need to delete cell data from time to time. The most basic method of doing this is to select the cell with the data you wish to remove and then press the **Delete** key. However, Excel also provides you with the **Clear** command, which gives you access to a number of options for removing cell content that doesn't always include removing everything from the cell. The **Clear** command is available in the **Editing** group on the **Home** tab.

The following table describes each of the **Clear** command options.

Clear Command Option	Clears
Clear All	Everything from the selected cell(s).
Clear Formats	Only formatting applied to the selected cell(s). The content is left in place, including any existing comments.
Clear Contents	Only the contents of the selected cell(s), but not the formatting.

Clear Command Option	Clears
Clear Comments	Only comments from the selected cell(s).
Clear Hyperlinks	Hyperlinks from cell contents. The formatting is left in place, including formatting applied to the text when the hyperlink was created.
Remove Hyperlinks	Hyperlinks and all formatting.

 Access the Checklist tile on your LogicalCHOICE course screen for reference information and job aids on How to Enter Data in Worksheet Cells.

ACTIVITY 1–4
Entering Cell Data

Data Files

C:\091018Data\Getting Started with Microsoft Office Excel 2010\my_new_products.xlsx

C:\091018Data\Getting Started with Microsoft Office Excel 2010\future_products.txt

Before You Begin

Excel 2010 is open.

Scenario

Your colleague emailed you a text file with some additional new products that My Footprint Sports will be adding to its catalog. In order to keep track of the new product lines all in one place, you decide to add the new items to the **my_new_products.xlsx** workbook file. Additionally, you want to start tracking sales of the new products weekly, so you decide to track that information on another worksheet in the same workbook.

---

1. Open the **my_new_products.xlsx** file.
   a) Select **File→Open**.
   b) In the **Open** dialog box, navigate to the **C:\091018Data\Getting Started with Microsoft Office Excel 2010 folder**.
   c) Select the **my_new_products.xlsx** file and then select **Open**.

2. Open the **future_products.txt** file.
   a) On the Windows 7 **taskbar**, select the **Windows Explorer** icon.
   b) In **Windows Explorer**, navigate to the **C:\091018Data\Getting Started with Microsoft Office Excel 2010 folder**.
   c) Double-click the **future_products.txt** file.

3. Copy and paste the new product names into the **my_new_products.xlsx** workbook.
   a) Select all of the text in the **future_products.txt** file.
   b) Press **Ctrl+C** to copy the text to the clipboard.
   c) Switch back to the **my_new_products.xlsx** workbook by selecting the Excel icon on the **taskbar**.
   d) Select cell **A4**, and then select **Home→Clipboard→Paste**.

e) Ensure the new product names are displayed in the worksheet.

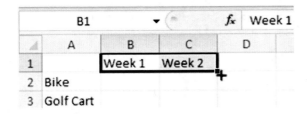

f) Close the **future_products.txt** file.

4. Copy and paste the product names to another worksheet.
   a) Select range **A2:A8** and then select **Home→Clipboard→Copy**.
   b) Along the bottom of the user interface, select the **Sheet2** worksheet tab.
   c) Select cell **A2** and then select **Home→Clipboard→Paste**.
   d) Ensure the product names appear in the range **A2:A8**.

5. Use the AutoFill feature to add entries for tracking the new product sales on a weekly basis.
   a) Ensure the **Sheet2** worksheet is selected, and then select cell **B1**.
   b) Type *Week 1* and press **Tab**.
   c) In cell **C1**, type *Week 2* and press **Tab**.
   d) Select the range **B1:C1**.
   e) Place the mouse pointer over the **fill handle** until it appears as a thin-stroked black plus symbol.

	A	B	C	D
1		Week 1	Week 2	
2	Bike			
3	Golf Cart			

f) Drag the fill handle until the range **B1:K1** is selected and then release the mouse button.
   g) Verify that Excel filled in the remaining cells through week 10 as expected.

6. Save and close the **my_new_products.xlsx** file.

TOPIC E

Use Excel Help

Learning how to master a new application, especially one as robust as Excel, can be daunting. As you become more familiar with some of Excel's more advanced functionality, you are likely to encounter commands you are unfamiliar with or have questions about how to perform certain tasks. When such issues arise, you could attempt to figure things out on your own, use a trial-and-error approach, or hit the Internet to find answers. However, it seems there should be an easier way to seek help when you need it. Fortunately, there is!

Excel 2010 comes packaged with its own Help system that can assist you in finding answers to your questions. As there is a staggering amount of functionality wrapped up in Excel, learning your way around the Help system may be the single greatest advantage you can give yourself in terms of eventual Excel mastery. Taking the time to learn how to use Excel Help now could save you countless hours of research down the road.

Microsoft Excel Help

Microsoft Excel Help provides you with access to a number of different resources that can answer your Excel questions and show you how to perform a number of tasks within the application. Excel Help combines local resources, which are installed on your computer when you install Excel, with access to various online resources to provide you with a central source for articles, websites, and videos you can use to discover answers to your Excel-related questions. In order to access the online resources, you must have an active Internet connection. To access the Excel Help system, select the **Microsoft Excel Help** button on the ribbon or press the **F1** key.

The Excel Help Window

When you open the Excel Help system, Excel displays the **Excel Help** window. You can use the **Excel Help** window to search for, browse through, and review a number of different help resources. By default, if you have an active Internet connection, the **Excel Help** window is configured to search for either online help or through the Help files that are installed with Excel. However, you have the option to tell Excel Help where you'd like to search.

There are several key elements to the Excel Help window that you will use to find answers to your questions.

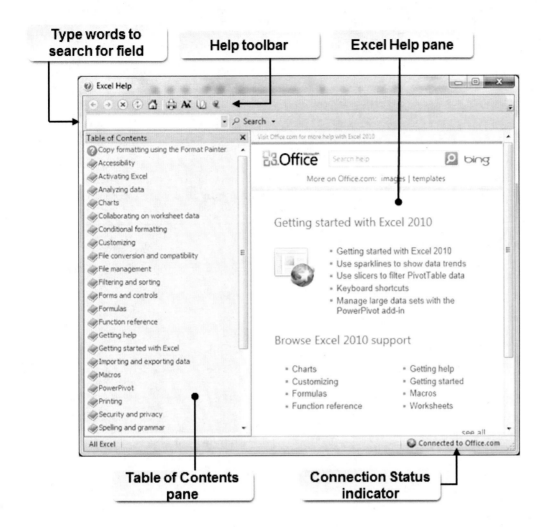

Type words to search for field   **Help toolbar**   **Excel Help pane**

Table of Contents pane   **Connection Status indicator**

Figure 1-26: The Excel Help window.

The following table details the function of the various Excel Help window elements.

Excel Help Window Element	Is Used To
Help toolbar	Access the commands you will use to navigate, print, and work with Excel Help resources.
Type words to search for field	Search for help resources either locally on your machine or online.
Search button	Execute search queries and select the type of resources Excel will return in search queries.
Search down arrow	Select the specific location in which to search for Help resources. You can temporarily override the current connection status by using the options available from the **Search down arrow**. For example, if you have the connection status set to **Offline**, if you have an active Internet connection, you can still search for online Help resources by selecting one of the options in the **Content from Office.com** section of the options menu.
Close button	Close the **Excel Help** window.

Excel Help Window Element	Is Used To
Table of Contents pane	Display lists of categorized links to help resources stored on your computer.
Search help field	Search for online help resources through Office.com. This field is displayed only in the Excel Help pane when the connection status is set to **Connected to Office.com**.
Excel Help pane	View and navigate search results and to display the contents of various help resources.
Connection Status indicator	Select whether Excel Help defaults to displaying local or online Help resources. The **Connection Status** indicator also displays the current selection.

The Toolbar Commands

You will use the Excel Help toolbar commands to navigate and print various help resources.

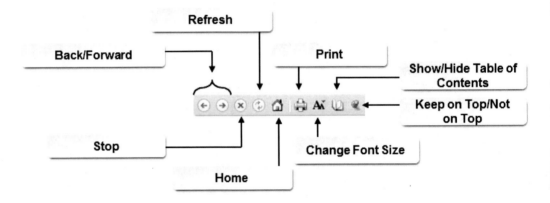

Figure 1-27: The Excel Help toolbar.

The following table details the functions of the Excel Help toolbar commands.

Excel Help Toolbar Command	Is Used To
Back	Navigate back to the previous screen in Excel Help. The **Back** button remains inactive until you navigate away from the Excel Help home screen.
Forward	Navigate forward to subsequent screens in the Excel Help window. The **Forward** button remains inactive until you use the **Back** button to navigate back.
Stop	Stop Excel Help from loading the current screen.
Refresh	Refresh the search results.
Home	Navigate back to the Excel Help home screen.
Print	Print the contents of the Excel Help pane.
Change Font Size	Increase or decrease the font size of Excel Help pane content.
Show/Hide Table of Contents	Open or close the **Table of Contents** pane.

Excel Help Toolbar Command	Is Used To
Keep On Top/Not On Top	Pin the **Excel Help** window so that it always remains in front of the Excel application window, or to unpin the **Excel Help** window so that you can view the Excel application window in front of it.

 Access the Checklist tile on your LogicalCHOICE course screen for reference information and job aids on How to Use Excel Help.

ACTIVITY 1-5
Using Excel Help

Before You Begin
Excel 2010 is open.

Scenario
As you've been working with Excel more and more, you have come across a few commands and features that you have some questions about. So, you decide to use the Excel Help system to find out more about the application.

---

1. Select the **Microsoft Excel Help** button 🄯 in the top-right corner of the ribbon to open Excel Help.

2. Select the **Show Table of Contents** button to display the **Table of Contents** pane.

3. Search for Excel Help articles stored on your computer.
   a) Select the **Connection Status** indicator.
   b) Select **Show content only from this computer**.

   c) Ensure the **Connection Status** indicator appears as **Offline**.
   d) In the **Table of Contents** pane, select **Getting help** to expand that section of Help topics.
   e) Scroll down slightly and select the **What and where is the Backstage view** link.
   f) Select the **Maximize** button to view the **Excel Help** window full-screen.
   g) Review the content about the Backstage view.
   h) On the **Help** toolbar, select the **Home** button. 🏠

4. Search for Help resources online.
   a) Select the **Connection Status** indicator.
   b) Select **Show content from Office.com**.
   c) Ensure the **Connection Status** indicator appears as **Connected to Office.com**.
   d) In the **Search help** field, type *compatibility checker* and press **Enter**.
   e) Review the search results and select a search result that links to a Help article.

> **Note:** Help articles will display the text **Article** below the search-result hyperlink, before the resource's description.

f) Review the article content and, on the **Help** toolbar, select the **Back** button.

g) Select a search result that links to a website.

> **Note:** Help websites will display the text **Link** below the search-result hyperlink, before the resource's description.

h) In your web browser, review the Help content.

5. Close your web browser and the **Excel Help** window.

Summary

In this lesson, you used some of the most basic Excel 2010 functionality, which laid the foundation you will need to begin developing your Excel knowledge and skills. You navigated the Excel user interface, used Excel commands, created and saved a basic worksheet, entered cell data, and used the Excel Help system. As you build upon these foundational skills, you will begin to unlock Excel's robust functionality and discover the power that lies within your organizational data.

How will your experience with other Microsoft Office applications translate to working with Excel 2010?

Do you think you'll prefer to use the mouse or the keyboard navigation options as you develop your workbooks?

 Note: Check your LogicalCHOICE Course screen for opportunities to interact with your classmates, peers, and the larger LogicalCHOICE online community about the topics covered in this course or other topics you are interested in. From the Course screen you can also access available resources for a more continuous learning experience.

2 | Performing Calculations

Lesson Time: 1 hour, 30 minutes

Lesson Objectives

In this lesson, you will perform calculations. You will:

- Create worksheet formulas.

- Insert functions.

- Reuse formulas.

Lesson Introduction

So far, you have navigated the Excel environment, created and saved basic workbooks, and entered data into cells. You've found your way around the Excel Help system in order to start finding answers to your Excel-related questions. Now what? You know the true power of Excel lies in its ability to help you analyze your organizational data. But, you may not quite know how to transform your raw data into actionable business intelligence. Excel contains an incredible array of functionality to help you do this. And, like many other business and organizational tasks, getting started boils down to just some basic math.

It should come as no surprise that most people no longer use a pencil and paper to perform calculations. After all, with calculators and computer applications there to help, why bother? And there are numerous pitfalls you can avoid by having a machine perform your calculations for you. Fortunately, Excel offers you these and a host of other benefits when you let it crunch your numbers. In order to take full advantage of everything Excel can do for you, you must first understand how Excel thinks, what it can do for you, and how to tell it what to do. In this lesson, you'll begin to do just that.

TOPIC A

Create Worksheet Formulas

Performing calculations by hand can be a tedious and time-consuming task. Manually performing calculations can lead to errors, which leads to erasing, which leads to sloppy documents, which leads to...well, you get the idea. Imagine also, trying to maintain a spreadsheet that contains important financial figures that constantly change. Every time a single value changes, you might have to change entire rows or columns of data. Keeping up with such calculations manually is not only impractical and tedious, but it is also unnecessary and, in some cases, nearly impossible.

In today's fast-paced, data-driven environment, you probably don't have the time to crunch numbers by hand and few organizations are able to tolerate the volume of errors sure to arise when people perform calculations manually. Why not have Excel do it for you? Performing calculations is one of the most critical, foundational functions Excel performs, forming the basis for nearly all of the data analysis you'll need to perform. By gaining a solid, clear understanding of how Excel performs such calculations, you'll save yourself valuable time, avoid a ton of headaches, and ensure a level of accuracy not possible when performing the same calculations on your own.

Excel Formulas

Excel *formulas* perform simple or complex mathematical computations in worksheets. You can use formulas to perform tasks such as adding up a row or a column of numbers, multiplying sales figures by commission rates, and applying tax to sales. One of the key benefits of using formulas in Excel is that you can change some of the values used in the formulas and, by default, Excel will automatically adjust the calculations accordingly.

It is important to remember that, in Excel, what you see isn't necessarily what you get. When you enter a formula into a worksheet cell, by default, Excel will display the result of calculating the formula in the cell, not the formula itself.

Excel can perform calculations by using fixed numbers or by referring to values in other cells. This is one of the truly powerful features of using Excel to perform calculations. Excel 2010 provides you with an incredible array of options for performing calculations in your workbooks and worksheets.

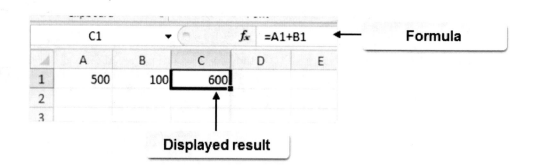

Figure 2-1: A formula in a worksheet cell.

The Formula Bar and the Name Box

You can enter Excel formulas directly into worksheet cells or you can use the *Formula Bar*. The **Formula Bar** is an element of the Excel application window that provides you with the ability to edit cell contents; quickly insert pre-existing formulas; and select, navigate to, and view the contents of selected cells. The **Formula Bar** is divided into three main sections: the **Name Box**, the function buttons, and the **Formula Bar**.

This terminology can be a bit confusing because both the text field that displays the content of the currently selected cell and the entire section of the application window below the ribbon and above the workbook window are commonly referred to as the **Formula Bar**. Technically speaking, the **Name Box** is a separate user interface element and the function buttons are a part of the **Formula Bar**.

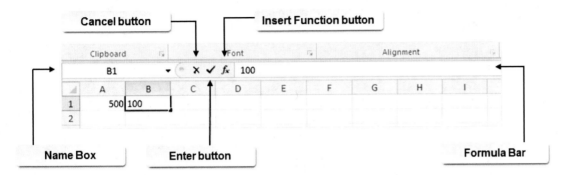

Figure 2-2: The Formula Bar.

The following table describes the **Formula Bar** elements in greater detail.

Formula Bar Element	Description
Name Box	The **Name Box** displays the cell reference for the active cell. If a range of cells is selected, the **Name Box** displays the cell reference for the currently active cell within the range. You can navigate to a cell by entering its reference in the **Name Box**. Excel also allows you to name cells or ranges. If your workbook contains named cells or ranges, you can use the **Name Box** down arrow to access a menu displaying all of the names. Selecting a name from this menu will select the named cell or range.
Cancel button	The **Cancel** button is displayed only when a cell is in Edit mode or Enter mode. Selecting the **Cancel** button will undo any changes you have made to a cell since selecting it and will keep that cell active. Basically, it reverts the call back to its state before you began editing it.
Enter button	The **Enter** button is essentially the same as pressing **Ctrl + Enter**. When you select the **Enter** button, Excel enters whatever content is in the active cell and keeps the cell active.
Insert Function button	The **Insert Function** button opens the **Insert Function** dialog box, providing you with access to a wide variety of pre-existing Excel formulas. You can also access the **Insert Function** button in the **Function Library** group on the **Formulas** tab.
Formula Bar	The **Formula Bar** displays the true content of the active cell, which can be different from what appears in the cell itself. When you place the insertion point in the **Formula Bar**, the active cell enters Edit mode, allowing you to add or edit cell content directly in the **Formula Bar**.

Elements of Excel Formulas

The first rule of using formulas in Excel is that all formulas begin with an equal sign. This may seem a bit counterintuitive at first as you are used to seeing figures on both sides of a formula when it's written out. But, Excel displays formula results in cells, which takes care of the result side of the equal sign. So, how do you write the expression side of formulas? You enter that after the equal sign.

To understand this better, let's first look at a basic mathematical formula. Formulas basically consist of an expression on one side of the equal sign and a result on the other. Expressions consist of a series of constants, variables, and mathematical operators. Operators indicate where to perform such basic computations as adding, subtracting, multiplying, dividing, calculating exponents, and so on. Here are the basic elements of a mathematical formula as written on paper.

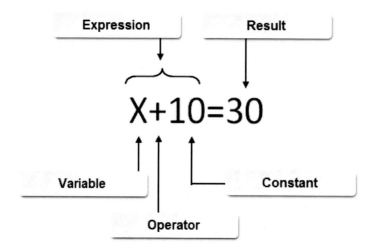

Figure 2-3: A basic mathematical formula.

Excel formulas work pretty much the same way. When you enter a formula in a worksheet cell, the cell displays the result. The equal sign and the mathematical expression make up the content that's actually entered in the cell. In Excel formulas, you can think of constants as numbers you manually enter into formulas and variables as references to other cells. When you manually type a number into an Excel formula, that number remains the same unless you manually edit it. When you enter a cell reference in an Excel formula, the result of the calculation will change if you change the value in the reference cell.

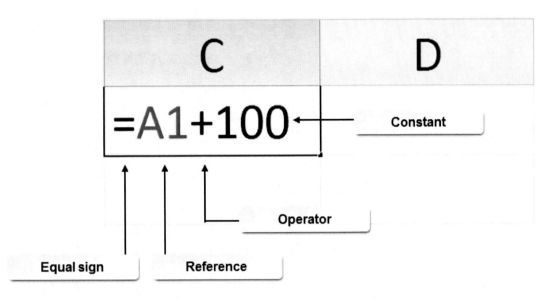

Figure 2-4: An Excel formula.

Basic Excel formulas consist of the following elements: the equal sign, constants, references, and mathematical operators.

Excel Formula Element	Description
Equal sign	The equal sign defines cell content as a formula. The equal sign tells Excel to perform a calculation based on the formula components and then to display the result of the calculation in the cell. All formulas in Excel must start with an equal sign.
Constants	Numbers or text that do not change unless manually entered.
References	Basically the variables in Excel formulas. When you include a reference to a cell or a range, the value(s) from that cell or range are used by Excel to perform the calculation.
Mathematical operators	Symbols that specify the kind of calculation that Excel should perform on the elements of a formula.

Common Mathematical Operators

Excel uses a set of the most commonly used mathematical operators to perform a wide variety of calculations. These are simply symbols Excel uses to identify the calculations it should perform.

Mathematical Operator	Symbol	Function
Parentheses	( )	Groups a set of constants, references, and operators into a single value within a formula.
Caret	^	Exponent
Asterisk	*	Multiplication
Forward slash	/	Division
Plus sign	+	Addition
Minus sign	-	Subtraction

The Order of Operations

Excel gives precedence to certain mathematical operators over others. So, it is important that you understand how Excel will compute a formula before you create one to ensure Excel will perform the calculation exactly as you want it to. Do you remember the acronym PEMDAS from middle school math? If so, you're already familiar with how Excel performs calculations. PEMDAS stands for: Parentheses, Exponents, Multiplication, Division, Addition, and Subtraction. This is the order in which Excel will perform calculations in all formulas. In Excel, multiplication and division, and addition and subtraction carry the same weight in the order of operations.

Note: A common method for remembering the order of operations is to memorize the expression "Please excuse my dear Aunt Sally."

In addition to the PEMDAS sequencing, it's important to understand that Excel also reads formulas from left to right. So, if two or more operators fall in the same order of precedence, such as in a formula with both the addition and the subtraction operators, Excel will perform the first calculation it encounters first.

Note: While often used for subtraction, the minus sign (−) can also be used to denote a negative value. In these cases, the minus sign takes greater precedence than exponents, allowing you to calculate the exponential value of a negative number. Percentage signs (%) also take higher precedence than exponents.

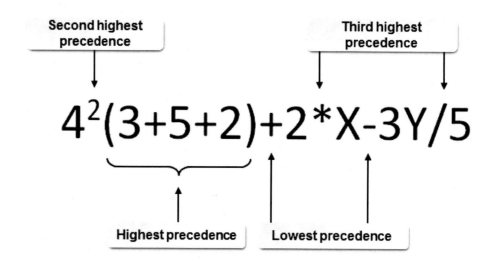

Figure 2-5: Excel performs mathematical computations in a specific order.

Reference Operators

Mathematical operators aren't the only type of operator you will use to work with the data in your workbooks. In fact, there are four different kinds of operators you can use to perform calculations. *Reference operators* are one of the most important. Reference operators tell Excel which cell or range values to use as variables in your formulas. There are three reference operators: the comma, the colon, and the space.

Reference Operator	Symbol	Function
Comma	,	The comma is used as a union operator, which tells Excel to include each reference in a series of references. This is similar to how you would use a comma when writing a serial list; you are telling Excel to include each of the references. So, A1,B3,C5 tells Excel to include the values in each of these three cells.
Colon	:	The colon is used as a range operator, which you've already seen when selecting a range of cells. The colon tells Excel to include all cells in a range between the cell references on either side of the colon. For example, A1:A10 tells Excel to include the values in every cell from A1 to cell A10.
Space	N/A	A blank space is an intersection operator. This tells Excel to look for a value in the cell where two ranges intersect. For example, C1:C5 A3:E3 tells Excel to look for the value in the cell where these two ranges intersect, which in this case would be the value in cell C3.

Note: Excel only reads a blank space as an intersection operator if no other operator is present between cell or range references. If you enter another reference operator in between the cell or range references, Excel will read the operator and ignore the spaces. So, A1:A3, A5, A6 is the same, to Excel, as A1:A3,A5,A6. Here, the spaces don't matter because of the commas. Excel will not look for the intersection, which in this case makes sense as the cells don't actually intersect.

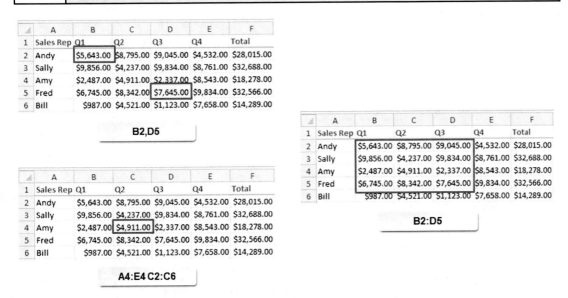

Figure 2-6: Reference operators and how Excel interprets them.

Access the Checklist tile on your LogicalCHOICE course screen for reference information and job aids on How to Create Formulas.

ACTIVITY 2-1
Creating Worksheet Formulas

Data Files

C:\091018Data\Performing Calculations\new_product_income_xlsx

Before You Begin

Excel 2010 is open.

Scenario

My Footprint Sports plans to introduce four new products. Company management wants you to analyze the projected sales figures to determine how much the company can plan to profit from the new items. You have entered the sales estimates into an Excel worksheet. Now, you must use Excel formulas to get Excel to perform the calculations for you.

---

1. Open the **new_product_income_xlsx** file.
   a) Select **File→Open**.
   b) In the **Open** dialog box, navigate to the **C:\091018Data\Performing Calculations** folder.
   c) Select the **new_product_income.xlsx** file and then select **Open**.

2. Calculate net sales based on the sales estimates for each product.
   a) Select cell **B10**.
   b) Type *=b6+b7+b8+b9* and press **Enter**.

6	Backpack	2886
7	Tent with screen room	6323
8	Knee pads	5334
9	Mountain bike	7597
10	Net Sales	22140
11		
12	Gross Sales	
13	Expenses	4585
14	Profit	

 Note: Although Excel displays cell and range references, and many other elements of formulas and functions, in all capital letters, it is not necessary to type them in all capital letters. Excel's functionality enables it to determine what is a formula or function and what is standard text based on the context of your cell data. Excel will automatically display formulas and functions in all capital letters, even if you type them as lowercase letters.

   c) Verify the sum of the values in the range **B6:B9** is displayed in cell **B10**.

3. Calculate gross sales by adding tax to the net sales.
   a) Select cell **B12**.
   b) Type *=b10+(b10*e5)* and press **Enter**.

c) Verify that Excel performed the calculation as expected.

5		Est. Sales
6	Backpack	2886
7	Tent with screen room	6323
8	Knee pads	5334
9	Mountain bike	7597
10	Net Sales	22140
11		
12	Gross Sales	23911.2
13	Expenses	4585
14	Profit	

4. Subtract expenses from net sales to calculate the estimated profit on the new product sales.
   a) Select cell **B14**.
   b) Type *=b10-b13* and press **Enter**.
   c) Verify that Excel performed the calculation as expected.

5		Est. Sales
6	Backpack	2886
7	Tent with screen room	6323
8	Knee pads	5334
9	Mountain bike	7597
10	Net Sales	22140
11		
12	Gross Sales	23911.2
13	Expenses	4585
14	Profit	17555
15		

5. Save the file as *my_new_product_income.xlsx* and close the workbook.
   a) Select **File→Save As**.
   b) In the **Save As** dialog box, in the **File name** field, type *my_new_product_income* and select **Save**.
   c) Close the workbook.

TOPIC B

Insert Functions

You've seen how using formulas in Excel can shift the burden of performing mathematical computations from you to the computer. And, it's easy to see how this functionality can be highly useful. But at some point, you will likely need to use some pretty complex formulas that involve numerous cell and range references. Even as a relative newbie to the Excel world, you can probably imagine that writing such formulas can be messy and complicated. And you'd be right. Additionally, there are likely to be formulas you use so frequently that you get sick and tired or writing the same formula over and over again. So, what should do in these cases?

Fortunately, Excel 2010 provides you with the ability to create complex formulas quickly and easily by using a massive set of built-in formulas. Excel includes functionality to help you fill in and interpret these formulas, allowing you to focus more on the information you need to extract from your data and less on building impossibly complex formulas. Taking the time to learn how to use this functionality now will save you time, effort, and possibly a few headaches.

Functions

In Excel, *functions* are simply built-in, predefined formulas that you can quickly and easily insert into worksheet cells. Like formulas, all functions begin with an equal sign. Unlike formulas, in functions the equal sign is followed by the function name and then a set of *arguments* in parentheses, which are separated by commas. Arguments can be cell references, constants, formulas, or even other functions or logical values. Functions use their arguments in specific ways to calculate a result. The function name is typically the name, or an abbreviated version, of the actual mathematical function. For example, you would use the SUM function to find the sum of a group of numbers and you would use the EXP function to calculate an exponential expression. Each function has its own specific structure and order of arguments. You can manually type functions into worksheet cells or you can enter them by using various commands and dialog boxes.

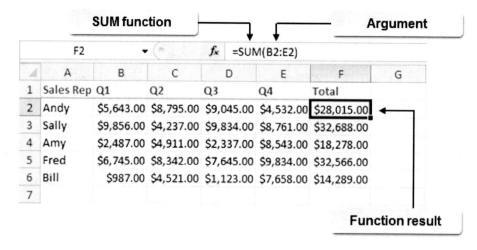

Figure 2-7: The SUM function with a single argument displayed.

The Function Library Group

Excel 2010 provides you with a central location for accessing all of its available functions: the **Function Library** group. The **Function Library** group contains a set of menus that organizes

Excel functions according to specific categories for ease of reference. The **Function Library** group also provides you with access to the **Insert Function** button, which is the same as the **Insert Function** button on the **Formula Bar**, and the AutoSum feature. You can access the **Function Library** group on the **Formulas** tab.

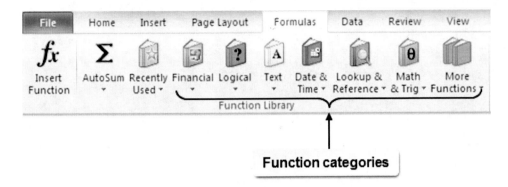

Function categories

Figure 2-8: The Function Library group.

The following table provides a brief description of the function categories in the **Function Library** group.

Category	Provides You with Access To
Recently Used	The functions you have most recently used. When you first install Excel, you can access a set of commonly used functions from this menu.
Financial	Functions used to perform business calculations, such as determining loan repayment figures, determining the future value or net present value of an investment, and calculating asset depreciation.
Logical	Functions that determine if an argument is true or false or if it meets other logical conditions.
Text	Functions that change text values, such as making text all capital letters or converting numbers into dollar amounts.
Date & Time	Functions that allow you to incorporate dates and times into calculations. You might use these, for example, to determine how many work days occur between two specific dates.
Lookup & Reference	Functions that allow you to look up a particular cell value or reference from a range or table given specific criteria.
Math & Trig	Formulas that perform any number of mathematical or trigonometric calculations.
More Functions	A set of menus that contain some higher-level and less commonly used functions, such as engineering and statistical functions.

The Insert Function Dialog Box

The **Insert Function** dialog box allows you to search for and insert into cells any of the available functions in Excel 2010. The **Insert Function** dialog box also displays a brief description of whatever function you have selected and provides a link to open the **Excel Help** window, which automatically displays help content on the currently selected function when you select the link. You can access the **Insert Function** dialog box by selecting the **Insert Function** button either on the **Formula Bar** or in the **Function Library** group.

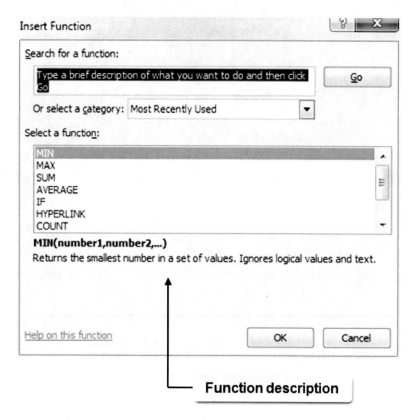

Figure 2-9: The Insert Function dialog box.

The following table describes the various elements of the **Insert Function** dialog box.

Insert Function Dialog Box Element	Use This To
Search for a function field	Enter a description of what you would like a function to do. For example, you could type "add numbers together" or "find the average of a set of numbers." The **Insert Function** dialog box will use this as a search query to find the appropriate function.
Go button	Execute a function search.
Or select a category drop-down menu.	Filter the available functions by category. If you perform a search, this menu defaults to the **Recommended** setting and the search results will appear in the **Select a function** menu. Even if you've entered a search query, if you change the setting here to any category other than **Recommended**, the **Select a function** menu displays all functions in the selected category, effectively ignoring the search query. Hence the word "or" in the name.
Select a function menu	View a list of available functions depending on your search query or your selection in the **Or select a category** drop-down menu.
Function description	View a brief description of the currently selected function.
Help on this function link	Open the **Excel Help** window to display an article about the currently selected function.

The Function Arguments Dialog Box

When you insert a function using the categorized menus in the **Function Library** group or the **Insert Function** dialog box, Excel displays the **Function Arguments** dialog box. You can use this dialog box to enter the required and optional arguments for the function, view descriptions of the function and its arguments, and view a preview of the function results given the currently entered arguments. The **Help on this function** link performs the same task here as it does in the **Insert Function** dialog box.

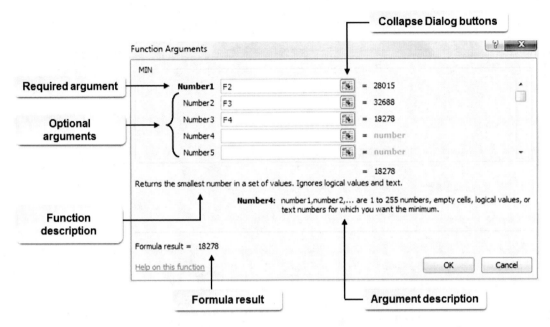

Figure 2-10: The Function Arguments dialog box assists you with the process of entering function arguments.

The following table describes the various elements of the **Function Arguments** dialog box.

Function Arguments Dialog Box Element	Use This To
Required argument fields	Enter the required arguments for the function. The required argument names are displayed in bold text.
Optional argument fields	Enter the desired optional arguments for the function. The optional argument names are displayed in non-bold text.
Collapse Dialog button	Minimize the **Function Arguments** dialog box to graphically select cell and range references directly on your worksheets. This command appears in numerous dialog boxes, wherever you have the option of manually selecting a cell or range.
Function description	View a brief description of the function.
Argument description	View a brief description of the currently selected argument.
Formula result	Preview the function result given the currently entered arguments.

Graphical Cell and Range Reference Entry

Excel 2010 provides you with a useful graphical method for entering cell and range references for a number of purposes, including for use in formulas and functions. Whenever you need to enter a cell or range reference, you have the option of typing the reference manually or selecting the reference graphically right from the worksheet. This is why the **Function Arguments** dialog box provides the

Collapse Dialog buttons . These minimize the dialog box, providing you with easier access to your worksheets for the purpose of graphically selecting references. To graphically select a reference, you can simply select the cell or the range with mouse clicks or by dragging the mouse (or by using the appropriate equivalent action on a touch-screen device), and then either press the **Enter** key or

select the **Expand Dialog** button in the minimized dialog box.

> **Note:** If you are manually typing a formula or function, once you've graphically selected a range, you can simply enter the next formula element or type a comma and then enter the next function argument.

After you graphically select a cell or range reference, Excel displays the "dancing ants" around your selection to help you verify that you have selected the correct cell or range. When you have finished entering the reference, the dancing ants go away.

Range entered in function

AVERAGE		X ✓ *fx*	=AVERAGE(B2:E5)		
	A	B	C	D	E	F
1	Sales Rep	Q1	Q2	Q3	Q4	Total
2	Andy	$5,643.00	$8,795.00	$9,045.00	$4,532.00	$28,015.00
3	Sally	$9,856.00	$4,237.00	$9,834.00	$8,761.00	$32,688.00
4	Amy	$2,487.00	$4,911.00	$2,337.00	$8,543.00	$18,278.00
5	Fred	$6,745.00	$8,342.00	$7,645.00	$9,834.00	$32,566.00
6	Bill	$987.00	$4,521.00	$1,123.00	$7,658.00	$14,289.00
7						

Graphically selected range

Figure 2-11: Graphically selecting cell and range references is a quick and easy alternative to typing them.

The AutoSum Feature

Adding up the values in a row or a column is the single most common mathematical calculation most people perform in Excel. As such, Excel provides you with a fast and easy way to do this: the AutoSum feature. The AutoSum feature allows you to calculate the total of the values in a row or a column simply by selecting a single button and then pressing **Enter** or **Tab**. Using the AutoSum feature inserts a SUM function in the active cell.

The AutoSum feature will automatically try to guess which cells you would like to add together if you use it on a cell in a row or a column that contains values. You can also manually edit the group of cells or the range that the AutoSum feature should include as arguments in the SUM function. If there are no values in the row and the column associated with a cell and you insert the SUM function, you must manually enter the arguments in the SUM function.

You can access the AutoSum feature by selecting **Formulas→Function Library→AutoSum** or by using the **Alt + =** keyboard shortcut. For ease of access purposes, Excel also displays the **AutoSum** button in the **Editing** group on the **Home** tab.

> **Note:** You do not have to use the AutoSum feature to insert a SUM function. You can also simply type the SUM function into a cell or access the SUM function from the **Math & Trig** menu in the **Function Library** group.

▲	A	B	C	D	
1	Sales Rep	Q1	Q2	Q3	
2	Andy	$5,643.00	$8,795.00	$9,045.00	
3	Sally	$9,856.00	$4,237.00	$9,834.00	
4	Amy	$2,487.00	$4,911.00	$2,337.00	
5	Fred	$6,745.00	$8,342.00	$7,645.00	
6	Bill	$987.00	$4,521.00	$1,123.00	
7		=SUM(B2:B6)			
8		SUM(**number1**, [number2], ...)			
9					

Figure 2-12: The AutoSum feature will try to guess which cells you want to include as arguments.

Other Commonly Used Functions

The **AutoSum** button in the **Function Library** group also provides you with quick access to some other commonly used Excel functions. When you select the **AutoSum** down arrow, Excel displays a menu that allows you to insert one of these other common functions into the active cell.

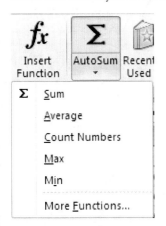

Figure 2-13: The other commonly used functions available from the AutoSum button.

You can use the functions available from the **AutoSum** down arrow to perform the following tasks.

Function	Use To
Sum	Add the values entered in the cells that are specified in the arguments.
AVERAGE	Calculate the average of the values entered in the cells specified in the argument.
COUNT	Find the number of cells, out of those that have been specified in the arguments, that contain numeric entries.
MAX	Find the largest single numeric value out of all of the values entered in the cells specified in the arguments.
MIN	Find the smallest single numeric value out of all of the values entered in the cells specified in the arguments.

Basic Function Syntax

In order to understand exactly how an Excel function works, you must understand its *syntax*. An argument's syntax is simply the structure necessary to properly express the function and to define its arguments. As stated earlier, all Excel functions begin with an equal sign followed by the function name. The function name is followed by a set of parentheses that contains the function's arguments; the arguments are separated by commas. Remember that depending on the particular function you are using, arguments can include constants, cell or range references, logical values such as TRUE or FALSE, formulas, and even other functions.

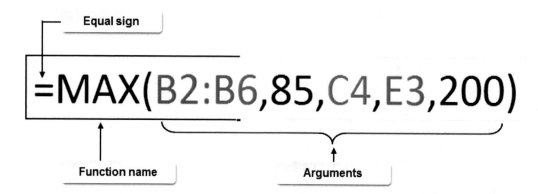

Figure 2-14: The basic elements of an Excel function.

Functions can contain both required and optional arguments. In function syntax, optional arguments are notated by using square brackets [ ]. The SUM function, as an example, contains one required argument and up to 254 optional arguments. Excel must have at least one number to return a result. Excel can sum up to 255 values with a single SUM function. So the first argument (value) is required, and the rest are optional.

Each function has a unique syntax and requires different specific arguments. If all of the arguments for a function are valid, the function will return a result in a cell. If one or more of the arguments in a function is invalid, Excel will return an error, which you will have to correct. Let's take a look at the syntax for each of the commonly used functions we've mentioned so far.

The SUM Function

Syntax: =SUM(number 1, [number 2], ...)

 Note: The ellipsis (...) in the SUM function syntax indicates that the same type of argument can carry out up to the maximum number of arguments for the function. In this case, it's up to 255 arguments, which is the maximum number of supported arguments in an Excel 2010 function.

Description: Adds the values specified by the arguments. For this function, the arguments can be constants, cell or range references, or both.

The following table includes examples of the SUM function in action.

To Add These Numbers	Enter This Function
5, 9, 11, and 20	=SUM(5, 9, 11, 20)
The values in cells A1 through A10	=SUM(A1:A10)
The values in cells A1 through A10, in cell B3, and in cell D17	=SUM(A1:A10, B3, D17)
The values in cells A1 through A10, in cell B3, in cell D17, and the numbers 14 and 7	=SUM(A1:A10, B3, D17, 14, 7)

The AVERAGE Function

Syntax: =AVERAGE(number 1, [number 2], ...)

Description: Adds the values specified by the arguments and then divides the total by the number of individual values. In other words, the AVERAGE function calculates the average (arithmetic mean) of the specified values. For this function, the arguments can be constants, cell or range references, or both.

The following table includes examples of the AVERAGE function in action.

To Find the Average of These Numbers	Enter This Function
5, 9, 11, and 20	=AVERAGE(5, 9, 11, 20)
The values in cells A1 through A10	=AVERAGE(A1:A10)
The values in cells A1 through A10, in cell B3, and in cell D17	=AVERAGE(A1:A10, B3, D17)
The values in cells A1 through A10, in cell B3, in cell D17, and the numbers 14 and 7	=AVERAGE(A1:A10, B3, D17, 14, 7)

The COUNT Function

Syntax: =COUNT(value 1, [value 2], ...)

Description: Counts the number of cells specified in the arguments that contain a numeric entry. For this function, the arguments can be cell or range references, or both.

The following table includes examples of the COUNT function in action.

To Count the Number of Numeric Entries in These Cells	Enter This Function
A1 through A10	=COUNT(A1:A10)
A1 through A10, B7, and F11	=COUNT(A1:A10, B7, F11)
All cells from A1 through D10	=COUNT(A1:D10)

 Note: The COUNT function will also count constants if you include them as arguments. However, it is more intended to count numeric cell entries.

The MAX Function

Syntax: =MAX(number 1, [number 2], ...)

Description: Returns the largest numeric value out of any numbers entered into the cells specified by the arguments and any constants specified in the arguments. For this function, the arguments can be constants, cell or range references, or both.

The following table includes examples of the MAX function in action.

To Return the Largest Numeric Value from These Sources	Enter This Function
Cells A1 through A10	=MAX(A1:A10)
Cells A1 through A10, B13, and C22	=MAX(A1:A10, B13, C22)
Cells A1 through A10, and the numbers 15, 22, and 78	=MAX(A1:A10, 15, 22, 78)

The MIN Function

Syntax: =MIN(number 1, [number 2], ...)

Description: Returns the smallest numeric value out of any numbers entered into the cells specified by the arguments and any constants specified by the arguments. For this function, the arguments can be constants, cell or range references, or both.

The following table includes examples of the MIN function in action.

To Return the Smallest Numeric Value from These Sources	Enter This Function
Cells A1 through A10	=MIN(A1:A10)
Cells A1 through A10, B13, and C22	=MIN(A1:A10, B13, C22)
Cells A1 through A10, and the numbers 15, 22, and 78	=MIN(A1:A10, 15, 22, 78)

 Note: If you want to know more about how Excel handles dates in calculations, view the LearnTO **Calculate Dates in Excel** presentation from the **LearnTO** tile on the LogicalCHOICE Course screen.

The Formula AutoComplete Feature

With the enormous array of functions available in Excel 2010, it may seem overwhelming to have to remember the names and the syntax of a large number of functions. And, perhaps you don't have the time to search through the various menus and submenus in the **Function Library** group. Additionally, what happens if you type the wrong function name, misspell the function, or make a mistake entering arguments? In large workbooks containing a lot of complex functions and formulas, navigating these scenarios could quickly become a nightmare. The good news is that Excel 2010 includes a feature that can help eliminate all of these issues: the Formula AutoComplete feature.

The Formula AutoComplete feature is a dynamic feature that enables you to select and enter functions without having to remember specific function names or worry about misspellings. When you type an equal sign into a cell, and then begin typing the name of a function, Excel displays a pop-up menu displaying all of the available functions that begin with the characters you have already typed. This allows you to select the desired function, and then simply enter the required arguments to complete it. The Formula AutoComplete feature also displays a tooltip that describes whatever function you select from the pop-up menu.

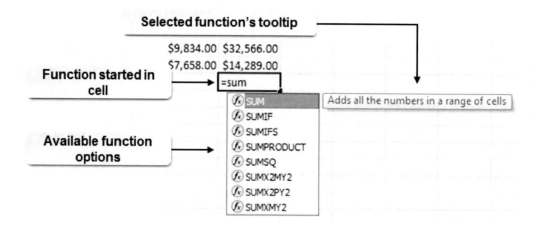

Figure 2-15: Excel displays the available function options and their descriptions as you type the function name.

The Formula AutoComplete feature also provides you with assistance when entering function arguments. As you enter the arguments for the selected formula, Excel displays a different tooltip that highlights the specific argument you're currently entering. This helps you keep track of which arguments you've entered and which ones you still need to enter. When you're done entering all necessary arguments, simply press **Enter** or **Tab**, and Excel will automatically add the closing parenthesis, enter the function, and navigate to the next cell.

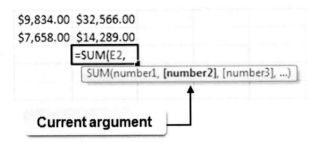

Figure 2-16: This tooltip highlights where you are within the function syntax.

 Access the Checklist tile on your LogicalCHOICE course screen for reference information and job aids on How to Insert Functions.

ACTIVITY 2-2
Inserting Functions

Data File

C:\091018Data\Performing Calculations\sales_contest.xlsx

Before You Begin

Excel 2010 is open.

Scenario

You've launched a sales contest to reward My Footprint Sports' best performing sales reps. To track their progress, you created a worksheet to store and perform calculations on the sales figures for each of the reps. You're trying to analyze the numbers to determine which sales reps will win prizes. You want to start by calculating each rep's total sales, average quarterly sales, and highest and lowest quarterly sales.

1. Open the **sales_contest.xlsx** workbook file.

2. Calculate the total sales for the first two sales reps: Del Prentice and Christina Chirillo.
    a) Select cell **F7**.
    b) Select **Formulas→Function Library→AutoSum**.
    c) Verify that the cell range **B7:E7** is selected on the worksheet and that it appears in the active cell and in the **Formula Bar**.
    d) Press **Enter**.
    e) Perform the same calculation for Christina Chirillo.

3. Calculate the average quarterly sales for the same two sales reps.
    a) Select cell **G7** and type *=av*
    b) From the **AutoComplete** pop-up menu, double-click **AVERAGE**.
    c) On the worksheet, select the range **B7:E7** and press **Enter**.
    d) Perform the same calculation for Christina Chirillo.

4. Determine the highest quarterly sales total for the same two sales reps.
    a) Select cell **H7**.
    b) Select **Formulas→Function Library→Insert Function**.
    c) In the **Insert Function** dialog box, in the **Search for a function** field, type *max* and select **Go**.
    d) In the **Select a function** menu, ensure **MAX** is selected, and then select **OK**.
    e) In the **Function Arguments** dialog box, to the right of the **Number 1** field, select the **Collapse Dialog** button.
    f) On the worksheet, select the range **B7:E7** and press **Enter**.

    > **Note:** You may need to move the **Insert Function** dialog box to select the range.

    g) In the **Function Arguments** dialog box, select **OK**.
    h) Repeat the process for Christina Chirillo.

5. Determine the lowest quarterly sales for the same two sales reps.

   a) Select cell I7.

   b) Select **Formulas→Function Library→AutoSum down arrow→Min**.

   c) On the worksheet, select the range **B7:E7** and press **Enter**.

   d) Ensure that cell I8 is selected and then select **Formulas→Function Library→More Functions→Statistical→MIN**.

   e) In the **Function Arguments** dialog box, to the right of the **Number 1** field, select the **Collapse Dialog** button.

   f) Select the range **B8:E8** and press **Enter**.

   g) In the **Function Arguments** dialog box, select **OK**.

6. Save the workbook to the **C:\091018Data\Performing Calculations** folder as *my_sales_contest.xlsx*

TOPIC C

Reuse Formulas

Those who work with Excel workbooks often find themselves regularly using the same formulas over and over. For example, if you're totaling rows of sales figures for individual sales associates to calculate their commissions, you will likely have to apply the same formula or function to each row. If your organization employs hundreds, or even thousands, of sales associates, this could be an incredibly lengthy, mundane process. Although the AutoSum feature may make part of this task simpler, you would still have to apply it to each row and then use another function to calculate commissions. Wouldn't it be far easier to create one set of formulas or functions and then apply those to all of the rows? You can do this in Excel.

Excel, much like a word processing application, provides you with a number of methods to reuse nearly any of your content, including formulas and functions, basically by using a variety of copy and paste techniques. This functionality represents one of the most useful features of Excel and will, with absolute certainty, save you time. By reusing your content, you can eliminate the hassle and reduce the likelihood of entering numerous errors in your workbooks. All of this will allow you to avoid repetitive tasks and hours of troubleshooting so you can focus on more important things.

Formulas and the Cut, Copy, and Paste Commands

As with other worksheet content, if you want to reuse your Excel formulas and functions, you can do so by using the **Cut**, **Copy**, and **Paste** commands. By default, if a cell contains a formula or a function and you cut or copy its content to the clipboard, when you paste the content to another cell, Excel pastes the formula in the destination cell. Although the destination cell will display the result of the formula or function, as it did in the source cell, the content is still the formula. This functionality forms the basis of how you can reuse your formulas and functions throughout your worksheets and workbooks.

Drag-and-Drop Editing

In addition to using the **Cut**, **Copy**, and **Paste** commands to move content, you can use Excel's drag-and-drop editing functionality. When you select a cell or a range, the cell or range is displayed with a solid black border around it. If you place the mouse pointer over the black border anywhere

other than above the **fill handle**, the mouse pointer is displayed with a move icon. When the move pointer appears, you can click and drag the selected cell or range and drop it in place anywhere else on the worksheet. This effectively cuts and pastes all content within the selection to the new location.

If you press and hold **Ctrl** while performing this procedure, the mouse pointer changes into the copy pointer. Using the copy pointer, you can drag a copy of the content in the selected cell(s) to a new location. This is the same as copying and pasting the content.

The Paste Options

Excel 2010 provides you with a number of different options for pasting copied content into other cells. This is because there will be occasions where you want to paste certain elements of a cell's content into another cell, but not the exact contents. Let's look at an example to clarify this. Remember that what is displayed in your worksheet cells isn't necessarily what's in the cells. If a cell contains a formula, it displays the result of the calculations, but its content is the formula itself. So, what if you want to paste the numerical value of the calculation's result in another cell simply as a number, without bringing the formula along for the ride? These types of situations are where Excel's paste options come in handy.

When you copy a cell's contents to the clipboard, a number of paste options become available from the **Paste** drop-down menu, which you can access from the **Paste** down arrow in the **Clipboard** group. These options are also available from the **Paste Options** button if you paste the content by using the **Paste** button or the **Ctrl+V** keyboard shortcut. If you access the paste options from the ribbon, placing the mouse pointer over the various option icons will display a temporary preview of what the content will look like if you select that option.

 Note: The paste options are not available if you cut a cell's content. They are available only when you copy and paste.

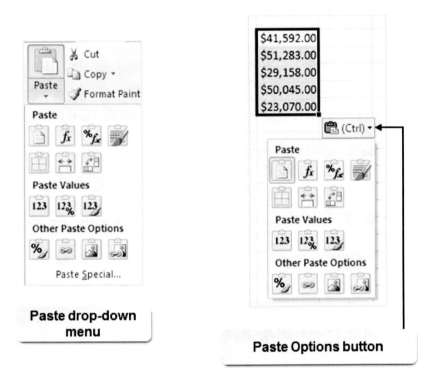

Figure 2-17: The paste options are available from both the ribbon and the Paste Options button.

The following table describes the various paste options.

Paste Option	Will Paste
Paste	All of a cell's contents.
Formulas	Just the formula from the copied cells.
Formulas & Number Formatting	The formula and any applied number formatting from the copied cells.
Keep Source Formatting	All of the copied cells' content along with all applied formatting.
No Borders	All of the copied cells' content and formatting except for the border formatting.
Keep Source Column Widths	All of the copied cells' content and formatting. This option will also adjust the column width for the column the destination cells are in to match the column width of the copied cell.
Transpose	All of the contents and formatting from a group of copied cells. This option will also switch rows to columns and vice versa.

Paste Option	Will Paste
Values	Just the values from the copied cells without formulas or formatting.
Values & Number Formatting	Just the values and any number formatting from the copied cells without formulas or other types of applied formatting.
Values & Source Formatting	Just the values and any applied formatting from the source cells without the formulas.
Formatting	Just the formatting from the copied cells without any cell content.
Paste Link	The content from the selected cells into the new cells and will create a link between the cells. If you make any changes to the copied cells, those changes will be reflected in the new cells. This option works only for certain types of content, such as formulas that contain absolute references.
Picture	The displayed content from the copied cells as a picture. The pasted content will no longer behave like values, formulas, functions, text, and so on.
Linked Picture	The displayed content from the copied cells as a picture and create a link between the picture and the copied cells. The pasted content will no longer behave like values, formulas, functions, text, and so on, but changes made in the copied cells will be reflected in the pasted picture.

Note: Some of the paste options described in this table cover features or options that have not yet been discussed. Most of these will be covered either later in this course or in other courses in the Excel 2010 series.

The Paste Special Options

Excel 2010 provides you with several other paste options that you can access by using the **Paste Special** dialog box. Here you will find many of the same paste options that have already been covered, but you will also find a few more. These include the ability to paste review markup such as comments and validation formatting (which restricts the type of data that a user can enter into cells) along with several options for performing basic mathematical operations. You can access the **Paste Special** dialog box by selecting **Home→Clipboard→Paste down arrow→Paste Special**.

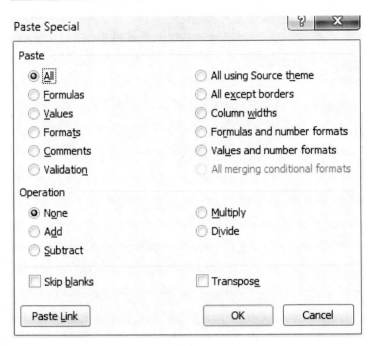

Figure 2-18: The Paste Special dialog box provides you with access to additional paste options.

The following table describes some of the Paste Special options that are not available with the other paste options.

Paste Special Option	Description
Add	Adds the value in the copied cell to the value entered in the destination cell.
Subtract	Subtracts the value in the copied cell from the value entered in the destination cell.
Multiply	Multiplies the value in the destination cell by the value in the copied cell.
Divide	Divides the value in the destination cell by the value in the copied cell.
Skip blanks	If the range you copy includes blank cells. These will be omitted when you paste the content to the destination range of cells.

Relative References

Before you explore how cutting, copying, and pasting relate to reusing formulas, you will first need to understand how cell and range references work. In Excel, there are three types of references: relative, absolute, and mixed. *Relative references* are the default in Excel. A relative reference is a cell or a range reference that will change when you move or copy a formula from one cell to another. In other words, the reference is relative to the location of the cell. To see how this works, take a look at this simple example.

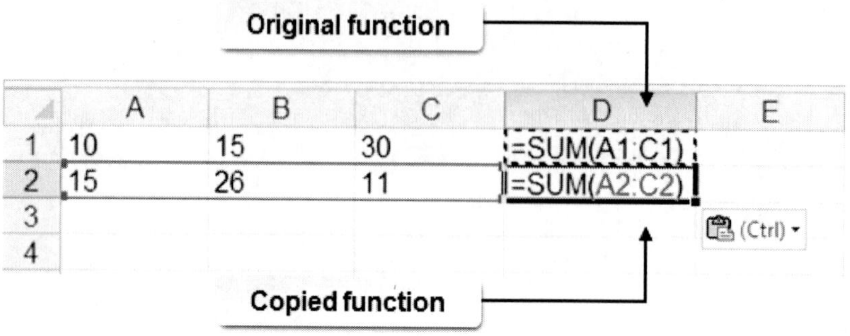

Figure 2-19: With relative references, when you move a formula or function, the cell references change.

In this example, the formula from cell D1 has been copied and pasted into cell D2. The formula in cell D1 adds the values in cells A1, B1, and C1. But because the range reference in the formula is a relative reference, what it's telling Excel is to look at the cell three spaces to the left of the formula, the cell two spaces to the left of the formula, and the cell one space to the left of the formula to find the values to add. So when you copy and paste the formula into cell D2, it still looks for the values in the cells three spaces to the left, two spaces to the left, and one space to the left. This is why the reference has changed from A1:C1 to A2:C2, as those are now the cells the correct number of spaces away from the formula. If you were to paste the same formula into cell D3, the range reference would change to A3:C3, and so on.

Relative references are one of the keys to understanding just how powerful and useful Excel can be. This forms the basis for how Excel can apply the same calculation to thousands of rows and columns of data.

Locating a reference cell In the formula bar, after clicking your reference cell, press F4.

Absolute References

As you've probably guessed, *absolute references* refer to particular cells and do not change when you move or copy formulas to other cells. In Excel, absolute references are indicated by using the dollar sign ($) before the row and column header. So, if A1 is a relative reference, then A1 is an absolute reference. You use absolute references whenever you want to apply a formula to multiple cells but still want part of the calculation to include a value entered into a single cell. Common examples of this include multiplying a sales figure by the sales tax rate or a sales rep's sales totals by the commission rate. Rather than having to enter the same multiplier in every row or column of data, you can simply place that value in a single cell on your worksheet, and then include an absolute reference to that cell in the formula. When you move or copy that formula to the other sales figures, each is now multiplied by the same value.

In the following example, the cells in column D contain formulas that contain relative references. These were copied from cell D2 to the other cells in the column. By default, the cells in column D would display the sales totals for each sales rep for the first two quarters. The formulas in column E are multiplying the sales totals from column D by a fixed rate. In this case, it's the sales commission rate in cell G4. Because the formula in cell E2 contains an absolute reference to cell G4, when copied to cell E3, the formula still references the same cell. Notice, however, that the formula is referencing the sales total in cell D3, not D2, because that is a relative reference in the formula.

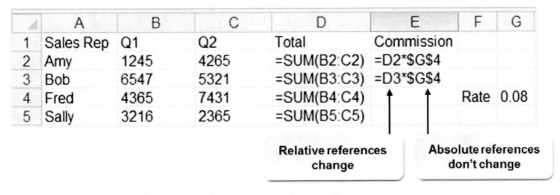

Figure 2-20: Absolute references do not change when copying or moving formulas.

Mixed References

Mixed references are cell or range references in which either the column or the row header is absolute, but the other reference is relative. So, the cell reference A$1 would be a mixed reference. In this example, the column header, A, is relative and will change if used in a formula that is copied or moved to another cell. But, the row header, $1, is absolute, so if you move the formula, it will reference different columns, but in the same row. Mixed references are typically used less than relative and absolute references but they can be quite handy. You would use a mixed reference when you need to copy a formula across multiple rows and columns and you need the formula to look, for example, for values in the same column but in different rows. Let's take a look at a simple example to see how this works.

In the following example, the worksheet contains historical sales figures for different types of vehicles for the years 2011 and 2012. In column B, we've entered a formula that will calculate the sales increase percentage from 2011 to 2012.

	A	B	C	D	E	F
1	Product	Percent Change	2011	2012	2013	2014
2	Cars	=(D2/C2)*100	3500000	3600000		
3	Trucks	=(D3/C3)*100	4000000	4250000		
4	RVs	=(D4/C4)*100	1500000	1750000		

Now, let's say you want to project the sales increases out across 2013 and 2014 based on the current sales trends. Because the percent increase is different for each type of vehicle, you would need the formula to keep looking in column B for the percent change, but you would also need it to change the row it's looking at so each vehicle type's sales are multiplied by the correct percentage. So the cell reference in the formula you enter in E2 would need to contain this reference: $B2. This reference tells the formula to always look in column B but to look in different rows.

	A	B	C	D	E	F
1	Product	Percent Change	2011	2012	2013	2014
2	Cars	=(D2/C2)*100	3500000	3600000	=D2*$B2	=E2*$B2
3	Trucks	=(D3/C3)*100	4000000	4250000	=D3*$B3	=E3*$B3
4	RVs	=(D4/C4)*100	1500000	1750000	=D4*$B4	=E4*$B4

Relative reference | Mixed reference

Figure 2-21: In mixed references, one reference is absolute whereas the other is relative.

Notice that as the formula from cell E1 is copied both across columns and rows, the relative reference changes both the row and the column references, while the mixed reference maintains the same column but changes row references.

 Note: To quickly cycle through relative, absolute, and mixed references in Excel formulas, select the cell with the formula, place the insertion point next to or within the reference in the formula in the **Formula Bar**, and press the **F4** key. If you press the key multiple times, the reference will cycle through all possible combinations.

AutoFill and Formulas

Now that you know how relative, absolute, and mixed references work, and how they affect the reuse of formulas, you're ready to discover one of the single most useful features Excel has to offer. You already know the AutoFill feature can make entering a pattern or a sequential list of alphanumeric characters quick and easy. You can also use the AutoFill feature to quickly and easily copy and paste a formula across columns and rows.

Let's say you have a worksheet that lists quarterly sales for your sales team. You want the final column to display the total sales for each sales rep for the entire year. So you enter a SUM function for the first sales rep in the **Total** column. Now you want to copy and paste that formula, by using relative references, all the way down the **Total** column. If your company has only 5 or 10 sales reps, copying and pasting would likely be just fine. But what if your organization has thousands of sales reps? Copying and pasting the formula could take hours. However, you can also simply select the cell containing the formula and, by using the **fill handle**, drag the formula down the entire column all at once. If there is one trick you remember about Excel, this should be it.

You can also double-click the **fill handle** to automatically fill all cells in a column with a formula or function. This feature does not work to fill across a row. Also, if there are any gaps in your data, the formula or function will not copy all the way down the column. If you have any empty rows in your data, Excel will fill in the column's cells only up to the first empty row.

	A	B	C	D	E	F	G
				fx	=SUM(B2:E2)		
1	Sales Rep	Q1	Q2	Q3	Q4	Total	
2	Andy	$5,643.00	$8,795.00	$9,045.00	$4,532.00	$28,015.00	
3	Sally	$9,856.00	$4,237.00	$9,834.00	$8,761.00	$32,688.00	
4	Amy	$2,487.00	$4,911.00	$2,337.00	$8,543.00	$18,278.00	
5	Fred	$6,745.00	$8,342.00	$7,645.00	$9,834.00	$32,566.00	
6	Bill	$987.00	$4,521.00	$1,123.00	$7,658.00	$14,289.00	
7							
8							

Figure 2-22: The AutoFill feature enables you to copy and paste multiple instances of a formula in one easy step.

Worksheet References

You've seen how Excel formulas can reference cells in various ways on a worksheet. But what if you want to include values from cells on another worksheet in one of your formulas? Excel workbooks often contain multiple worksheets. It would be a waste of time and effort to have to copy and paste data from one worksheet just to be able to use that data in calculations on another. Fortunately, you don't have to. Excel 2010 allows you to create references to cells on other worksheets for use in a number of different ways, including as references in functions and formulas.

Creating a reference to cells on another worksheet is as simple as adding the worksheet name and an exclamation point directly before the cell or range reference. Let's look at a simple example using the default worksheet names you would find in a new blank workbook. If you have a formula on Sheet1 and you would like that formula to reference cell D3 from the worksheet Sheet2, you would include the following reference in the formula: Sheet2!D3. Excel allows you to rename your worksheets, so be sure to include the correct worksheet name when creating references to cells on other worksheets.

Note: You can also graphically select cells and ranges on other worksheets for use as references in formulas. You do the same as you would for references on the same worksheet, except you switch to the correct worksheet to select the cell or range.

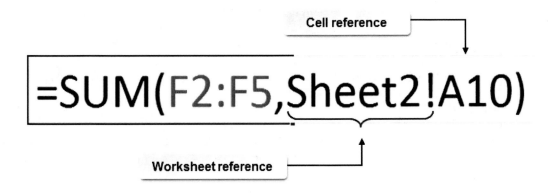

Figure 2-23: A reference to a cell on another worksheet.

Access the Checklist tile on your LogicalCHOICE course screen for reference information and job aids on How to Reuse Formulas and Functions.

ACTIVITY 2-3
Reusing Functions

Before You Begin

The my_sales_contest.xlsx file is open.

Scenario

You need to complete your analysis of the sales figures for all sales reps so you can announce the sales contest winners at an upcoming meeting. You decide to reuse the functions you have already created for Del Prentice and Christina Chirillo for the remaining sales reps rather than create new functions for each one. Because you also need to provide commission payment figures to the payroll department before the meeting, you decide to use the same worksheet to perform the commission calculations.

---

1. Use the existing functions to calculate the total and average quarterly sales for the remaining sales reps.
   a) Select cell **F8**.
   b) Press **Ctrl+C** to copy the cell's contents to the clipboard.
   c) Select the range **F9:F30** and then press **Ctrl+V** to paste the function to the selected range of cells.
   d) Verify that the function has been copied into the remaining cells in the column.
   e) Select cell **G8**.

   f) Place the mouse pointer over the **fill handle** until it displays as a thin black plus symbol. +

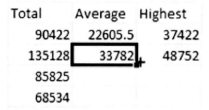

   g) Drag the **fill handle** down the column until the selected range is **G8:G30** and then release the mouse button.
   h) Verify that the function has been copied into the remaining cells in the column.

2. Use the AutoFill feature to drag the functions for the highest and lowest quarterly sales figures down to fill the remaining cells in columns **H** and **I**.

3. Calculate the annual sales commission figure for Del Prentice by using the commission rate in cell **M6**.
   a) Select cell **J7**.
   b) Type *=f7*m6* and press **Enter**.

4. Reuse the formula to calculate the commission for Christina Chirillo.
   a) Select cell **J7**.
   b) Drag the fill handle down to copy the formula to cell **J8**.
   c) Verify the figure that appears in cell **J8** is **0**.

5. Modify the commission formula to include an absolute reference to the commission rate in cell **M6**.

    a) Select cell **J7**.

    b) In the **Formula Bar**, place the insertion point immediately before or after **M6** in the formula.

    c) Press the **F4** key to switch the relative reference to an absolute reference.

    d) Ensure that **M6** is now displayed as **M6** in the **Formula Bar** and press **Enter**.

6. Copy and paste the modified formula from cell **J7** into cell **J8**.

7. Ensure that the formula now returns the appropriate value.

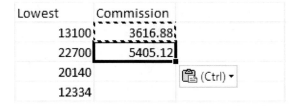

Lowest	Commission
13100	3616.88
22700	5405.12
20140	
12334	

8. Use the AutoFill feature to drag the formula down to the remaining cells in column **J**.

9. Save and close the workbook file.

Summary

In this lesson, you created Excel formulas, inserted functions into cells, and reused formulas and functions in other cells. These basic tasks will form the foundation of your ability to work with and analyze your organizational data. This will enable you to extract actionable organizational intelligence from your data so that you can make sound business decisions.

Which formulas and functions do you see yourself using most in your daily life? How does that relate to your current role?

How do you see the AutoFill feature saving you time and effort? Can you think of uses for it not covered so far?

Note: Check your LogicalCHOICE Course screen for opportunities to interact with your classmates, peers, and the larger LogicalCHOICE online community about the topics covered in this course or other topics you are interested in. From the Course screen you can also access available resources for a more continuous learning experience.

3 Modifying a Worksheet

Lesson Time: 45 minutes

Lesson Objectives

In this lesson, you will modify a worksheet. You will:

- Insert, delete, and adjust cells, columns, and rows.

- Search for and replace data.

- Use proofing and research tools.

Lesson Introduction

From time to time, you'll need to make changes to your worksheets and workbooks. What if the changes you need to make go beyond simply re-entering a formula or updating a value? What if you need to add a whole new column or row to your worksheet? What if that column or row is in the middle of existing data? Also, what if you discover you've made the same mistake over and over? Or, what if you need to check your spelling throughout all worksheets in a workbook?

These days, changes occur rapidly. You'll need to be able to react quickly to keep your workbooks and your worksheet data up-to-date and accurate. And you don't want to waste any of the effort you've already put into developing your workbooks to do so. Excel 2010 provides you with a wide variety of options for making significant changes to your worksheets. This functionality allows you to do so without disturbing the work you've already done. Understanding how this functionality works will help you keep your documents updated without throwing away all of the valuable work you've already done.

TOPIC A

Insert, Delete, and Adjust Cells, Columns, and Rows

Cells, columns, and rows make up the very fabric of Excel worksheets. This is where you store and organize your data, perform calculations, and present results to other people. You'll want to be able to configure the cells, columns, and rows in your worksheets to suit your needs. For example, the amount of text you need to display in a cell may be more than the cell can hold. Or, perhaps, your organization will create a new metric by which certain figures are tracked. To include information on the new metric, you may have to add a row or a column right in the middle of existing data. Or, perhaps, you want to view your data in a different way to focus more on one element of a system that another.

When situations like this arise, you'll need to be able to modify your worksheets to accommodate the need. Fortunately, Excel 2010 provides you with a number of commands and features that allow you to make these kinds of changes. Excel worksheets are dynamic, which allows them to keep up with the changing needs of a wide variety of organizations. Taking the time to learn how to make these kinds of changes will allow you to stay on top of your data and react to an ever-changing world.

The Insert and Delete Options

Adding new information at the end of a column or row is easy. But, what if you need to add a cell, a row, or a column in the middle of existing data? Actually, it's a pretty easy process, and Excel provides you with ready access to the commands to do so. The **Cells** group on the **Home** tab provides you with access to the **Insert** and **Delete** commands. These commands allow you to add a single cell, a group of cells, or even entire rows or columns anywhere you need them.

If you select either the **Insert** or the **Delete** button, Excel will insert or delete whatever you currently have selected. If you select a cell or a group of cells and then select **Insert**, Excel will insert a cell or a group of cells. If you select an entire row and then select **Delete**, Excel will delete the entire row. Excel defaults to pushing cells or rows down to make room for new ones when adding cells or rows. It defaults to pushing them up to fill in the space when you delete them. Excel also defaults to pushing columns to the right to make room for new columns, and pushing them to the left to fill in the space when you delete columns.

The **Insert** and **Delete** options, which you can access by selecting the **Insert down arrow** or the **Delete down arrow** in the **Cells** group, provide you with additional functionality for inserting and deleting cells. If you insert or delete a cell or a group of cells by using either the **Insert Cells** or the **Delete Cells** commands from the drop-down menus, Excel displays either the **Insert** dialog box or the **Delete** dialog box. These provide you with options for shifting cells in a particular direction or inserting or deleting an entire row or column even if you've only selected a cell or group of cells.

 Note: You can also access the **Insert** and **Delete** dialog boxes by right-clicking a selected cell or range, and then selecting either **Insert** or **Delete**.

Figure 3–1: The Insert and Delete dialog boxes give you greater control over how Excel inserts and deletes cells.

Width and Height Adjustments

There will, undoubtedly, be instances in which you need to enter data or formulas in worksheet cells that spill over beyond cell borders. When this happens, you'll need to adjust the size of the cells in your worksheets. To adjust cell sizes, you must either adjust row heights, column widths, or both. Excel 2010 provides you with several options for adjusting cell sizes in your worksheets.

The first method is to simply click and drag row or column borders to adjust them manually. To do this, place the mouse pointer directly over the desired border in either the row or column headers until it appears as a dark line with a double arrow ✚. Then click and drag the border until the row or the column is the desired height or width. When you adjust row and column heights manually, drag either the bottom border of the desired row or the right-hand border of the desired column.

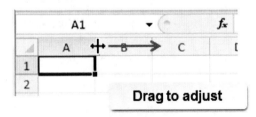

Figure 3–2: Click and drag column or row borders to manually adjust cell size.

You can also manually auto-fit row heights or column widths to match cell content. To do this, double-click the appropriate row or column border in the row and column headers. When you use this method, Excel will auto-fit the row or the column to accommodate the greatest amount of cell content in the row or column. As with manually dragging rows or columns to the desired size, when you double-click to auto-fit them, you double-click the lower border for a row and the right-hand border for a cell.

Note: You can auto-fit all columns or rows in a worksheet at the same time. To do this, select the **Select All** ◢ button where the column and the row headers intersect to select all cells in the worksheet, and then double-click on any column or row border in the headers.

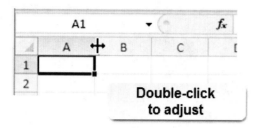

Figure 3-3: When the mouse pointer is displayed as a line with a double arrow, you can double-click row or column borders to auto-fit them to cell content.

You can also use the AutoFit feature in Excel to automatically adjust row height or column width to match cell content. You can access the AutoFit commands by selecting the **Format** button in the **Cells** group on the **Home** tab. To use the AutoFit feature, select any cell within the row or the column that you would like to adjust and then select either the **AutoFit Row Height** or the **AutoFit Column Width** command from the **Format** drop-down menu.

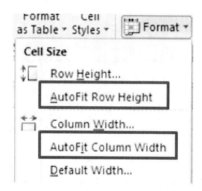

Figure 3-4: The AutoFit feature adjusts row height or column width to match cell content.

Finally, you can use the **Row Height** and **Column Width** dialog boxes to adjust cell size. To adjust cell size by using this method, simply select a cell in the desired row, open the appropriate dialog box, enter the desired height or width, and then select **OK**. You can access the **Row Height** and the **Column Width** dialog boxes from the **Format** drop-down menu in the **Cells** group.

Figure 3-5: The Row Height and the Column Width dialog boxes.

The Hide and Unhide Commands

The **Hide** and **Unhide** commands allow you to suppress the visibility of particular rows or columns in your worksheets. These commands can come in handy in large worksheets with more rows or columns than can fit on the screen at once, or if your worksheets contain sensitive information that is not appropriate for all audiences. When you hide rows or columns, they remain in the worksheet and all references to cells in the hidden rows or columns remain intact. You can access the **Hide** and **Unhide** commands by selecting **Home→Cells→Format→Hide & Unhide**.

> **Note:** You can also access the **Hide** and **Unhide** commands by selecting a row, a column, or multiple rows or columns, right-clicking anywhere within the selection and then selecting either **Hide** or **Unhide**.

	A	F	G
1	Sales Rep	Total	
2	Andy	$28,015.00	
3	Sally	$32,688.00	
4	Amy	$18,278.00	
5	Fred	$32,566.00	
6	Bill	$14,289.00	

Figure 3-6: Hidden rows or columns are not displayed until you unhide them. Cell content is not affected.

> Access the Checklist tile on your LogicalCHOICE course screen for reference information and job aids on How to Insert, Delete, and Adjust Cells, Columns, and Rows.

ACTIVITY 3-1
Adjusting Cells, Columns, and Rows

Data File

C:\091018Data\Modifying a Worksheet\sales_data.xlsx

Scenario

You have been asked to present data about your sales team to company leadership at an important, upcoming meeting. They would like to gauge the performance of individual members of your sales team. You have prepared an Excel worksheet you will use to present the information to attendees. But, as you're reviewing the worksheet, you feel some of the information isn't necessary to present, so you decide to hide some of the columns. You also feel some of the columns take up too much space for the data in them, so you want to adjust their widths. In addition, one of your sales reps recently left the company for another opportunity, so you'll need to delete his information.

1. Open the **sales_data.xlsx** workbook.

2. Adjust the column widths for columns **A** and **B**.
   a) Select the column header for column **A** to select the entire column.
   b) Select **Home→Cells→Format→AutoFit Column Width**.
   c) In the column headers, place the mouse pointer over the border between columns **B** and **C** until it is
      displayed as a vertical line with two arrows. ⟷
   d) Double-click the border between columns **B** and **C** to AutoFit the column width to the cell contents.

3. Hide the columns containing the quarterly sales data.
   a) Select the column header for column **C**, press and hold **Shift**, and then select the column header for column **F**.
   b) Ensure the range **C:F** is selected.
   c) Select **Home→Cells→Format→Hide & Unhide→Hide Columns**.
   d) Verify column headers **B** and **G** now displayed beside each other with nothing in between.

4. Delete the row containing information for the former employee.
   a) Select any cell within row **13**.
   b) Select **Home→Cells→Delete down arrow→Delete Sheet Rows**.

5. Save the workbook to the **C:\091018Data\Modifying a Worksheet** folder as *my_sales_data.xlsx*

TOPIC B

Search for and Replace Data

You've just put the finishing touches on your Excel workbook, and you're ready to share some of your insights with other people in your organization. Just as you're getting ready to send an email with your workbook attached, you receive a message that some key information has changed. Or perhaps, you just realize you made a mistake entering some data. Worse, you realize you repeated the same mistake over and over throughout the workbook. Sending out the wrong data can lead to errors, a loss of credibility among your peers, and a loss of credibility among your customers. You'll need to hunt down and fix these errors, and fast. But how?

If your worksheets contain only a few lines of data, this would be a relatively simple change. But, if your worksheets contain thousands of rows and columns worth of data, you could be spending the night at the office. Having to find and correct multiple errors in a workbook can be a painstaking, time-consuming process, and you have neither the time nor the desire to do so. You're in luck. Excel 2010 includes a number of options to help you find and correct mistakes throughout your workbooks quickly and easily. Taking advantage of this functionality will save you countless hours of manually scanning worksheets and can help maintain your data integrity and your reputation.

The Find Command

You can use the **Find** command to locate particular specific content within your worksheets and workbooks. When you select the **Find** command, Excel opens the **Find and Replace** dialog box with the **Find** tab automatically selected. From the **Find** tab, you can search your workbooks and worksheets for a number of different types of content including values, formulas, formatting, and review markup. You can search for individual instances of the content you're searching for or view a list of all instances of content matching your search query at once. Excel provides you with a number of options for configuring your search queries to find the precise information you're looking for. To access the **Find** command, select **Home→Editing→Find & Select→Find** or press **Ctrl+F**.

 Note: You can direct Excel to search only within a particular range by selecting that range before selecting the **Find** command.

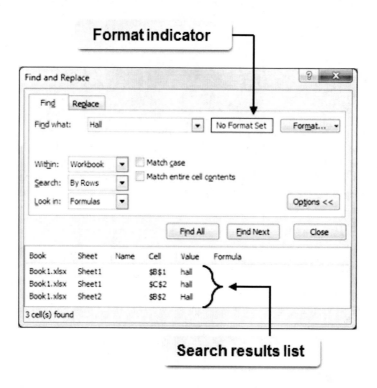

Figure 3-7: The Find and Replace dialog box with the options expanded.

The following table describes the various elements of the **Find** tab in the **Find and Replace** dialog box.

Find Tab Element	Use This To
Find what field	Enter your search query. This is the content Excel will search for in the workbook or worksheet.
Format indicator	View which type of formatting is currently selected when performing searches for content with specific formatting.
Format button	Select the type of formatting you wish to search for. Selecting the **Format** button opens the **Find Format** dialog box, which allows you to select the type of formatting you wish to search for. Selecting the **Find** down arrow gives you the option to manually select a worksheet cell to set the desired formatting to search for or to clear formatting from the search query.
Within drop-down menu	Decide between searching the current worksheet or the entire workbook.
Search drop-down menu	Choose whether to search by row or by column.
Look in drop-down menu	Tell Excel to search within cells containing values, formulas, or comments.
Match case check box	Require an exact casing match in order for Excel to return search results.
Match entire cell contents check box	Require an exact content match within a cell in order for Excel to return a search result.
Options button	Expand or collapse the options section of the **Find and Replace** dialog box.

Find Tab Element	Use This To
Find All button	Display a list of all instances of content matching your search query at the bottom of the **Find and Replace** dialog box. When you select a search result from the list, Excel automatically navigates to and selects the matching cell.
Find Next button	Cycle among all cells with content matching the search query. Excel automatically navigates to and selects each cell containing matching content in the order it finds them.
Search results list	Review search results when you use the **Find All** command and to select cells containing content that matches the search query.

The Replace Command

Like the **Find** command, the **Replace** command will also search for specific content within your workbooks and worksheets. But, you can also use the **Replace** command to switch out the old, incorrect data with the updated or correct data. Excel provides you with the same options for configuring your searches by using the **Replace** command, with the additional option of entering the content you would like to replace the incorrect content with. As with the **Find** command, you can apply the **Replace** command for one instance of your search query at a time or for all matching instances at once. They keyboard for the Replace command in **Ctrl+H**.

 Note: As with the **Find** command, you can direct the **Replace** command to only search for and replace content within a particular range by first selecting the range and then selecting the **Replace** command.

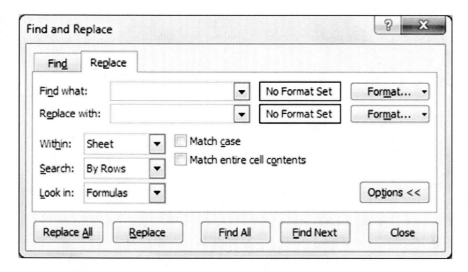

Figure 3-8: The Replace tab is a near match for the Find tab; the only difference is the ability to specify the content you want to replace the old content with.

The Go To Dialog Box

You can use the **Go To** dialog box to quickly navigate to and select any cell within a workbook or worksheet. This works in much the same way as using the **Name Box** to navigate. You simply enter the desired cell reference and then select **OK** to navigate to a cell. If you would like to navigate to a cell on a different worksheet within the same workbook, include the name of the desired worksheet followed by an exclamation point (!) before the cell reference. Although this isn't really necessary in smaller worksheets, if you have thousands of rows and columns in a large worksheet, this can make navigation far easier.

The main advantage of using the **Go To** dialog box over the **Name Box**, is that the **Go To** dialog box saves a list of the cells to which you have previously navigated. This way, if you use particular cells often in a worksheet, you can quickly jump back to them when you need to edit data. And, once you use the **Go To** dialog box to navigate within a workbook, it displays a reference back to cell A1 so you can quickly navigate back to the beginning of a worksheet. The list of cells that is displayed in the **Go To** dialog box is specific to the current workbook, so Excel will remember your navigation history for each workbook file. You can access the **Go To** dialog box by selecting **Home→Editing→Find & Select→Go To** or by pressing the **F5** key.

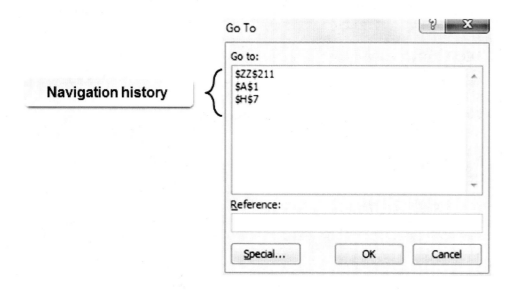

Figure 3-9: The Go To dialog box remembers your navigation history.

The Go To Special Dialog Box

The Go To Special feature is far more powerful than the Go To feature. Whereas the **Go To** dialog box allows you to navigate directly to a particular cell, the **Go To Special** dialog box allows you to select multiple cells that all meet particular criteria. This feature is particularly handy when you want to avoid manually navigating through a large worksheet to select multiple cells by pressing and holding down the **Ctrl** key. But the feature also works well for finding a single cell in a worksheet that meets the desired search criteria or for selecting a contiguous range of cells that all meet the criteria. The Go To Special feature works only on the currently selected worksheet.

When you use this feature, selected cells behave as they normally do when you select a range. So you can add formatting to all of the cells at once, delete the content of all of the cells, or use the **Tab** and **Enter** keys to navigate among the selected range to enter data one cell at a time. You can access the Go To Special dialog box by selecting **Home→Editing→Find & Select→Go To Special** or by accessing the **Go To** dialog box and selecting the **Special** button.

Figure 3-10: The Go To Special dialog box.

The **Go To Special** dialog box provides you with a wide array of criteria for selecting cells and ranges.

Option	Select This To
Comments radio button	Select all cells containing comments.
Constants radio button	Select all cells containing constants. You can restrict the search to select only cells containing numbers, only cells containing text, or only cells containing the logical statements TRUE or FALSE. This option will not select instances of TRUE or FALSE that are the result of a logical function, only cases in which you've typed TRUE or FALSE as text. Also, Excel differentiates TRUE and FALSE from all other text when using this option.
Formulas radio button	Select cells containing formulas. You can restrict the search to select only cells containing formulas that return numbers, formulas that return text, formulas that return a logical value, or formulas that return an error.
Numbers check box	Restrict the **Constants** option to select only cells containing constants that are numbers or to restrict the **Formulas** option to select only cells containing numbers returned by a formula.
Text check box	Restrict the **Constants** option to select only cells containing text constants or to restrict the **Formulas** option to select only cells containing text returned by a formula.
Logicals check box	Restrict the **Constants** option to select only cells containing the text TRUE or FALSE if you manually typed the text into the cells, or to restrict the **Formulas** option to select only cells containing logical values returned by a formula.
Errors check box	Restrict the **Formulas** option to select only cells containing errors returned by a formula.

Option	Select This To
Blanks radio button	Select all blank cells in a worksheet.
Current region radio button	Select all cells in the same region as the currently selected cell.
Current array radio button	Select all cells in the same array as the currently selected cell, if the selected cell is part of an array.
Objects radio button	Selects all objects on the worksheet. This option does not select worksheet cells, only objects on the worksheet.
Row differences radio button	Select all cells in the same row as the selected cell that do not contain the same content as the selected cell.
Column differences radio button	Select all cells in the same column as the selected cell that do not contain the same content as the selected cell.
Precedents radio button	Selects all cells that contain data feeding the formula in the selected cell.
Dependents radio button	Selects all cells that contain formulas that the currently selected cell is feeding.
Direct only radio button	Restrict the **Precedents** option or the **Dependents** option to select only those cells directly feeding or fed by the currently selected cell.
All levels radio button	Set the **Precedents** option or the **Dependents** option to select all cells feeding or fed by the currently selected cell.
Last cell radio button	Select the last cell containing data or formatting in a worksheet.
Visible cells only radio button	Select all non-hidden cells.
Conditional formats radio button	Select all cells containing conditional formatting or all cells containing the same conditional formatting as the currently selected cell.
Data validation radio button	Select all cells containing data validation or all cells containing the same data validation as the currently selected cell.
All radio button	Set the **Conditional formats** option to select all cells containing conditional formatting or to set the **Data validation** option to select all cells containing data validation.
Same radio button	Restrict the **Conditional formats** option to select only cells containing the same conditional formatting as the currently selected cell, or to restrict the **Data validation** option to select only cells containing the same data validation criteria as the currently selected cell.

 Access the Checklist tile on your LogicalCHOICE course screen for reference information and job aids on **How to Search for and Replace Data.**

ACTIVITY 3-2
Searching for and Replacing Data

Before You Begin
The my_sales_data.xlsx file is open.

Scenario
You have received notification from the human resources department that one of your sales reps has been transferred to a different region, and another was recently married and has changed her name. You decide to use the **Find** command to locate the employee information without having to manually search the worksheet so you can update the records. Additionally, My Footprint Sports has recently consolidated the sales teams from two regions into one. You realize it would be easier to use the **Replace** command to update all of the records at once rather than to do so one at a time.

---

1. Change the regional information for the transferred employee.
   a) Select **Home→Editing→Find & Select→Find**.
   b) In the **Find and Replace** dialog box, ensure that the **Find** tab is selected.
   c) In the **Find what** field, type *trowns* and select **Find Next**.
   d) Ensure that Excel navigated to cell **A20**.
   e) Select cell **B20**, type *Southwest* and press **Enter**.

    Note: You can leave the **Find and Replace** dialog box open when you edit cell B20.

2. Update the married sales rep's last name.
   a) If you previously closed the **Find and Replace** dialog box, select **Home→Editing→Find & Select→Find**, and then ensure that the **Find** tab is selected.
   b) In the **Find what** field, type *silvis* and press **Enter**.
   c) Ensure that Excel navigated to cell **A15**.
   d) Close the **Find and Replace** dialog box, type *Kertz* in cell **A15**, and then press **Enter**.

3. Change all instances of **West** region entries to *Southwest*.
   a) Select the range **B7:B23**.
   b) Select **Home→Editing→Find & Select→Replace**.
   c) In the **Find and Replace** dialog box, ensure that the **Replace** tab is selected.
   d) In the **Find what** field, type *West*.
   e) In the **Replace with** field, type *Southwest*
   f) Select the **Options** button.
   g) Check the **Match entire cell contents** check box and select **Find Next**.
   h) Ensure that Excel selected an instance of **West** in the **Region** column and select **Replace**.
   i) Verify that Excel changed the previous instance of **West** to **Southwest**, and then selected another instance of **West** in the **Region** column.
   j) To change all other instances of **West** to **Southwest**, select **Replace All**.
   k) In the **Microsoft Excel** dialog box, select **OK** and close the **Find and Replace** dialog box.

4. Save the workbook.

TOPIC C

Use Proofing and Research Tools

Although you may not always be asked to do so, it's likely that at some point you will have to share your workbooks with your colleagues. After all, what good is organizational data if you can't share it with others in your organization? Whether you're presenting your workbooks in front of a live audience, sharing some data with colleagues in a meeting, or emailing your workbook files to other people, you'll want to make sure all of your content is correct before doing so. One of the easiest ways to lose credibility with an audience is to present content that's riddled with mistakes. In addition to ensuring you have the correct data and formulas in your worksheets, you'll want to make sure everything is spelled correctly and that you're using all terminology correctly. This is why Excel 2010 includes spelling check and other functionality you can use to ensure your content is ready to present to others. Understanding how to use this functionality can help you make sure your worksheets are accurate and look professional, and it just may help preserve your credibility with others.

The Spelling Dialog Box

You can use the **Spelling** dialog box to inspect your worksheets for spelling errors. Excel 2010's spelling check feature flags as spelling errors any text that Excel doesn't recognize and then lets you decide how to resolve the errors. Excel uses a set of built-in dictionaries to compare the text in your worksheets to. If a word is not in the currently selected dictionary, Excel will flag it as an error. Keep in mind, however, not all words that aren't in the dictionary are actual spelling errors, such as proper nouns. If a word that Excel believes is an error is similar to other words in the dictionary, the **Spelling** dialog box displays a list of suggested corrections that you can choose from to replace the misspelling.

 Note: Unlike some other applications, such as Microsoft Office Word, Excel does not mark spelling errors with red underlines. Don't rely on on-screen markup to flag spelling errors in your worksheets. You must run spelling check manually.

You can also add words to the dictionary so that Excel no longer flags them as spelling errors. This can be useful if you include a lot of names in your worksheets, which may be the case for people who manage sales or HR, or if you use a lot of job-related jargon or terminology in your worksheets. You can inspect only one worksheet at a time using the **Spelling** dialog box.

You can access the **Spelling** dialog box by selecting **Review→Proofing→Spelling** or by pressing the **F7** key. You can direct Excel to check the spelling in only a particular range by first selecting it and then opening the **Spelling** dialog box.

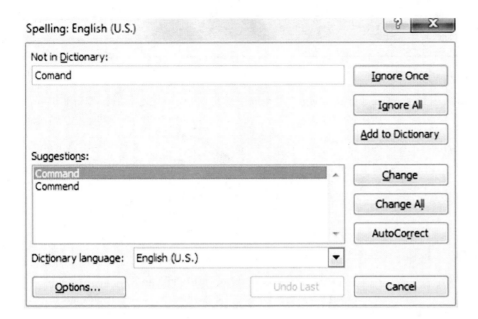

Figure 3-11: The Spelling dialog box helps you find and correct spelling errors.

The **Spelling** dialog box contains a number of commands and options you can use to configure exactly how you search for and resolve spelling errors.

Spelling Dialog Box Element	Description
Not in Dictionary field	Displays the word that the spelling checker does not recognize and has flagged as a possible error.
Suggestions list	Displays a list of suggested alternatives for the flagged word from the currently selected dictionary.
Dictionary language drop-down menu	Allows you to select the desired dictionary against which Excel checks for spelling errors.
Ignore Once button	Ignores the currently selected instance of a misspelled word.
Ignore All button	Ignores all instances of the currently selected misspelled word throughout a worksheet.
Add to Dictionary button	Adds the term in the **Not in Dictionary** field to the currently selected dictionary so Excel no longer flags it as a misspelling.
Change button	Replaces the currently selected instance of the word in the **Not in Dictionary** field with the word selected in the **Suggestions** list.
Change All button	Replaces all instances of the word in the **Not in Dictionary** field throughout a worksheet with the word selected in the **Suggestions** list.
AutoCorrect button	Adds the word in the **Not in Dictionary** field to the AutoCorrect feature so that, whenever you type the flagged word, Excel automatically replaces it with the word selected in the **Suggestions** list.
Options button	Opens the **Excel Options** dialog box with the **Proofing** tab selected.
Undo Last button	Reverts the last corrected instance of a word back to its original spelling.

Spelling Dialog Box Element	Description
Cancel button	Cancels the current spelling check and closes the **Spelling** dialog box.

The AutoCorrect Feature

Excel 2010 also includes a feature that can help you avoid spelling errors as you type them, the *AutoCorrect feature*. The AutoCorrect feature automatically changes common misspellings to the correct spelling as you type. For example, if you type *teh* in a cell, Excel will automatically change it to *the*. The AutoCorrect feature can also automatically format text as you type it, such as creating a hyperlink when you type a Web address or an email address, and insert certain mathematical symbols when you type particular keystrokes. When you install Excel 2010, the AutoCorrect feature is preconfigured with a set of terms it will automatically correct, but you can customize this to suit your needs.

The Research Task Pane

Excel 2010 can also help you perform research from a number of built-in and online resources. The **Research** task pane can help you look up word spellings and definitions, synonyms and antonyms, and reference articles and other online resources. You can select which particular resources you want it to search through, and you can look for and add further resource options to those available by default. You can access the **Research** task pane by selecting **Review→Proofing→Research** or **Review→Proofing→Thesaurus**. When you select the **Thesaurus** button, the **Research** task pane automatically opens with the default thesaurus selected as the reference source.

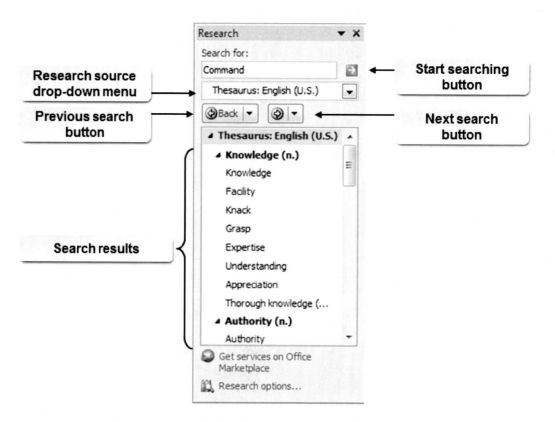

Figure 3-12: The Research task pane.

The following table describes the functions of the various **Research** task pane elements.

Research Task Pane Element	Use This To
Search for field	Enter the word or the phrase you'd like to search for.
Start searching button	Execute a search.
Research source drop-down menu	Select the desired research source.
Previous search button	Navigate back through your research trail. This command only becomes active once you've navigated away from the original search results.
Next search button	Navigate forward through your research trail. This command only becomes active once you've navigated back through your research trail using the **Previous search** button.
Search results	View and select search results.
Get services on Office Marketplace link	View a list of and select links to popular research services.
Research options link	Open the **Research Options** dialog box, which you can use to add or remove items from the **Research Source** drop-down menu.

 Access the Checklist tile on your LogicalCHOICE course screen for reference information and job aids on **How to Check a Worksheet's Spelling and Perform Research.**

ACTIVITY 3-3
Checking the Spelling in a Worksheet

Before You Begin
The my_sales_data.xlsx workbook file is open.

Scenario
You would like to both project your worksheet to attendees at the upcoming meeting and create printed handouts. Before you do, you want to make sure there are no spelling errors in the file. You decide to use the spelling check feature to check the worksheet for you.

1. Prepare to check the spelling in the worksheet.
   a) Select cell **A1** so Excel begins spell checking from the beginning of the sheet.
   b) Select **Review→Proofing→Spelling** to open the **Spelling** dialog box.

2. Check the worksheet's spelling.
   a) In the **Spelling** dialog box, in the **Not in Dictionary** field, verify that Excel has identified **Comission** as a misspelled word.
   b) In the **Suggestions** list, ensure that **Commission** is selected, and then select **Change**.

   > **Note:** You may need to relocate the **Spelling** dialog box on screen to view which cells Excel is identifying as having misspelled words.

   c) Verify that Excel has flagged another instance of the misspelling **Comission**.
   d) To correct all instances of **Comission**, select **Change All**.
   e) Verify that Excel has flagged **Chirillo** as a misspelled word.
   f) As this is a proper noun, and you do not wish to correct it, select **Ignore All**.
   g) Select **Ignore All** for **Kertz**, as this is also a proper noun.
   h) Verify that Excel flags **Southweest** as a misspelled word.
   i) In the **Suggestions** list, ensure **Southwest** is selected, and then select **Change**.
   j) Select **Ignore All** for the remaining flagged terms.
   k) In the **Microsoft Excel** dialog box, select **OK**.

3. Save and close the workbook.

Summary

In this lesson, you modified worksheets by inserting, deleting, and adjusting cells, columns, and rows; searching for and replacing cell data; and performing a spelling check. Understanding how to work with and modify your worksheets will give you the flexibility you'll need to build upon existing workbooks without having to start from scratch whenever significant changes are needed. This means you'll always be able to produce and develop functional, professional-looking workbooks without wasting your valuable time. And, you can help ensure your organization is able to react to the nearly constant change in available data that is becoming more and more the norm in today's information-driven environment.

Identify some situations in which the ability to adjust or hide columns and rows would come in handy.

How has some of Excel's search-and-replace, research, or proofing functionality made previous tasks you've performed easier?

 Note: Check your LogicalCHOICE Course screen for opportunities to interact with your classmates, peers, and the larger LogicalCHOICE online community about the topics covered in this course or other topics you are interested in. From the Course screen you can also access available resources for a more continuous learning experience.

4 | Formatting a Worksheet

Lesson Time: 1 hour, 30 minutes

Lesson Objectives

In this lesson, you will format a worksheet. You will:

- Modify fonts.

- Add borders and colors to worksheets.

- Apply number formats.

- Align cell contents.

- Add styles and themes.

- Apply basic conditional formatting.

- Create and use templates.

Lesson Introduction

The ability to enter your data into Excel worksheets and to use Excel's powerful mathematical capabilities to your advantage forms the foundation you'll need to extract actionable intelligence from your organizational data. Excel can also help you do so much more. Large worksheets with thousands, or perhaps millions, of data entries can be difficult to read. This can be especially true if you're working with a variety of numeric data types, such as dollar amounts, percentages, and figures with varied numbers of decimal places. Plus, you may need to organize your data according to department, region, job role, or other important distinctions. And, some data is simply more important than other data and should stand out even at first glance. In other words, you could potentially have a limitless need to present data in a wide variety of formats. Fortunately, Excel 2010 allows you to do just that.

Excel provides you with a staggering variety of formatting options that can help you present your data in precisely the right way to suit your needs. Understanding how to use, and, perhaps more importantly, when and why to use these formatting options will help you make your worksheets easy to read, professional in their appearance, and simply more useful. Additionally, you can avoid the hassle of the wasted time, frustration, and headaches that can accompany trying to force data to behave the way you want it to when it's not properly formatted.

TOPIC A

Modify Fonts

When you pick up a newspaper or a magazine, one of the first things that likely stands out is that the headline and article title text is larger and more prominent than the rest of the text. This is meant to draw your eye to the most important information first. It also allows you to easily skim pages to locate the exact story you're looking for with ease. You'll find similar use of font sizes and even font colors in advertisements, on signs and billboards, and, really, just about everywhere else. This is because differences in letter size, color, and style make it easy for the eye to pick out particular information in what is often a sea of clutter. And, this is really no different with spreadsheets.

Excel 2010 provides you with a number of options for formatting the text in your worksheets. This functionality will help you create spreadsheets that are easy to read and interpret and that allow the important information to stand out from the crowd. This will also help you add a level of visual appeal, which can facilitate a greater level of engagement when you present your data to others that would simply not be possible by using a single, monotonous type of font.

Fonts

When people talk about *fonts* and typefaces, there is often a lot of confusion surrounding the topic. Essentially, a font is a physical collection of characters, whether that be a computer file or a collection of metal pieces to be used in a printing press, and the typeface is the overall design and appearance of the characters in a font. In this course, the word font may be used interchangeably to refer to both a physical font and the typeface design. What's really important to remember is that when you change the font in your worksheets, letters, numbers, punctuation, and other characters will look different.

You can use different fonts and different font sizes to change the appearance of the text and data in your worksheets for a number of reasons. Differing fonts and font sizes can help distinguish certain content from other content, give certain data prominence over other data, or simply make your worksheets more visually pleasing. In addition to changing the design of the text in your worksheets, changing fonts can also affect the spacing between characters.

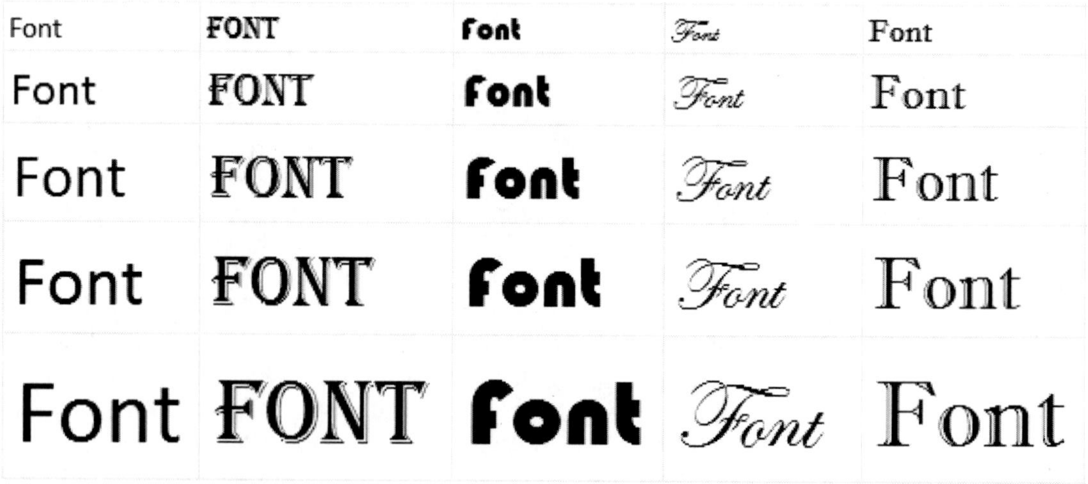

Font	FONT	Font	Font	Font
Font	FONT	Font	Font	Font
Font	FONT	Font	Font	Font
Font	FONT	Font	Font	Font
Font	FONT	Font	Font	Font

Figure 4–1: The same text repeated in different fonts and sizes.

The Font Group

The **Font** group on the **Home** tab provides you with access to the most commonly used commands for adjusting the fonts in your worksheets. From here you can change the font type, size, and color of the font in your worksheets. You will also find commands in the **Font** group for applying particular formatting to your fonts, such as bolding, italics, and underlining.

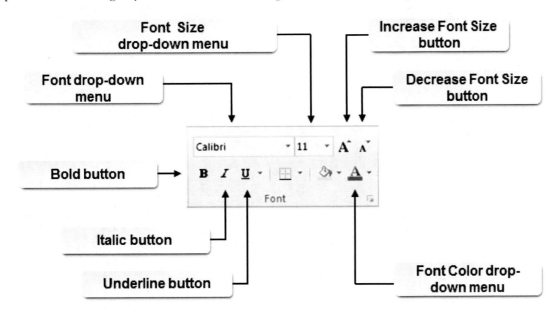

Figure 4-2: The Font group on the Home tab.

Use the commands in the Font group to configure the text in your worksheets.

Font Group Command	Use This To
Font drop-down menu	Change the font type.
Font Size drop-down menu	Change the font size. You can either select one of the predefined font sizes from the drop-down menu or manually type the desired font size.
Increase Font Size button	Cycle up through the predefined font sizes to make your worksheet font bigger.
Decrease Font Size button	Cycle down through the predefined font sizes to make your worksheet font smaller.
Bold button	Bold the currently selected text.
Italic button	Italicize the currently selected text.
Underline button	Underline the currently selected text.
Font Color drop-down menu	Change the color of the currently selected text.

Live Preview

Live Preview is a dynamic feature of Excel 2010 that allows you to see what a particular formatting change will look like before you actually apply it. This feature can help you quickly assess which particular formatting you would like to apply to the content and objects in your worksheets. The Live Preview feature works with a number of different formatting options including font formatting, table formatting, and **Paste** command options.

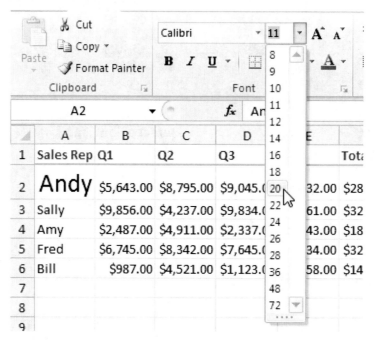

Figure 4-3: Live Preview displays formatting options before you apply them.

The Format Cells Dialog Box

You can access all of the commands and options for formatting your worksheet fonts, along with a wide variety of other formatting options, in the **Format Cells** dialog box. Think of the **Format Cells** dialog box as an extension of the common formatting commands you will find in the various ribbon groups. It is divided into six tabs that are grouped by specific categories of cell content formatting. You can access the **Format Cells** dialog box by selecting the dialog box launcher in either the **Font**, the **Alignment**, or the **Number** group on the **Home** tab.

 Note: Alternately, you can open the **Format Cells** dialog box by right-clicking a selected cell, and then selecting **Format Cells**.

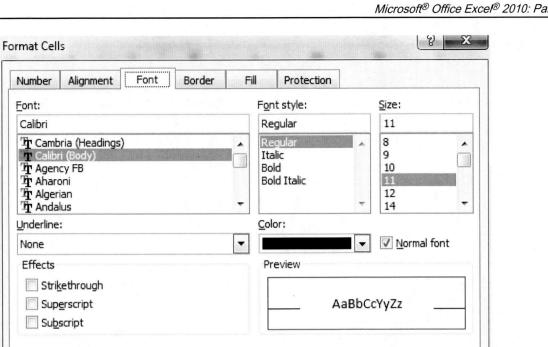

Figure 4-4: The Format Cells dialog box.

The following table identifies the types of formatting commands and options you will find on the **Format Cells** dialog box tabs.

Format Cells Dialog Box Tab	Contains Commands For
Number	Formatting numeric data for a wide variety of purposes. Number formatting configures the display and behavior of numbers for figures such as monetary amounts, dates, times, percentages, and fractions.
Alignment	Controlling the placement of data within cells. You can use these commands to align data with a particular cell border, to center content within a cell, to display text at different angles, and to control the relationship between the content and the cell borders.
Font	Applying a variety of formatting to your worksheet fonts. You can use these commands to change the type, size, and color of your fonts, and to add effects such as bolding, underlining, and italics.
Border	Applying a variety of formatting to your cell borders. You can use these commands to configure the width, color, and style of your cell borders.
Fill	Adding color, gradient shading, or patterns as cell backgrounds.
Protection	Protecting your cell content.

The Colors Dialog Box

In addition to the common font colors available from the **Font Color** drop-down menu, a wider range of color options or the ability to customize your font color is available in the **Colors** dialog box. The **Colors** dialog box is divided into two tabs: the **Standard** tab and the **Custom** tab. The **Standard** tab provides you with access to a wide range of pre-configured color and grayscale options, while the **Custom** tab lets you customize color options by using two different color models. In addition to using the **Colors** dialog box to customize your font color, you can use it to apply color formatting to a number of other items, such as cell backgrounds and borders. You can access the **Colors** dialog box by selecting **More Colors** from any of the color drop-down menus.

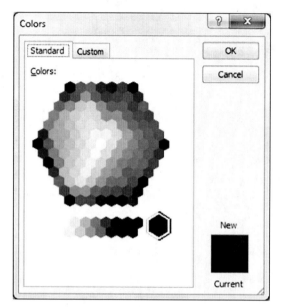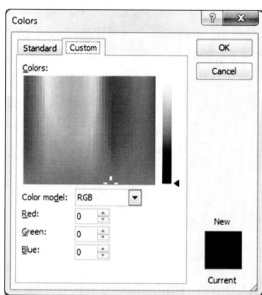

Figure 4-5: The Standard and Custom tabs on the Colors dialog box.

 Access the Checklist tile on your LogicalCHOICE course screen for reference information and job aids on How to Modify Fonts.

Hyperlinks

Hyperlinks can be thought of as a type of font or text formatting, but there is an important distinction to make here. While font formatting typically affects only the display of text, a hyperlink adds an element of functionality as well. A hyperlink is simply a link within a document that, when selected, performs a particular action, such as navigating to a different location within the document, opening another document, creating a new document, navigating to a web page, or starting an email. In Excel 2010, you can create a hyperlink within a worksheet cell or out of an object. When you select the cell or object, Excel performs the designated action.

One other important distinction to make here is that, in many applications, you create a hyperlink out of specific text, so the text itself is the hyperlink. In Excel, selecting the cell, not the text, initiates the action. So, the cell acts as the hyperlink, not the text. However, by default, Excel does automatically format the text in cells containing hyperlinks so workbook users can tell which cells contain them. The default text formatting for hyperlinks in Excel 2010 is blue, underlined text. You can modify the formatting, however, to suit your needs.

Note: When you wish to select a cell containing a hyperlink, it's a best practice to select a nearby cell, and then use keyboard navigation to select it. This is because simply selecting the cell manually will activate the hyperlink action.

6	Bill	$987.00	$4,521.00	$1,123.00	$7,658
7					
8	Click here for additional sales information				
9					

Figure 4-6: Worksheet text formatted as a hyperlink.

The Insert/Edit Hyperlink Dialog Box

You will use the **Insert Hyperlink** dialog box and the **Edit Hyperlink** dialog box to create and modify hyperlinks in your worksheets. These are, essentially, the same dialog box; the only differences are that the **Insert Hyperlink** dialog box opens when the active cell does not already contain a hyperlink, and the **Edit Hyperlink** dialog box opens when the active cell contains a hyperlink, also displaying the **Remove Link** button. The buttons in the **Link to** section of the **Insert Hyperlink** and **Edit Hyperlink** dialog boxes provide access to the various commands and options needed to create, configure, and modify worksheet hyperlinks. You can access the **Insert Hyperlink** and **Edit Hyperlink** dialog boxes by selecting **Insert→Links→Hyperlink**.

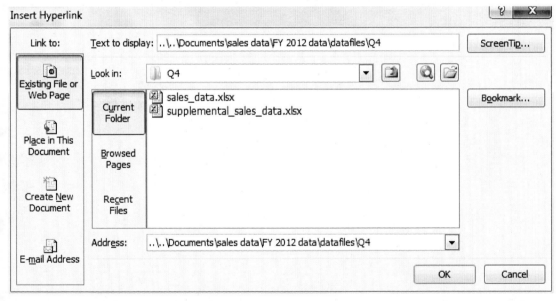

Figure 4-7: The buttons in the Link to section of the Insert Hyperlink and Edit Hyperlink dialog boxes act like tabs, displaying a variety of different commands so you can create a variety of different hyperlinks.

Although most of the commands available in the **Insert Hyperlink** and **Edit Hyperlink** dialog boxes change depending on the type of hyperlink you're creating, there are a few elements that are always displayed.

Dialog Box Element	Use This To
Link to section buttons	Select the type of hyperlink you wish to create or edit. Selecting each of these will display a different set of commands for configuring the hyperlink.

Dialog Box Element	Use This To
Text to display field	Enter the text you want to display in the cell once you create or edit the hyperlink. If there is already text in the cell, Excel automatically displays it here. Any changes you make here will overwrite the existing cell text.
ScreenTip button	Open the **Set Hyperlink ScreenTip** dialog box, which allows you to enter text that will appear in a small pop-up box when a user points the mouse pointer at the cell or object containing the hyperlink.

 Access the Checklist tile on your LogicalCHOICE course screen for reference information and job aids on How to Insert and Edit Hyperlinks.

ACTIVITY 4-1
Modifying Fonts and Adding Hyperlinks

Data Files

C:\091018Data\Formatting a Worksheet\sales_data.xlsx

C:\091018Data\Formatting a Worksheet\supplemental_sales_data.xlsx

Before You Begin

Excel 2010 is open.

Scenario

You have updated and checked the spelling of the worksheet you plan to present at the upcoming meeting. Your supervisor requested that you include all sales data in your presentation, so you have already unhidden the hidden sales data columns. Now, you would like to make the worksheet more visually appealing and easier to read for the meeting attendees. You decide to start by making some text formatting changes to the worksheet text. Also, you want to include a link to a document containing supplemental sales data. You plan on emailing a copy of the workbook file to everyone attending the meeting, and you feel the additional information may be helpful.

1. Open the **sales_data.xlsx** workbook file.

2. Change the worksheet font.
   a) At the intersection of the row and column headers, in the top-left corner of the worksheet, select the
      Select All button ◣ to select the entire worksheet.
   b) Select **Home→Font→Font down arrow** and, from the **Font** drop-down list, select **Arial**.

3. Format the worksheet title so it stands out from the rest of the text.
   a) Select cell **G5**.
   b) Select **Home→Font→Font Color down arrow**, and then, in the **Standard Colors** section, select **Blue**.
   c) Select **Home→Font→Bold**.
   d) Select **Home→Font→Font Size** down arrow, and then select **16**.

4. Format the column labels to distinguish them from the cells containing data and increase the font size for the sales rep names.
   a) Select the range **A6:L6**.
   b) Change the font size to **12** and make the text **Bold**.
   c) Select the range **A7:A24** and change the font size to **12**.
   d) Adjust the column widths for columns **H:L** to accommodate the column labels.

5. Add a hyperlink to the **supplemental_sales_data.xlsx** workbook.
   a) In the **sales_data.xlsx** workbook, select cell **N11**.
   b) Select **Insert→Links→Hyperlink**.
   c) In the **Insert Hyperlink** dialog box, in the **Link to** section, ensure that **Existing File or Web Page** is selected.
   d) In the **Text to display** field, type *Click here for additional sales data*
   e) Select the **ScreenTip** button.
   f) In the **Set Hyperlink ScreenTip** dialog box, in the **ScreenTip text** field, type *Supplemental Sales Data* and select **OK**.

g) In the **Current Folder** list, select the **supplemental_sales_data.xlsx** file and select **OK**.

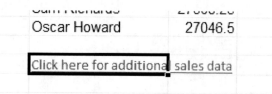

6. Verify the newly added hyperlink works as expected.

   a) Select cell **N11**.

   b) Verify that the **supplemental_sales_data.xlsx** workbook file opens and close the workbook.

7. Save the **sales_data.xlsx** file to the **C:\091018Data\Formatting a Worksheet** folder as *my_sales_data.xlsx*

TOPIC B

Add Borders and Colors to Worksheets

You know that by formatting the text in your worksheets you can make them easier to read, differentiate among various types of data, and make your data more visually appealing. But, you may not want too much variety in your worksheet text. Too many differences can actually make your worksheets look busy and cluttered, and could make them harder to read. So, you'll likely want to use other methods of organizing and formatting your worksheets to make them easier to read and more visually appealing.

Advertisers know how to use a variety of colors and design layouts to catch your eye and get you to focus on key elements of their messages. In much the same way, you can apply particular types of formatting to your worksheet borders and cells to help draw your audience to the important information in your workbooks. By doing so, you can reduce clutter on your worksheets and organize your content visually, while maintaining a professional, polished look.

Border Options

It's easy to distinguish one cell from another on an Excel worksheet; by default, they are displayed with light blue gridlines that define them. You may wish to distinguish particular areas of your worksheets from others and you may not always want to have empty spaces in between them to do so. Fortunately, Excel 2010 allows you to apply a variety of border formatting options to your worksheet cells to help highlight and define various sections of your data. Excel allows you to define the color and style of your cell borders. You can select from a number of quick-configuration border formatting options, manually draw borders on worksheets, or format a selection of cells by using the **Border** tab on the **Format Cells** dialog box.

Sales Rep	Q1	Q2	Q3	Q4	Total
Andy	$5,643.00	$8,795.00	$9,045.00	$4,532.00	$28,015.00
Sally	$9,856.00	$4,237.00	$9,834.00	$8,761.00	$32,688.00
Amy	$2,487.00	$4,911.00	$2,337.00	$8,543.00	$18,278.00
Fred	$6,745.00	$8,342.00	$7,645.00	$9,834.00	$32,566.00
Bill	$987.00	$4,521.00	$1,123.00	$7,658.00	$14,289.00

Sales Rep	Q1	Q2	Q3	Q4	Total
Juanita	$5,643.00	$8,795.00	$9,045.00	$4,532.00	$28,015.00
Janet	$9,856.00	$4,237.00	$9,834.00	$8,761.00	$32,688.00
Oscar	$2,487.00	$4,911.00	$2,337.00	$8,543.00	$18,278.00
Betty	$6,745.00	$8,342.00	$7,645.00	$9,834.00	$32,566.00
Fabiola	$987.00	$4,521.00	$1,123.00	$7,658.00	$14,289.00

Sales Rep	Q1	Q2	Q3	Q4	Total
Joe	$5,643.00	$8,795.00	$9,045.00	$4,532.00	$28,015.00
Alan	$9,856.00	$4,237.00	$9,834.00	$8,761.00	$32,688.00
Courtney	$2,487.00	$4,911.00	$2,337.00	$8,543.00	$18,278.00
Samantha	$6,745.00	$8,342.00	$7,645.00	$9,834.00	$32,566.00
Sal	$987.00	$4,521.00	$1,123.00	$7,658.00	$14,289.00

Sales Rep	Q1	Q2	Q3	Q4	Total
Chan	$5,643.00	$8,795.00	$9,045.00	$4,532.00	$28,015.00
Seth	$9,856.00	$4,237.00	$9,834.00	$8,761.00	$32,688.00
Faith	$2,487.00	$4,911.00	$2,337.00	$8,543.00	$18,278.00
Jalen	$6,745.00	$8,342.00	$7,645.00	$9,834.00	$32,566.00
Scott	$987.00	$4,521.00	$1,123.00	$7,658.00	$14,289.00

Figure 4–8: Cell borders help you define areas of your worksheets for easier data viewing and analysis.

The Borders Drop-Down Menu

To quickly apply border formatting to your worksheet cells, you can use the options in the **Borders** drop-down menu. It is important to note that selecting most of these options will apply border formatting to the selected cells based on the color and style options currently selected in the **Line Color** and **Line Style** menus, which are located near the bottom of the **Borders** drop-down menu. The only exception to this is the bottom group of border options in the **Borders** section of the **Borders** drop-down menu. These options apply predefined border formatting.

The command button for the **Borders** drop-down menu, which is located in the **Font** group on the **Home** tab, will display as the last option you selected from the **Borders** drop-down menu. This makes it easy to quickly apply the same formatting to multiple sections of a worksheet.

The **Borders** drop-down menu also provides you with access to the commands you can use to manually draw borders on your worksheets. These are located in the **Draw Borders** section. The options selected in the **Line Color** and **Line Style** menus also apply to manually drawn borders.

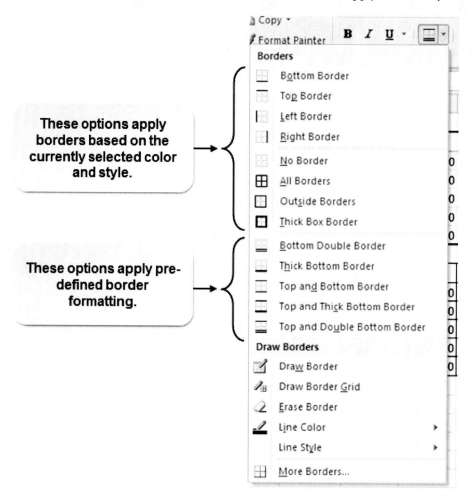

Figure 4–9: Quickly apply border formatting or manually draw borders by using the commands in the Borders drop–down menu.

The Border Tab

You can access a few more options for formatting your worksheet borders on the **Border** tab of the **Format Cells** dialog box. From here, you can apply all of the same formatting options you can access from the **Borders** drop-down menu, and you can add diagonal borders that split cells in half. It is important to remember, however, that diagonal borders do not actually create two separate cells. You need to format your text manually to display it properly, and Excel cannot distinguish between the two halves for calculating. The **Border** tab also displays a border preview, so you can configure and adjust your border formatting as necessary.

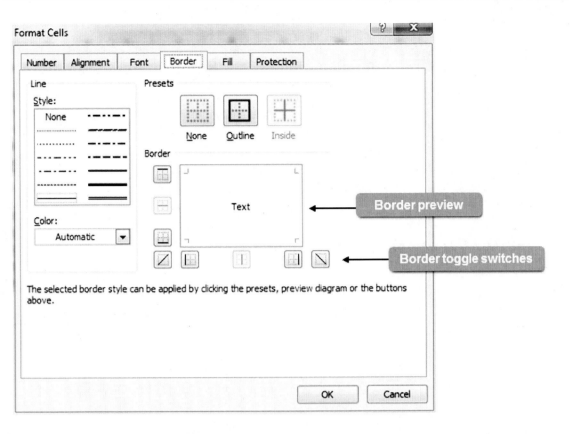

Figure 4-10: The Border tab on the Formal Cells dialog box.

The commands on the **Border** tab allow you to customize and modify your worksheet borders.

Border Tab Element	Allows You To
Style menu	Select the desired border style.
Color drop-down menu	Select the desired border color. You can select from a set of common, predetermined colors or use the **Colors** dialog box to customize your border colors.
None button	Remove all borders from the currently selected cell or range.
Outline button	Apply a border around the outer edge of the currently selected cell or range.
Inside button	Apply a border to all internal cell borders in the currently selected range. Basically, this applies a border to any lines not along the outer edge of a range.
Border toggle switches	Apply formatting to or remove formatting from any of the particular lines within the currently selected cell or range.
Border preview	View the result of your currently selected border options.

Fill Options

Another, more colorful, way to draw attention to particular sections of your worksheets is by applying a *fill*. A fill is a type of worksheet formatting that allows you to add colors, patterns, and gradient shading to the background of a cell or a range. Excel 2010 allows you to select from a predefined set of colors, create custom colors, and blend colors to create gradient effects for use as cell backgrounds. You can also select from a set of predefined pattern backgrounds and select a color to apply to the patterns. The **Fill Color** drop-down menu in the **Font** group on the **Home** tab provides you with quick access to solid color fill options, whereas the **Fill** tab on the **Format Cells** dialog box provides you with access to all of the commands you can use to format cell fills.

Sales Rep	Q1	Q2	Q3	Q4	Total
Andy	$5,643.00	$8,795.00	$9,045.00	$4,532.00	$28,015.00
Sally	$9,856.00	$4,237.00	$9,834.00	$8,761.00	$32,688.00
Amy	$2,487.00	$4,911.00	$2,337.00	$8,543.00	$18,278.00
Fred	$6,745.00	$8,342.00	$7,645.00	$9,834.00	$32,566.00
Bill	$987.00	$4,521.00	$1,123.00	$7,658.00	$14,289.00

Figure 4–11: Fills help you define worksheet areas, draw attention to important data, and add visual appeal to your worksheets.

The Fill Tab

Use the commands on the **Fill** tab of the **Format Cells** dialog box to customize your worksheet fills. From here, you can add pattern and gradient fills, which are not available from the **Fill Color** drop-down menu on the ribbon.

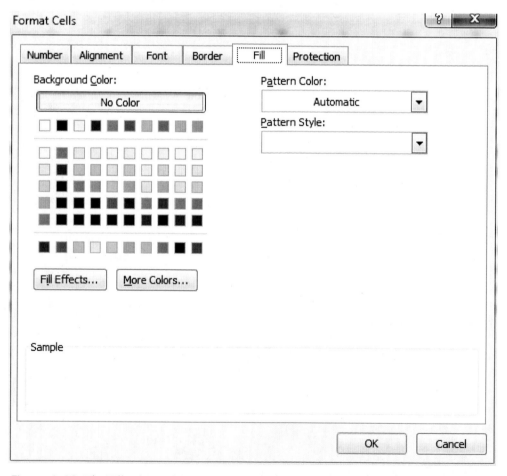

Figure 4–12: The Fill tab provides you with a number of additional options for adding fills to cells.

The following table describes the functions of the various elements on the **Fill** tab.

Fill Tab Element	Use This To
Background Color section	Select a solid color fill for worksheet cells.
Fill Effects button	Open the **Fill Effects** dialog box, which you can use to configure multi-color shading and gradient fill effects.
More Colors button	Open the **Colors** dialog box, which you can use to create custom fill colors.
Pattern Color drop-down menu	Select a color to apply to a pattern fill.
Pattern Style drop-down menu	Select a specific pattern to apply to cells as a fill.
Sample section	View the results of your currently selected fill options.

The Format Painter

You can probably already tell that applying a variety of different formatting to a large number of cells throughout a worksheet can quickly become a tedious, painstaking task. Excel 2010 includes a tool that can help make this process easier: the **Format Painter**. You can think of the **Format Painter** much as you would a standard paint brush. Whatever color you dip a paintbrush into is the color you can paint on a canvas. When you use the **Format Painter**, you are dipping the brush into the formatting of whatever cell you select, and then painting that formatting onto another cell or range.

The **Format Painter** essentially copies and pastes just the formatting from one cell or range to another cell or range. The content of the affected cells remains intact. You cannot select which type of formatting you wish to transfer to the new cell or cells; whatever formatting is applied to the source cell is fully applied to the destination cells. If you double-click the **Format Painter** command, the **Format Painter** enters sticky mode. When in sticky mode, you can apply the copied formatting to any number of other cells. You must exit sticky mode to be able to select another cell or range without applying the copied formatting.

By using the **Format Painter**, you can reapply existing formatting to other cells on the same worksheet, to other worksheets in the same workbook, and in other open workbook files. You can access the **Format Painter** from the **Clipboard** group on the **Home** tab.

Figure 4-13: The Format Painter allows you to quickly and easily apply formatting to any number of cells in your workbooks.

Sheet Backgrounds

Excel 2010 also provides you with the ability to add a picture to act as a worksheet background. Sheet backgrounds are background images that are not technically a part of your worksheets. Sheet backgrounds are for display purposes only and will not print when you print your worksheets. Although they are not a part of your worksheets and won't print, sheet backgrounds are saved along with the rest of the workbook file. You can use sheet backgrounds to enhance the visibility of your worksheets when presenting data in front of a live audience. You may need to toggle off the visibility of cell gridlines if you use these. If the image is not large enough to fill the entire sheet, Excel will repeat, or tile, the image until the entire worksheet is filled. You can add a sheet background by selecting **Page Layout→Page Setup→Background**.

 Note: To learn more about adding background images to your worksheets, view the LearnTO **Add a Non-Tiling Background to a Worksheet** presentation from the **LearnTO** tile on the LogicalCHOICE Course screen.

Figure 4-14: An Excel worksheet with a sheet background.

Formatting and the Paste Options

As you begin to add more and more formatting to your worksheets, it will be important to keep some of the paste and Paste Special options in mind as you move content around on your worksheets. As a reminder, the following table lists some of the more commonly used paste and Paste Special options and describes how they affect cell formatting.

Paste/Paste Special Option	Has This Effect on Formatting
Paste	Pastes all formatting from the source cell or range, along with all cell content, in the destination cell or range. This will overwrite any existing formatting in the destination cells.
Formulas & Number Formatting	Pastes the number formatting and the formulas from the source cell or range in the destination cell or range. This will not affect other existing formatting in the destination cell or range, but will overwrite cell data.
Keep Source Formatting	Pastes all content and formatting from the source cell or range in the destination cells. This will overwrite any existing formatting and data in the destination cells.

Paste/Paste Special Option	Has This Effect on Formatting
No Borders	Pastes all data and most formatting from the source cells in the destination cells, but will not paste border formatting in the destination cells. Existing border formatting in the destination cells is preserved.
Values	Pastes only values from the source cells in the destination cells. Existing formatting in the destination cells is preserved.
Values & Number Formatting	Pastes only values and number formatting from the source cells in the destination cells. All existing formatting, other than number formatting, in the destination cells is preserved.
Values & Source Formatting	Pastes all values and formatting from the source cells in the destination cells. All existing formatting in the destination cells is overwritten.
Formatting	Pastes only formatting from the source cells in the destination cells. All data in the destination cells is preserved. This is the same as using the **Format Painter** to copy and paste cell formatting.

 Access the Checklist tile on your LogicalCHOICE course screen for reference information and job aids on How to Add Borders and Color to Worksheets.

ACTIVITY 4–2
Adding Borders and Colors to Worksheets

Before You Begin

The my_sales_data.xlsx workbook file is open.

Scenario

You have finished formatting the text in your worksheet for the upcoming meeting. Now you would like to add background color to some of the worksheet cells and add a border around the top-employee information to help worksheet viewers differentiate among the various types of content.

---

1. Add a light red background to the worksheet title.
   a) Select cell **G5**.
   b) Select **Home→Font→Fill Color down arrow**.
   c) From the **Fill Color** menu, in the **Theme Colors** section, select **Red, Accent 2, Lighter 80%**.

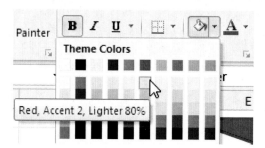

2. Add a light blue background to the column labels.
   a) Select the range **A6:L6**.
   b) Select **Home→Font→Fill Color down arrow**.
   c) From the **Fill Color** menu, in the **Standard Colors** section, select **Light Blue**.

3. Apply the column label formatting to the **Top 3 Employees** section of the worksheet.
   a) Ensure at least one of the cells in the range **A6:L6** is selected.
   b) Select **Home→Clipboard→Format Painter**.
   c) Select the range **N5:O9** and release the mouse button.
   d) Ensure that Excel pasted the formatting as expected.

4. Use the **Format Cells** dialog box to add a border around the top-employee information.

   a) Ensure the range **N5:O9** is still selected, select **Home→Font**, and select the dialog box launcher.
   b) In the **Format Cells** dialog box, select the **Border** tab.

c) In the **Line** section, from the **Style** menu, select the thin double-line border style.

d) From the **Color** drop-down menu, in the **Standard Colors** section, select **Red**.

e) In the **Presets** section, select the **Outline** button.

f) In the **Border** section, ensure that the **Top**, **Bottom**, **Left**, and **Right** border buttons are toggled on and that the preview displays a thin, red, double-line border around the text.

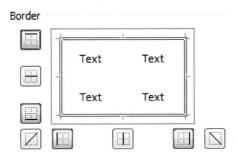

g) Select **OK**.

5. Deselect the range **N5:O9** to verify that Excel applied the desired border.

6. Save the workbook.

TOPIC C

Apply Number Formats

Numeric data comes in all shapes and sizes. People who work with data in Excel worksheets will, naturally, need to express and work with that numeric data in a variety of ways. For example, an accountant may want all numbers to appear with a dollar sign, or other currency symbol, and only show two decimal places. An engineer may need to work with far more decimal places to achieve a higher level of accuracy for sensitive calculations. Someone who manages a team of people and is in charge of work schedules and coordinating paid leave will need to be able to work with dates and times.

Excel 2010 provides an almost staggering array of options when it comes to expressing numeric values. In order for a spreadsheet application to be truly effective, it must be able to display and perform calculations on numeric values in a variety of ways. One of the truly powerful features of Excel is its ability to do just that. By understanding how these different number formats work, and by knowing how and when to apply them, you'll give yourself the flexibility needed to work with and analyze all of your numeric data.

Number Formats

Number formats change the display of numeric data in Excel worksheets. By applying number formatting to your worksheet cells, you can control the display of such items as currency figures, dates and times, fractions, decimal places, and negative numbers. It's important to remember that, as with much of what is displayed in worksheet cells, number formatting affects only how data is displayed, not what data is actually stored in the cells. Excel 2010 includes a variety of preset number formatting options and provides you with the ability to create custom number formats. You can access all of the number formatting options on the **Number** tab of the **Format Cells** dialog box. Additionally, you can format cells by using the default settings for any of the number format categories by selecting the desired format category from the **Number Format** drop-down menu.

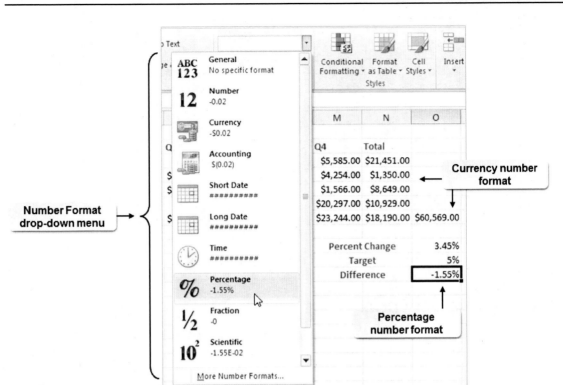

Figure 4-15: Various number formats applied to worksheet cells.

Number Format Categories

Excel 2010's number formatting options are arranged by categories, which are grouped according to function, for ease of use.

Number Format Category	Allows You To
General	Display numeric data in cells exactly as you enter it. This is the default number formatting in Excel worksheets and, essentially, applies no specific number formatting to your data.
Number	Control how many decimal places are displayed, how negative numbers are displayed, and whether or not Excel uses commas to separate degrees of 1,000.
Currency	Control how many decimal places are displayed, whether or not to display currency symbols, and how Excel displays negative numbers.
Accounting	Control how many decimal places are displayed and whether or not to display currency symbols.
Date	Display dates by using a variety of long and short date formats.
Time	Display times by using a variety of time formats. This can include military time and whether or not to display AM and PM to distinguish morning and night time values from each other.
Percentage	Automatically display numeric values as a percentage and control the number of decimal places that are displayed. Basically, this format multiplies the cell value by 100 and adds the percent sign.

Number Format Category	Allows You To
Fraction	Display decimal values as fractions, control how many digits are displayed in the numerator and the denominator, and round non-whole number values to the nearest fraction value.
Scientific	Display large numeric values in scientific notation and control the number of decimal places that are displayed.
Text	Treat numeric data as textual data. Numbers will be displayed exactly as you enter them but cannot be used in calculations.
Special	Display specific numeric data types, such as phone numbers, Social Security numbers, and zip codes, in the correct format. Special formatting is also useful for working with lists and database tables.
Custom	Specify the exact number formatting you require.

Custom Number Formats

If one of the existing number formatting options won't fit your particular needs, you can create and apply custom number formatting. Excel uses strings of code to create number formats. By selecting the **Custom** category on the **Number** tab in the **Format Cells** dialog box, you can view the code strings for the predetermined number formats. To create your own custom format, you can start with one of the existing code strings and modify it to suit your needs. Custom formats are saved along with the workbook file and will not be available in other workbooks. You cannot delete or alter the existing, pre-defined formats; when you create a custom format, you are working with a copy of the original code.

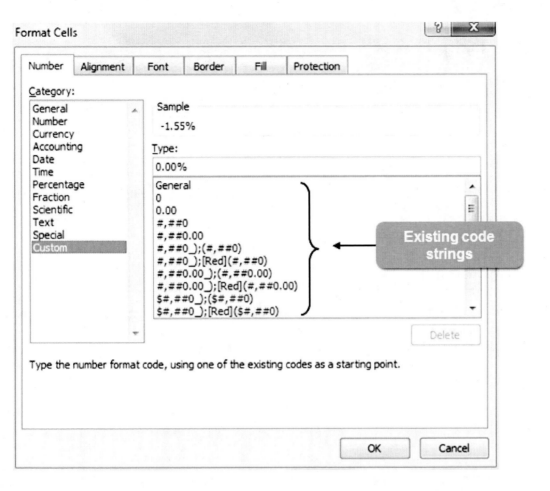

Figure 4-16: You can modify the existing number formatting code strings to create custom number formats.

Note: The full range of options for customizing number formats and in-depth coverage of the formatting code is beyond the scope of this course. For more information on customizing number formats, visit office.microsoft.com.

Access the Checklist tile on your LogicalCHOICE course screen for reference information and job aids on How to Apply Number Formats.

ACTIVITY 4–3
Applying Number Formats

Before You Begin
The my_sales_data.xlsx workbook file is open.

Scenario
Your sales data worksheet is looking better and better. But you still see opportunities to make it easier to read. You decide that the worksheet would be easier to interpret if you applied the currency format to the dollar amounts. Also, you feel that adding the date to the worksheet will help give meeting attendees a better idea of how current the information is.

1. Format the quarterly and total sales data as currency with no decimal places displayed.
   a) Select the range **C7:G24**.
   b) Select **Home→Number** and select the dialog box launcher.
   c) In the **Format Cells** dialog box, ensure that the **Number** tab is selected.
   d) In the **Category** section, select **Currency**.
   e) Set the **Decimal places** spin box to **0** and then select **OK**.

2. Format the remaining sales data as currency with two decimal places displayed.
   a) Select the range **H7:K24**.
   b) Select **Home→Number** and select the dialog box launcher.
   c) In the **Format Cells** dialog box, on the **Number** tab, in the **Category** section, select **Currency**.
   d) Ensure that the **Decimal places** spin box is set to **2** and then select **OK**.
   e) Use the **Format Cells** dialog box to apply the same formatting to the range **O7:O9**.
   f) Adjust the width of column **O** to accommodate the new formatting.

3. Add the date to the worksheet and apply date formatting to suit your needs.
   a) Select cell **N1**.
   b) Enter the current date in the mm/dd/yyyy format, and then press **Ctrl+Enter**.
   c) Select **Home→Number** and select the dialog box launcher.
   d) In the **Format Cells** dialog box, on the **Number** tab, in the **Category** section, ensure that **Date** is selected.
   e) In the **Type** list, scroll to the bottom, select **14-Mar-2001** and then select **OK**.
   f) Ensure that Excel applied the date formatting to cell **N1**.

4. Save the workbook.

TOPIC D

Align Cell Contents

So far, you have formatted worksheets by applying formatting to objects such as text, numbers, and borders. But, you may also want to consider making your worksheets easier to read and interpret by controlling where data is displayed within cells. What if you need to enter several sentences' worth of text in a single cell? Should that be displayed as one long cell or would you rather keep the current column width and have the text be displayed on different lines? Would it be easier to view row totals if the numbers were displayed to the left or the right of the final cell? Should a worksheet title be displayed centered along the top of the worksheet or all the way to the left?

The answer to these and other similar questions will largely depend on your particular needs. These questions highlight the importance of such considerations. It's easy to see how the placement of cell data can affect how easy your worksheets are to read and how people interpret them. Taking the time to familiarize yourself with the text alignment options available in Excel 2010 will give yet another weapon in your arsenal when it comes to keeping your organizational data orderly, readable, and functional.

Alignment Options

If you look at a new blank worksheet, it may not at first be obvious how aligning cell content could make a significant difference in how visually appealing and readable your worksheets are. As you modify the size of cells and rows or if you enter a large amount of information in a single cell, it soon becomes apparent. Excel 2010 provides you with the ability to control where your content is displayed horizontally and vertically within your worksheet cells. By default, Excel aligns numeric data to the right side and along the bottom of worksheet cells, and textual data is aligned to the left side and along the bottom of worksheet cells.

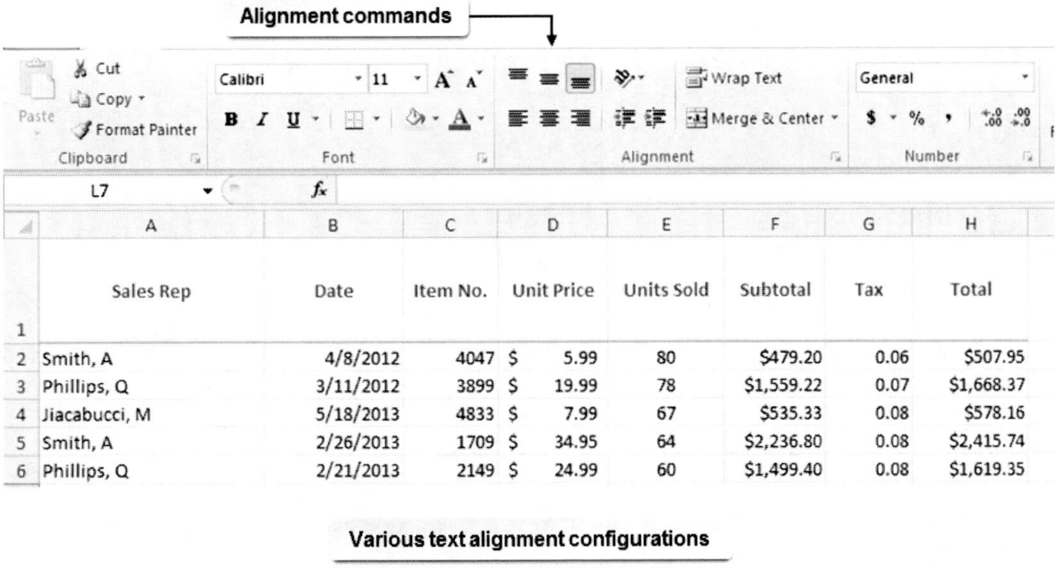

Figure 4-17: By default, Excel aligns the various data types in particular ways, but you can configure text alignment to suit your needs.

There are six basic alignment options in Excel, which display in the **Alignment** group on the **Home** tab.

Alignment Option	Command Button	Aligns Text
Top Align	≡	Vertically along the top of the cell.
Middle Align	≡	Centered vertically in the cell.
Bottom Align	≡	Vertically along the bottom of the cell.
Align Text Left	≣	Horizontally to the left side of the cell.
Center	≣	Centered horizontally in the cell.
Align Text Right	≣	Horizontally to the right side of the cell.

The Indent Commands

You can use the Indent commands to increase or decrease the amount of space between cell data and cell borders. If your cell content is aligned to the left side of cells, selecting the **Increase Indent** command will move the content to the right, increasing the amount of space between the left cell border and the content. Selecting the **Decrease Indent** command will move the content to the left. The opposite is true of content aligned to the right side of cells. If your content is centered within the cell, selecting the **Decrease Indent** command has no effect, while selecting the **Increase Indent** command will automatically change the alignment to left aligned and then increase the amount of space between the left border and the content.

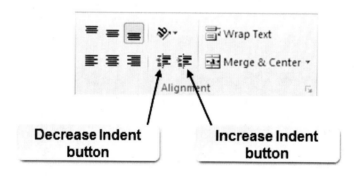

Figure 4-18: The Indent commands control the amount of space between the cell borders and the cell content.

The Wrap Text Command

By default, when a cell contains a large amount of text, the text spills over into the next column if the adjacent cells are empty. Excel truncates the display of the text if the adjacent cells are populated. Often, neither of these options is what worksheet users are looking for. You can use the **Wrap Text** command to automatically adjust row height to accommodate large amounts of text while preserving column width. When the **Wrap Text** command is enabled on a cell, and the textual content in that cell exceeds the column width, Excel automatically drops the text down to the next line by increasing the row height of the row containing the cell. This feature enables you to preserve your worksheet layout while still allowing worksheet users to view all of the content in cells.

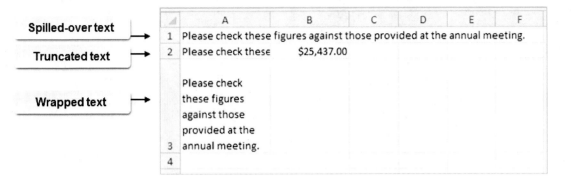

Figure 4-19: Use the Wrap Text command to preserve the layout of your worksheets while allowing users to view your content.

Manual Line Breaks

You can also simulate wrapped text by inserting manual line breaks in your cell content. To do so, place the insertion point in the desired location and press **Alt+Enter**. This isn't typically the best solution, however, as any text that happens to exceed the column width will still either spill over into adjacent columns or display as truncated text. You may decide to use this option if you're not satisfied with how Excel wraps your text automatically.

Orientation Options

In order to display data in a worksheet legibly, you may need to change the orientation of some of your text. For example, if a column's header text takes up more horizontal space than the data in the column's cells, you might want to change the display angle to avoid having to make the column too wide. Not only does this make your worksheet layout more visually appealing, but it can also help you fit more columns on the same screen or printed page. Excel 2010 provides you with a number of preset orientation options or it allows you to specify an exact orientation angle by using the commands in the **Orientation** section on the **Alignment** tab in the **Format Cells** dialog box. Changing cell orientation can affect row height and column width.

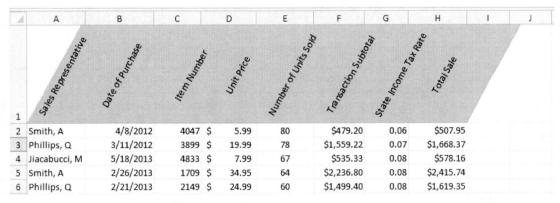

Figure 4-20: Use the orientation options to fit more content in the same amount of horizontal space or to add visual appeal to your worksheets.

You can access the preset orientation options from the **Orientation** button in the **Alignment** group on the **Home** tab. These options cannot be used in conjunction with one another, and are not configurable. Essentially, you can toggle these on or off, or switch from one orientation preset to another. You can, however, use orientation and alignment options in conjunction with one another to achieve the desired text placement.

Orientation Preset Option	Description
Angle Counterclockwise	Rotates the text in the selected cell or range 45 degrees counterclockwise.
Angle Clockwise	Rotates the text in the selected cell or range 45 degrees clockwise.
Vertical Text	Orients the text in the selected cell or range vertically from top to bottom, but keeps the letters, numbers, and symbols upright.
Rotate Text Up	Rotates the text in the selected cell or range 90 degrees counterclockwise.
Rotate Text Down	Rotates the text in the selected cell or range 90 degrees clockwise.
Format Cell Alignment	Opens the **Format Cells** dialog box with the **Alignment** tab automatically selected. From here, you can set more precise orientation configurations.

The Merge & Center Options

Excel 2010 provides you with the ability to merge multiple, contiguous cells across either rows or columns into a single cell, and to revert merged cells back to individual cells. It is important to note, however, that this can have a significant effect on the data in those cells. Excel will display a warning message if you attempt to merge cells in such cases. If you revert a merged cell back to individual cells, lost data will not be recovered. You can, however, use the **Undo** command to restore the data if you mistakenly merge cells.

	Percent Change	3.45%	
	Target	5%	
	Difference	-1.55%	

Figure 4–21: Merged cells on a worksheet.

You can access the Merge & Center options from the **Merge & Center** down arrow in the **Alignment** group on the **Home** tab.

Merge & Center Option	Description
Merge & Center	Merges all selected cells across rows and columns into a single cell and centers the text horizontally in the new, larger cell. Only the data in the top-leftmost cell is retained.
Merge Across	Merges selected cells together one row at a time. Only the data from the leftmost cell in each row is retained.
Merge Cells	Merges all selected cells across rows and columns into a single cell. Only the date in the top-leftmost cell is retained.
Unmerge Cells	Reverts a merged cell back into the original, individual cells. Data that was lost in the processing of merging is not restored.

> Access the Checklist tile on your LogicalCHOICE course screen for reference information and job aids on How to Align Cell Contents.

ACTIVITY 4–4
Aligning Cell Contents

Before You Begin
The my_sales_data.xlsx workbook file is open.

Scenario
Your worksheet is coming along nicely. You have formatted the text, added backgrounds and borders, and applied number and date formatting to make it easier to read and interpret. But you still feel some of the text doesn't line up quite right, and you would like to make adjustments. Specifically, you want to align some of the column labels with the cell content for their respective columns, ensure the title formatting applies to all of the title text, center the worksheet title above the worksheet data, and use the **Wrap Text** command to make one of the cells seem less crowded.

1. Right-align some of the column labels.
   a) Select the range **C6:L6**.
   b) Select **Home→Alignment→Align Text Right**.

2. Merge and center the title text over the sales data.
   a) Select the range **A5:L5**.
   b) Select **Home→Alignment→Merge & Center**.
   c) Adjust the height of row **5** to better accommodate the title text.

3. Revise the text in cell **N3** and then wrap the text to better fit the column width.
   a) Select cell **N3**, type *Total number of employees* and press **Enter**.
   b) Verify the text now spills over into the next cell and that Excel truncates the display of the text in cell **N3**.
   c) Select cell **N3** and then select **Home→Alignment→Wrap Text**.

4. Align the date text in cell **N1** to the left to better match the surrounding text.

5. Save the workbook.

TOPIC E

Apply Styles and Themes

Having the ability to apply formatting to the text, numbers, borders, and cells in your worksheets allows you to create professional-looking worksheets that are easy to read, work with, and interpret. But, if you create and analyze data in a number of large worksheets on a regular basis, you'll quickly find individually applying formatting to the various sections, data types, and worksheet elements to be a massive, tedious chore. This sense of monotony and wasted effort will only grow as you create multiple worksheets with the same type of formatting requirements over and over. Shouldn't there be an easier way to apply a variety of formatting combinations to your worksheet contents so users can instantly recognize common types of worksheet data at a glance? The answer, of course, is yes.

The good news is that Excel provides you with a number of options for quickly applying a variety of formatting options to your worksheet cells. This will not only save you time and effort, but can also help you consistently present data to your audiences in ways that are clear and instantly recognizable.

Cell Styles

If you looked at a large number of Excel worksheets from a number of different organizations in a variety of fields, you would probably quickly notice that a lot of them contain very similar data types. Sales figures, column and row totals, calculations, and column and row labels are just a few of these. Because a fairly small variety of data types appear over and over in many, if not most, worksheets, it would make sense to have a way to distinguish these data types from other types of data quickly and easily. There is, and that's by using *cell styles*.

A cell style is a unique set of formatting options that you can apply to a cell or a range on a worksheet. Styles can include any type of formatting options, and you can select from a wide arrange of predefined cell styles or create custom styles. Once you have created a custom cell style, you can access it in the **Custom** section at the top of the **Cell Styles** gallery. In addition to visual formatting options, styles can include cell protection options to prevent people from altering your important organizational data. You can access the commands you will use to apply cell styles to your worksheets and create new styles from the **Cell Styles** command in the **Styles** group on the **Home** tab.

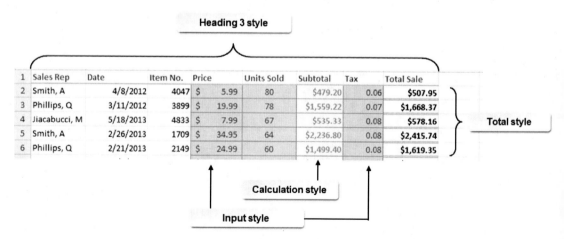

Figure 4–22: Cell styles make it easy to differentiate among common data types on worksheets.

Galleries

For many types of formatting options, Excel 2010 and other Office 2010 applications present you with a more visually oriented type of menu for making selections: *galleries*. Galleries behave very much like standard drop-down or pop-up menus but, instead of simply listing your options in the form of text, galleries present your options in the form of thumbnail images or icons that give you an indication of what the formatting options will look like once applied. Most galleries also use the Live Preview feature, so when you place the mouse pointer over an option in a gallery, Excel displays a temporary preview of what the formatting will look like on the selected cells. **Cell Styles** and **Themes** are just two types of formatting options that are displayed within galleries.

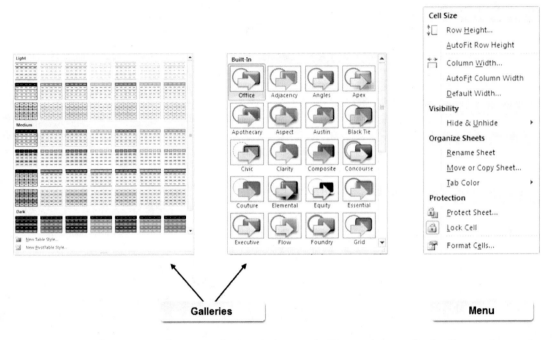

Figure 4–23: Galleries provide you with visual clues to indicate what particular formatting options will look like on your worksheets.

The Style Dialog Box

You will use the **Style** dialog box to modify existing cell styles and create custom cell styles. The **Style** dialog box contains a set of formatting option check boxes that you can use to quickly toggle particular formatting options on and off. From the **Style** dialog box, you can also access the **Format Cells** dialog box where you can make more detailed changes to your cell styles. You can access the **Style** dialog box by selecting **Home→Styles→Cell Styles→New Cell Style** or by selecting **Home→Styles→Cell Styles** and then right-clicking an existing cell style.

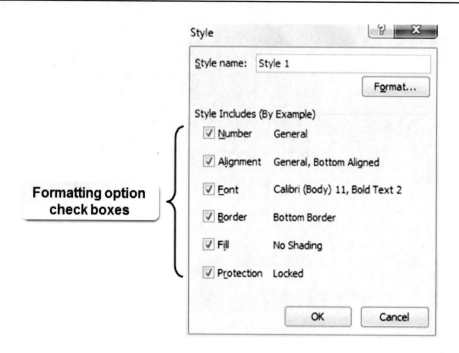

Figure 4-24: The Style dialog box.

The Merge Styles Dialog Box

By default, Excel saves custom cell styles with the associated workbook file and they are not available in other workbooks. However, Excel 2010 provides you with a tool you can use to import custom styles from existing workbooks into other workbooks: the **Merge Styles** dialog box. The **Merge Styles** dialog box searches all open workbook files for custom styles that you can merge into the active workbook file. You can access the **Merge Styles** dialog box by selecting **Home→Styles→Cell Styles→Merge Styles**.

Figure 4-25: The Merge Styles dialog box.

 Access the Checklist tile on your LogicalCHOICE course screen for reference information and job aids on How to Work with Cell Styles.

ACTIVITY 4-5
Applying Cell Styles

Before You Begin
The my_sales_data.xlsx workbook file is open.

Scenario
You like the progress you have made formatting the sales data worksheet, but you think it's important for the people who will be viewing the worksheet at the sales meeting to be able to distinguish between raw data and data that has been calculated using formulas and functions. You'd also like to set off the sales rep's names a bit more from the rest of the worksheet data. So, you decide to apply cell styles to differentiate among the various data types. You also feel it would be a good idea to modify the default **Title** cell style to align more with your current formatting. You want to use the modified cell style in other workbooks to ensure consistency.

---

1. Apply the **Title** cell style to the worksheet title.
   a) Select cell **A5**.
   b) Select **Home→Styles→Cell Styles**.
   c) In the **Cell Styles** gallery, in the **Titles and Headings** section, select **Title**.

2. Modify the **Title** cell style to include the background color you used in this workbook.
   a) Select **Home→Styles→Cell Styles**, and then right-click the **Title** cell style and select **Duplicate**.
   b) In the **Style** dialog box, in the **Style name** field, type *Footprint Title*
   c) Select **Format**.
   d) In the **Format Cells** dialog box, select the **Fill** tab.
   e) In the **Background Color** section, select the light red color that is in the second row of the sixth column.

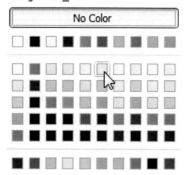

   f) Select **OK**.
   g) In the **Style** dialog box, ensure the **Fill** check box is checked, uncheck the **Number** check box, and then select **OK**.

3. Verify that Excel saved the modified cell style.
   a) Select **Home→Styles→Cell Styles**.

    b) In the **Cell Styles** gallery, in the **Custom** section, place the mouse pointer over the modified cell style to view its screen tip.

    c) Verify the screen tip displays as **Footprint Title**.

    d) Select anywhere on screen outside the **Cell Styles** gallery to close it.

4. Apply a cell style to the items in the **Name** column.

    a) Select the range **A7:A24**.

    b) Select **Home→Styles→Cell Styles**, and then, in the **Themed Cell Styles** section, select **Accent2**.

5. Apply a cell style to the raw sales data.

    a) Select the range **C7:F24**.

    b) From the **Cell Styles** gallery, in the **Data and Model** section, select the **Input** cell style.

6. Apply a cell style to cells containing formulas or functions.

    a) Select the range **G7:K24**.

    b) From the **Cell Styles** gallery, in the **Data and Model** section, select the **Calculation** cell style.

    c) Deselect the range to view the newly applied cell style.

7. Save the workbook.

Themes

Themes are collections of formatting options that you can apply to an entire workbook, as opposed to a particular cell or range. Theme formatting includes colors, fonts, and effects but, unlike cell styles, does not include number formatting, cell protection, alignment, or fill formatting. There are a number of predefined themes included with Excel 2010, and you can manually set the formatting of a workbook and then save it as a new custom theme.

You can use Excel themes to create numerous workbooks that all have a consistent, professional look. Customizing themes allows you to apply organizational branding across all of your spreadsheet documents. You can access the **Themes** gallery by selecting **Page Layout→Themes→Themes**. By default, all new, blank workbooks have the Office theme applied to them.

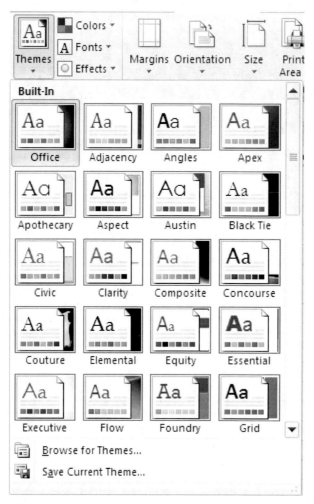

Figure 4–26: Themes make it easy for you to create multiple workbooks that all have a consistent look and feel.

Theme Components

As previously mentioned, Excel themes consist of colors, fonts, and effects. More specifically and more accurately, Excel themes contain combinations of multiple fonts and colors and a predefined set of theme effects. In order to fully understand how changing theme formatting will affect your worksheets, let's take a closer look at what each of the formatting components does.

Theme Colors

All Excel themes, both pre-existing and custom, contain a set of 10 colors: 4 text and background colors, 6 accent colors, and 2 hyperlink colors. The colors that are displayed on the **Colors** button in the **Themes** group on the **Page Layout** tab represent the text and background colors for the currently applied theme. When you select the **Colors** button, the gallery that is displayed allows you to view the accent and the hyperlink colors for all of the included themes and your custom themes. If you select **Page Layout→Themes→Colors→Create New Theme Colors**, Excel displays the **Create New Theme Colors** dialog box, which enables you to customize the theme colors and lets you view what, exactly, is affected by each color selection.

 Note: Applying various themes to your workbooks will also change the available colors in the **Theme** section of both the **Fill Color** and the **Font Color** drop-down menus.

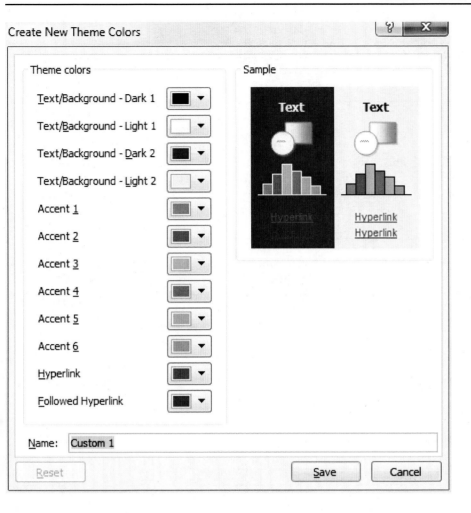

The following table describes in detail what each of the theme colors affects.

Theme Color Element	Description
Text/Background - Dark 1	Defines the default text color for the workbook. This will be the text color for all data displayed in cells unless otherwise formatted, along with the color of text displayed on light-colored backgrounds in graphical objects such as charts and in cells with light-colored fills.
Text/Background - Light 1	Defines the default color of text displayed on dark backgrounds in graphical objects and in cells with dark-colored fills.
Text/Background - Dark 2	Defines the default dark background color for graphical objects.
Text/Background - Light 2	Defines the default light background color for graphical objects.
Accent 1-6	Defines the color of graphical objects such as the individual bars or lines on a graph that represent different sets of data.
Hyperlink	Defines the default color of hyperlink text for the theme.
Followed Hyperlink	Defines the color of hyperlink text once it's been selected.

Theme Fonts

All Excel themes, both pre-existing and custom, contain two fonts: a heading font and a body font. The heading font defines the default font type for the **Title** cell style, and the body font defines the font type for labels, titles, and other text on some graphical objects, such as charts. You can access the theme fonts by selecting **Page Layout→Themes→Fonts**.

 Note: The theme fonts do not affect the default font type for cell data. That is an application-wide setting, which is also customizable. The default font type for cell data is Arial.

Theme Effects

All Excel themes contain a set of effects that define how graphical elements, such as line styles, line weights, object shading, and drop shadows, are displayed on worksheets. You cannot customize theme effects in Excel, but Excel 2010 includes a gallery of 40 predefined theme effect configurations. You can access the theme effects by selecting **Page Layout→Themes→Effects**.

Custom Themes Considerations

You have already seen that Excel themes can be customized. But there are a few important points to keep in mind when it comes to creating custom themes. The first is that you may want to find an existing theme that contains some of the formatting options you desire and then make the necessary changes to tweak the theme to suit your needs. This is far easier than trying to build one from scratch. Also, Excel saves all themes to a default folder that is installed along with Excel. Do not save your custom themes in any other folders. Excel will look for custom themes only in the default directory.

Excel allows you to create custom sets of theme colors and custom theme fonts as well as entire custom themes. Each will be displayed at the top of their respective galleries in a section called **Custom** once saved.

 Access the Checklist tile on your LogicalCHOICE course screen for reference information and job aids on How to Apply and Manage Themes.

ACTIVITY 4-6
Applying a Theme to a Workbook

Before You Begin
The my_sales_data.xlsx workbook file is open.

Scenario
You've asked your supervisor to review the sales data worksheet ahead of the upcoming sales meeting. He generally likes the overall layout and formatting that you've configured. But he suggested that the colors are a bit informal. He asked you go with a slightly more subtle color palette for the worksheet. You decide to apply a different theme to the workbook to consistently change the color palette throughout.

1. Preview several themes to determine how they will affect the overall look of your workbook.
   a) Select **Page Layout→Themes→Themes** to display the **Themes** gallery.
   b) In the **Themes** gallery, point the mouse pointer at various themes to preview them.

2. Select the **Black Tie** theme to apply it to the workbook.

3. Save the workbook.

TOPIC F

Apply Basic Conditional Formatting

As your Excel skill level increases and you begin to perform more and more data analysis with the information in your workbooks, you may find yourself looking for a way to make certain bits of information stand out. For example, if you're analyzing sales figures for your sales reps, you may find it helpful to display figures for reps who reached their sales targets in one color and figures for those who missed their targets in another. Or, you may wish to highlight departments or projects that have gone over budget. After all, your data is most useful when you can quickly glean important information from it at a glance. So, is there a way to make particular points of data stand out on your worksheets? Yes!

Excel 2010 allows you to specially format particular data that meets particular criteria. This kind of functionality can transform enormous, seemingly random bits of data into useful organizational intelligence that you can use to make sound decisions. Understanding how this functionality works and how you can tailor it to suit your needs will elevate your worksheets from glorified calculators to critical information and intelligence sources.

Conditional Formatting

One of the key benefits to using Excel is that it can help you find answers to questions you may ask of your data; answers that are often hidden in thousands of rows and columns of information. *Conditional formatting* is one of the features that can find you the answers you seek. When you apply conditional formatting to your worksheets, Excel displays data that meets specified criteria with the specified formatting applied. For example, on a budget worksheet, you may want all line items that are still under budget to appear in green text and line items that are over budget appear in red text. Or, perhaps you want to highlight in yellow all product lines on a sales summary that have increased in sales by more than 5 percent. Conditional formatting can perform these, and many other, tasks for you.

	A	B	C	D	E	F	G	H
1	Sales Rep	Date	Item No.	Price	Units Sold	Subtotal	Tax	Total Sale
2	Smith, A	4/8/2012	4047	$5.99	80	$479.20	6.00%	$507.95
3	Phillips, Q	3/11/2012	3899	$19.99	78	$1,559.22	7.00%	$1,668.37
4	Jiacabucci, M	5/18/2013	4833	$7.99	67	$535.33	8.00%	$578.16
5	Smith, A	2/26/2013	1709	$34.95	64	$2,236.80	8.00%	$2,415.74
6	Phillips, Q	2/21/2013	2149	$24.99	60	$1,499.40	8.00%	$1,619.35
7	Anderson, Z	12/5/2012	4806	$13.49	87	$1,173.63	6.00%	$1,244.05
8	Toner, R	3/7/2012	4728	$19.99	64	$1,279.36	5.50%	$1,349.72
9	Smith, A	1/3/2012	3215	$7.99	90	$719.10	5.50%	$758.65
10	Phillips, Q	3/7/2012	5089	$34.95	30	$1,048.50	6.00%	$1,111.41
11	Jiacabucci, M	12/6/2013	4932	$5.99	95	$569.05	7.00%	$608.88
12	Smith, A	9/29/2012	1884	$19.99	30	$599.70	8.00%	$647.68
13	Smith, A	5/19/2013	3250	$7.99	6	$47.94	8.00%	$51.78
14	Phillips, Q	2/9/2013	2151	$34.95	87	$3,040.65	8.00%	$3,283.90
15	Anderson, Z	1/29/2012	1042	$24.99	73	$1,824.27	6.00%	$1,933.73
16	Toner, R	11/1/2013	2255	$13.49	29	$391.21	5.50%	$412.73
17	Smith, A	5/19/2013	4291	$19.99	41	$819.59	8.00%	$885.16
18	Phillips, Q	7/30/2012	2561	$7.99	59	$471.41	6.00%	$499.69
19	Jiacabucci, M	9/30/2013	3265	$34.95	57	$1,992.15	5.50%	$2,101.72
20	Smith, A	9/29/2013	4492	$24.99	55	$1,374.45	8.00%	$1,484.41

Figure 4–27: Conditional formatting makes data that meets a specified criteria stand out from the rest of your data.

The Conditional Formatting Dialog Boxes

Each of the conditional formatting options covered in this topic has its own dialog box. These are all basically the same with a few minor exceptions for option-specific considerations. For example, the **Between** dialog box has two fields for values whereas the **Greater Than** and **Less Than** dialog boxes have only a single value field. And each of the dialog boxes is labeled with its corresponding conditional formatting option as the name.

The conditional formatting dialog boxes allow you to both select the criteria by which Excel analyzes the selected data and the formatting it will apply. You can select from among a small array of preconfigured formatting options or access the **Format Cells** dialog box to configure more specific formatting.

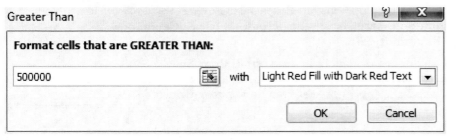

Figure 4–28: The Greater Than dialog box.

The Highlight Cells Rules

One of the most common types of conditional formatting that Excel users perform is highlighting cells that contain data meeting specific numeric criteria. To do this, you can select one of the options from the **Highlight Cells Rules** menu. These options allow you to select the criteria by which you wish to format your cell data and the specific formatting options you wish to apply to the

data that meets the criteria. You can access the **Highlight Cells Rules** menu by selecting
Home→Styles→**Conditional Formatting**→**Highlight Cells Rules**.

	A	B	C	D	E	F	G	H
1	Sales Rep	Date	Item No.	Price	Units Sold	Subtotal	Tax	Total Sale
2	Smith, A	4/8/2012	4047	$5.99	80	$479.20	6.00%	$507.95
3	Phillips, Q	3/11/2012	3899	$19.99	78	$1,559.22	7.00%	$1,668.37
4	Jiacabucci, M	5/18/2013	4833	$7.99	67	$535.33	8.00%	$578.16
5	Smith, A	2/26/2013	1709	$34.95	64	$2,236.80	8.00%	$2,415.74
6	Phillips, Q	2/21/2013	2149	$24.99	60	$1,499.40	8.00%	$1,619.35
7	Anderson, Z	12/5/2012	4806	$13.49	87	$1,173.63	6.00%	$1,244.05
8	Toner, R	3/7/2012	4728	$19.99	64	$1,279.36	5.50%	$1,349.72
9	Smith, A	1/3/2012	3215	$7.99	90	$719.10	5.50%	$758.65
10	Phillips, Q	3/7/2012	5089	$34.95	30	$1,048.50	6.00%	$1,111.41

Figure 4-29: Cells conditionally formatted to highlight all values greater than $1,200.

There are seven conditional formatting options in the **Highlight Cells Rules** menu.

Highlight Cells Rules Options	Applies the Selected Conditional Formatting To
Greater Than	Cells with values greater than the specified value.
Less Than	Cells with values less than the specified value.
Between	Cells with values between the two specified values.
Equal to	Cells with values equal to the specified value.
Text that Contains	Cells that contain the exact text or value specified.
A Date Occurring	Cells that contain a date that falls within the specified time range.
Duplicate Values	Cells in a range that contain the same value as other cells in the selected range.

The Top/Bottom Rules

Another common use of conditional formatting involves highlighting cells that contain either the highest or the lowest values in a particular range or cells that are above or below average for the selected cells. The options in the **Top/Bottom Rules** menu can help you do just that. You can access the **Top/Bottom Rules** menu by selecting Home→Styles→**Conditional Formatting**→**Top/Bottom Rules**.

There are six conditional formatting options in the **Top/Bottom Rules** menu.

Top/Bottom Rules Option	Applies the Selected Conditional Formatting To
Top 10 Items	The cells in the selected range containing the 10 largest values.
Top 10%	The 10 percent of cells in the selected range containing the largest values.
Bottom 10 Items	The cells in the selected range containing the 10 smallest values.
Bottom 10%	The 10 percent of cells in the selected range containing the smallest values.
Above Average	All cells in the selected range with values that are greater than the average of all values in the selected range.

Top/Bottom Rules Option	Applies the Selected Conditional Formatting To
Below Average	All cells in the selected range with values that are less than the average of all values in the selected range.

Note: The top and bottom 10 and the top and bottom 10-percent criteria are default settings that you can modify when applying conditional formatting to cells.

Access the Checklist tile on your LogicalCHOICE course screen for reference information and job aids on **How to Apply Basic Conditional Formatting.**

ACTIVITY 4-7
Applying Basic Conditional Formatting

Before You Begin

The my_sales_data.xlsx workbook file is open.

Scenario

Your supervisor had another suggestion after reviewing the sales data worksheet. He asked you to highlight all sales figures greater than $30,000 for each quarter and to highlight the bottom 25 percent of sales reps based on sales totals for the year and average quarterly sales. You decide that the easiest way to accomplish this is to apply conditional formatting to the worksheet columns.

1. Highlight all quarterly sales figures of $30,000 or more.
   a) Select the range **C7:F24**.
   b) Select **Home→Styles→Conditional Formatting→Highlight Cells Rules→Greater Than**.
   c) In the **Greater Than** dialog box, in the **Format cells that are GREATER THAN** field, type *30000*
   d) From the **with** drop-down menu, select **Green Fill with Dark Green Text** and then select **OK**.
   e) De-select the range to verify that Excel applied the formatting as expected.

2. Highlight the lowest 25 percent of performers in total sales and average quarterly sales.
   a) Select the range **G7:G24**.
   b) Select **Home→Styles→Conditional Formatting→Top/Bottom Rules→Bottom 10%**.
   c) In the **Bottom 10%** dialog box, in the **Format cells that rank in the BOTTOM *X*%** spin box, set the value to **25**.
   d) From the **with** drop-down menu, select **Light Red Fill** and then select **OK**.
   e) Apply the same conditional formatting to the cells in the **Average** column.
   f) Deselect the **Average** column's cells to verify that Excel applied the formatting.

3. Save the workbook.

TOPIC G

Create and Use Templates

For many Excel users, it's not uncommon to create and work with pretty much the same workbook over and over again with few, if any, significant changes. You may, for example, have to generate the same data for every quarter or month. Or your organization may use Excel worksheets to track project management goals and milestones. So, your project managers will likely start with the same basic worksheet and modify it to suit a particular project. Paid time off often resets every calendar year, so HR associates may need to start with a clean slate each year, but still be tracking data for the same set of employees. In these cases, it may seem like a waste of time to have to lay out the basic framework of your worksheets every time you create a new workbook. And, quite frankly, it is.

Fortunately, Excel allows you to leverage your existing workbooks to create similar new workbooks for subsequent accounting periods, projects, calendar years, and other reuse purposes. By taking advantage of this functionality, you can essentially store all the time, effort, and research that went into creating your workbooks for future use. This will not only save you time and effort, but will also ensure a level of consistency and quality that may not otherwise be attainable. After all, you've already ironed out the wrinkles in your current spreadsheet files, why risk missing something next time?

Templates

An Excel template is a file that contains a number of pre-formatted workbook elements, such as formatting, formulas, themes, and functions, that you can use to create and work with new workbooks. Essentially, templates are files that contain the desired structure for future workbook files. Excel 2010 comes preloaded with a small handful of templates. You can also search for and download thousands of Excel template files from office.com and a number of other websites or create your own custom templates to suit your needs.

The default file format for Excel 2010 template files is the XLTX file format. You can access your local Excel template files and search for others from office.com on the **New** tab in the Backstage view. Excel template files are saved to a default folder on your computer, so downloaded and custom templates will always be available to you if you use Excel on the same computer. You can transfer template files to other machines or simply re-download them from office.com when you have to work with Excel on a different computer.

Office.com Templates   Search Office.com for templates

G & A expense budget   Manufacturing overhead budget   Forecast of sales goals   Quarterly marketing budget   Expense budget spreadsheet

Event budget   Marketing budget plan estimates   Marketing budget plan   Business trip budget   Training budget

Figure 4-30: Office.com templates in the Backstage view.

 Access the Checklist tile on your LogicalCHOICE course screen for reference information and job aids on How to Create and Use Templates.

ACTIVITY 4-8
Creating a Template

Before You Begin
The my_sales_data.xlsx workbook file is open.

Scenario
You're nearly done developing the worksheet you will present during the upcoming sales meeting. As you are likely to need the same sales data for future periods and other meetings, you decide to save the current workbook as an Excel template from which to create future workbooks. Because you don't want to include all of the current sales data in the template, you decide to delete most of the worksheet data before saving the file as a template.

1. Delete cell content not needed in the template file.
   a) Select the range **A7:F24** and press **Delete**.
   b) Delete the employee ID entries in the **Employee ID** column.
   c) Delete the cell content in the following ranges and cells: **O3:O4**, **N7:O9**, **N1**, and **N11**.

    Note: Do not select cell **N11** directly, as that will activate the link. Instead, select a cell near it and use the arrow keys to navigate to it.

2. Save the workbook as an Excel template file.
   a) Select **File→Save As**.
   b) In the **Save As** dialog box, ensure that Excel is saving the template file to the default **Templates** folder; do not navigate away from this folder.
   c) In the **File name** field, type *my_sales_data_template*
   d) In the **Save as type** drop-down menu, verify that **Excel Template (*.xltx)** is selected and select **Save**.

3. Verify that the template file name appears in the **title bar** with the .xltx file extension and close the template file.

4. Verify that the template is available for future use.
   a) Select **File→New**.
   b) In the **Available Templates** section, select **My templates**.
   c) In the **New** dialog box, verify that the **my_sales_data_template.xltx** file is displayed and select **Cancel**.
   d) Select any tab to exit the Backstage view, and then close the workbook.

Summary

In this lesson, you formatted text, numbers, borders, and cells; aligned content within worksheet cells; applied cell styles and themes to worksheets; applied conditional formatting to cells; and created Excel template files. This robust set of formatting functionality will help you create highly functional, professional-looking workbooks time and time again without the need to spend countless hours tweaking and adjusting numerous settings. Being able to quickly generate high-quality workbooks will allow you to forget about tedious, small details, and get back to focusing on what's really important: what your data can tell you about your organization.

What are some of the ways you will use conditional formatting in your workbooks?

Can you think of reasons you would create custom templates for use within your organization?

 Note: Check your LogicalCHOICE Course screen for opportunities to interact with your classmates, peers, and the larger LogicalCHOICE online community about the topics covered in this course or other topics you are interested in. From the Course screen you can also access available resources for a more continuous learning experience.

5 | Printing Workbooks

Lesson Time: 30 minutes

Lesson Objectives

In this lesson, you will print a workbook. You will:

- Preview and print a workbook.
- Define the page layout.

Lesson Introduction

You put a lot of hard work into creating, populating, and formatting your workbook. Now it's time to share the final product with your colleagues, supervisor, or organizational leaders. This time you may simply need to email your workbook file to the necessary recipients or project it in front of a live audience; this will not always be the case. For any number of reasons, you may need to print hard copies of your workbooks to share with others. Your workbooks may contain multiple worksheets, each of which could contain thousands of data entries, formulas, and results. Do you really want to print that many pages to distribute to your audience? What information should you include and what do you do if you need to print a bit from here and a bit from there?

Fortunately, Excel provides you with a wide array of options when it comes to printing hard copies of your workbooks. Understanding how to set your worksheets up for printing and how to print only what you need will allow you to deliver only the necessary critical information to your audience. This will not only save your organization paper and money, but it will also prevent your document recipients from having to sift through mounds of irrelevant data.

TOPIC A

Preview and Print a Workbook

Although most everything you do these days is driven by computers, digital information, and electronic communication, your situation may require a hard copy of a document. Spreadsheets are not the same as most other documents. They can contain nearly any number of rows and columns: Workbooks can contain a number of worksheets and the amount of data you can include on worksheets can be staggering. So, what, exactly, defines a page for printed workbooks, largely depends on your preferences.

You'll want to be able to identify what is going to print when you print your worksheets. You'll likely want to print some, but not all, of the content in your workbooks for different situations. This is why Excel 2010 includes a variety of basic options for printing your workbooks. Knowing what these are and how they work means you'll be able to quickly generate hard copies of your data, exactly as you need to, quickly and easily.

The Print Tab

You can access all of the commands and setting you will need to print your workbooks on the **Print** tab in the Backstage view. From here you can select a printer, adjust numerous print settings, and view a preview of what your printed pages will look like based on the current settings. You can access the **Print** screen in the Backstage view by selecting **File→Print**.

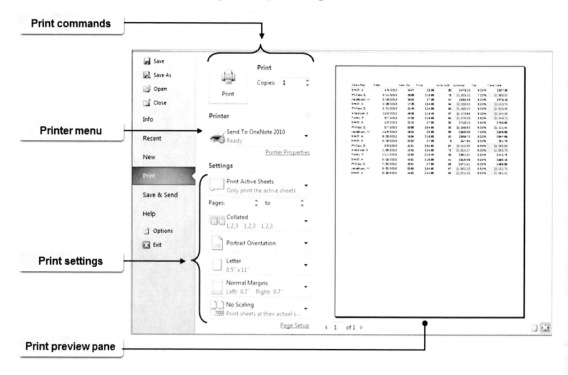

Figure 5-1: The Print tab in the Backstage view provides you with numerous options for determining how your workbooks will print.

The following table describes the functions of the various elements on the **Print** tab.

Print Tab Element	Allows You To
Print section	Access commands for selecting the number of copies you wish to print and for executing a print job.
Printer menu	Select the printer, device, or printer driver you wish to use.
Printer Properties link	Access the **Properties** dialog box for your selected printer, device, or printer driver.
Settings section	Configure general print settings, such as which worksheets to print, how to orient the printed pages, and what magnification level to use.
Page Setup link	Access the **Page Setup** dialog box, which allows you to configure the page layout of your worksheets.
Print preview pane	View a preview of how your workbook pages will look once printed.

The Print Settings

To ensure that your printed pages look exactly as you want them to, you'll likely need to adjust some of the print settings before you print. The **Settings** section of the **Print** tab contains all of the commands you will use to configure general print settings for your workbook. It is important to keep in mind that the print setting buttons are displayed with different text depending on your current selection, so the command buttons will not always match the following figure.

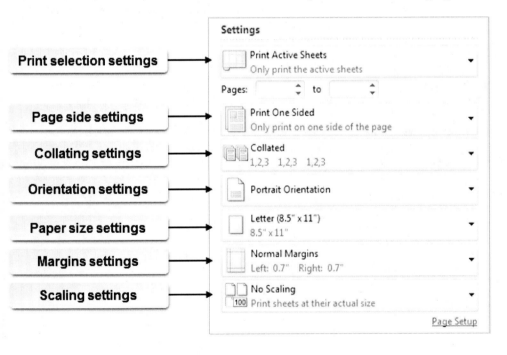

Figure 5-2: The Settings commands are displayed differently depending on your current selections.

The **Settings** commands give you control over the final printed copies of your workbooks.

Print Settings Command	Allows You To
Print selection settings	Decide among printing all worksheets in a workbook, printing the currently selected worksheet, or printing the currently selected cell or range. If you have defined a print area, you can also choose to ignore that in favor of whatever setting you select from this command.
Pages and **to** spin boxes	Select which range of pages to print. The content that appears on each page and the number of printable pages for a workbook depend on your other print settings.
Page sides settings	Decide between printing on one or both sides of the paper, if that's possible with your selected printer.
Collating settings	Decide between collating and not collating your pages. Collated print jobs print each copy of a multiple-page document in sequential order, so each copy is in the correct page order. Non-collated print jobs print all copies of the first page and then all copies of the second page, and so on.
Orientation settings	Decide between the portrait and landscape orientations for your printed pages.
Paper size settings	Decide what size paper to print on. These settings depend on your printer's capabilities.
Margins settings	Set the margin size for your printed pages.
Scaling settings	Determine whether or not Excel changes the magnification level of your printed data and how it applies magnification to printed pages.

Print Preview

With so many options when it comes to printing your workbooks, you'll want to be sure you have configured your print setting properly before you print. It would be a significant waste of paper and cost to repeatedly reprint workbooks because you didn't have the settings configured just right. Excel 2010 provides you with the ability to view a preview of your workbook print jobs before you print. The print preview is displayed in the right pane of the **Print** tab in the Backstage view. You can access this by selecting **File→Print** or by selecting either the **Print** or the **Print Preview** button in the **Page Setup** dialog box.

Preview image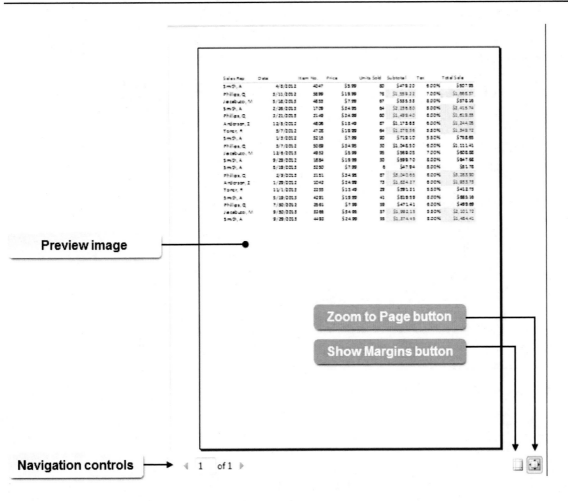

Navigation controls

Figure 5-3: A workbook document displayed in print preview.

The commands in the print preview pane enable you to inspect each page of a print job before printing.

Print Preview Element	Description
Preview image	Displays how the currently selected page will print on paper.
Navigation controls	Enables you to navigate through and inspect each page in the current print job.
Show Margins button	Toggles the display of page margins on and off.
Zoom to Page button	Toggles between two magnification levels for viewing the print preview.

 Access the Checklist tile on your LogicalCHOICE course screen for reference information and job aids on How to Preview and Print a Workbook.

ACTIVITY 5-1
Configuring and Previewing a Print Job

Data File

C:\091018Data\Printing Workbooks\sales_data_final.xlsx

Before You Begin

Excel 2010 is open.

You have a printer driver installed and available.

Scenario

Due to a request from senior managers, you've included a number of other sales teams' data in you workbook. Your workbook is now complete, and you're ready to print copies for attendees at the upcoming sales meeting. Before you do, you want to make sure the content will print correctly. You decide to configure and preview the print settings before you print actual hard copies.

1. Open the **sales_data_final.xlsx** workbook file.

2. Select **File→Print**.

3. In the left pane, in the **Settings** section, configure print settings.
   a) Set the collating settings to **Uncollated**.
   b) Set the scaling settings to **Fit all Rows on One Page**.

4. Preview the print job.
   a) In the right pane, review the first page of the print preview.
   b) Use the navigation controls to view the second page of the preview and then navigate back to page 1.
   c) In the bottom-right corner of the right pane, under the scroll bar, select the **Show Margins** button to view the page content in reference to the margins.
   d) Select the **Show Margins** button again, to toggle the margin view off.

5. Save the workbook to the **C:\091018Data\Printing Workbooks** folder as *my_sales_data_final.xlsx*

TOPIC B

Define the Page Layout

Although the general print settings provide you with a solid base of common printing options to configure your workbook print jobs, they are just the tip of the iceberg when it comes to what you can do in terms of printing in Excel. As mentioned, workbook printing can be highly complex for a large number of reasons. You will, from time to time, need to be able to fine-tune how to print your workbook pages. You may wish to add further information to your pages depending on why you need hard copies of your worksheets. For example, if you're creating handouts for a presentation, you may wish to number the pages, include a document title, or include your organization's name and branding images to your printouts.

Fortunately, Excel 2010 provides you with the ability to precisely configure your print jobs for nearly any imaginable circumstance. Knowing what configurations are available and how to set them will give you complete control over printing your worksheets and will allow you to create professional-looking printouts that focus your document recipients' attention on only the most important, pertinent information.

The Page Setup Dialog Box

The **Page Setup** dialog box provides you with more options for configuring your workbooks for printing than the print settings in the Backstage view. The **Page Setup** dialog box is organized into four tabs that contain task-related commands and settings for configuring your workbooks to print. You can access the **Page Setup** dialog box either by selecting the **Page Setup** link at the bottom of the **Settings** section on the **Print** tab in the Backstage view or by selecting any of the dialog box launchers on the **Page Layout** ribbon tab.

 Note: The **Print** and **Print Preview** buttons are displayed on the **Page Setup** dialog box only if you open it from the dialog box launcher on the **Page Layout** ribbon tab. You can also access most of Excel's print settings in the command groups on the **Page Layout** tab.

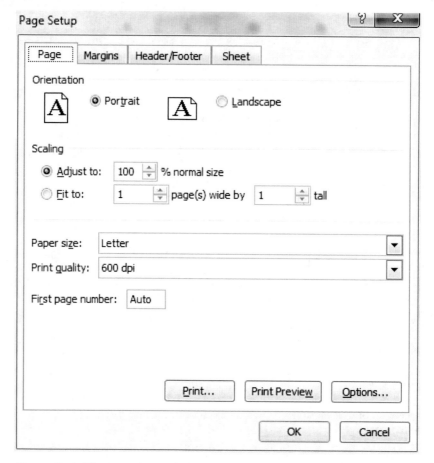

Figure 5-4: The Page Setup dialog box displaying the Print and Print Preview buttons.

The following table identifies the commands you will find on the various Page Setup dialog box tabs.

Page Setup Dialog Box Element	Provides You with Access To
Page tab	Commands to set page orientation and magnification level, the paper size, the print quality, and which page to start printing from.
Margins tab	Commands to adjust page, header, and footer margins and to determine how to center content on printed pages.
Header/Footer tab	Commands for inserting, modifying, and deleting headers and footers.
Sheet tab	Commands for defining a print area, determining which rows and columns print on every page, determining which page elements print on paper, and defining the order in which pages print.
Options button	The **Properties** dialog box for the currently selected printer, device, or printer driver.

Page Orientation

Page orientation is a page layout setting that determines the general, overall layout of each printed page. This setting specifies whether pages should print in portrait orientation or landscape orientation. In portrait orientation, page height is greater than page width; this enables you to fit more rows of data, but fewer columns, than landscape orientation. Landscape orientation is just the opposite; the page width is greater than the page height, allowing for more columns, but fewer rows, than portrait orientation.

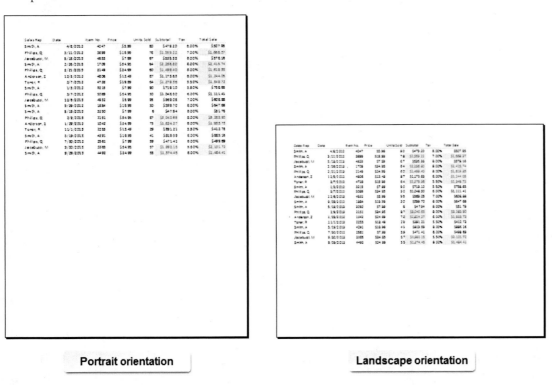

Portrait orientation   **Landscape orientation**

Figure 5-5: The same worksheet printed in both the portrait and landscape orientations.

Margins

Page margins are invisible boundaries that define where particular content is located on printed worksheets. Margins determine how much space there is between the worksheet content and the edge of the paper. Excel provides you with a set of common margin configurations from which to choose, and it allows you to customize margin sizes to suit your needs. Margins can define where worksheet data, headers, and footers are arranged on printed pages. The **Margins** tab on the **Page Setup** dialog box also provides you with options for centering your content vertically or horizontally on the page.

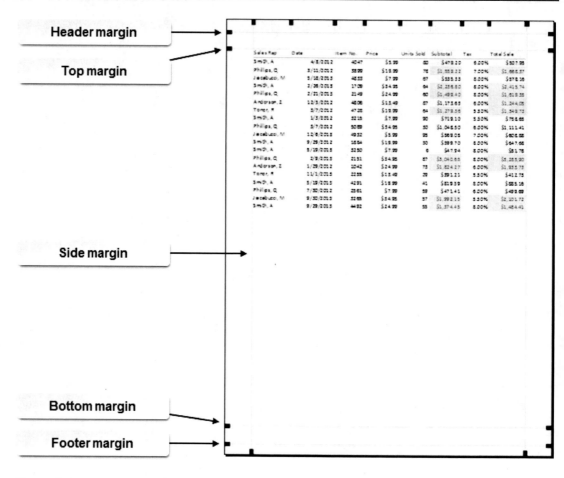

Figure 5-6: Page margins displayed on a worksheet page in print preview.

Headers and Footers

Headers and *footers* are small content placeholders that display additional information or images in certain Excel views and on printed pages. Headers appear along the top of the page, whereas footers are displayed along the bottom. They are not considered part of the worksheets themselves and cannot be referenced by formulas and functions. Headers and footers are worksheet-specific, so you have to configure them for each worksheet in a workbook individually.

Excel 2010 includes a number of preconfigured headers and footers and you also have the option of creating custom headers and footers. Headers and footers can contain text or images and can be placed to the left or right, or centered, along the top or the bottom of the page. You can also create different headers and footers for odd and even pages and exclude them from the first printed page or create unique headers and footers for the first page. Common items included in headers and footers include page numbers, the date, the name of the person who created the worksheet, the name of your organization, and organizational logos.

Headers

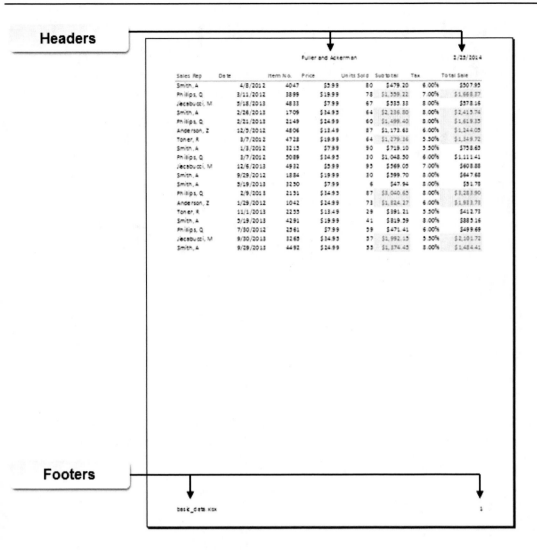

Footers

Figure 5-7: Headers and footers on an Excel worksheet.

Contextual Tabs

Contextual tabs are specialized, temporary ribbon tabs that display commands for working with a particular type of worksheet content. Contextual tabs appear when you select the associated content type, such as a graph or an image, and they close when you change your selection. Contextual tabs can contain one or multiple other tabs that contain command groups like any of the other ribbon tabs.

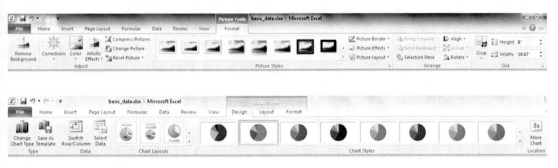

Figure 5-8: The Picture Tools contextual tab contains only one tab, whereas the Chart Tools contextual tab contains three.

The Header & Footer Tools Contextual Tab

In addition to the commands and settings on the **Header/Footer** tab in the **Page Setup** dialog box, you can access the commands for creating and modifying headers and footers in the **Text** group on the **Insert** ribbon tab. Selecting the **Header & Footer** button switches Excel to the Page Layout view and displays the **Header & Footer Tools** contextual tab. From here, you have access to the commands you can use to work with headers and footers in the ribbon environment. This may be a better option for you if you prefer working with ribbon commands. Working with headers and footers in the **Page Layout** view allows you to utilize all of the same options and commands in a more graphically oriented environment.

> **Note:** Page views will be covered in greater detail in the next lesson.

Figure 5-9: The Header & Footer Tools contextual tab displays all of the same commands as the Header/Footer tab in the Page Setup dialog box.

Header and Footer Options

There are several header and footer options that warrant covering in a bit more detail. These options provide you with a greater level of control over configuring your worksheet headers and footers. You can access these settings either in the **Page Setup** dialog box or in the **Options** group on the **Header & Footer Tools** contextual tab.

Header and Footer Option	Description
Different odd and even pages	Tells Excel that you want to configure your headers and footers differently for odd and even pages. You can configure the different headers and footers in either the **Page Layout** view or in the **Header** and **Footer** dialog boxes.
Different first page	Tells Excel that you want to configure unique headers and footers for the first page of your document. This is useful, for example, if you want to include a document title. You can configure this unique header in either the **Page Layout** view or in the **Header** and **Footer** dialog boxes.
Scale with document	Selecting this option tells Excel to scale header and footer text up or down when scaling other worksheet content.
Align with page margins	Selecting this option automatically aligns headers and footers with the left and right page margins.

The Header and Footer Dialog Boxes

The **Header** and **Footer** dialog boxes are displayed when you create custom headers and footers from the **Page Setup** dialog box. These allow you to enter specific text or images to create unique customized headers. If you check either the **Different odd and even pages** or the **Different first page** check box, or both, the **Header** and **Footer** dialog boxes will display additional tabs allowing you to create unique headers and footers for each option selected. You can access the **Header** and **Footer** dialog boxes by selecting the **Custom Header** and **Custom Footer** buttons, respectively.

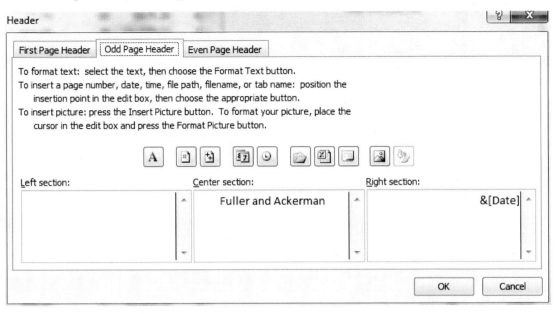

Figure 5-10: Use the tabs in the Header and Footer dialog boxes to create different headers and footers for various document pages.

The Print Area

The *print area* feature allows you to select specific cells and ranges to print from your workbooks. Once you've set a print area, only those cells within the print area will print. Cells within the print area display surrounded by a dashed-line marquee. You can expand the print area by adding cells to it and you can clear the print area to print the entire workbook or any other areas you designate via other methods. You cannot add objects, such as graphs, to print areas. Once you've set a print area, it is saved along with the workbook; it won't affect other workbook files.

Print areas are worksheet-specific, so you have to configure them for each worksheet individually. If you select the **Print Entire Workbook** option from the print settings, any worksheets on which you have set print areas will print only those areas, while worksheets without print areas will print in their entirety. You can access the **Print Area** options by selecting **Page Layout→Page Setup→Print Area**.

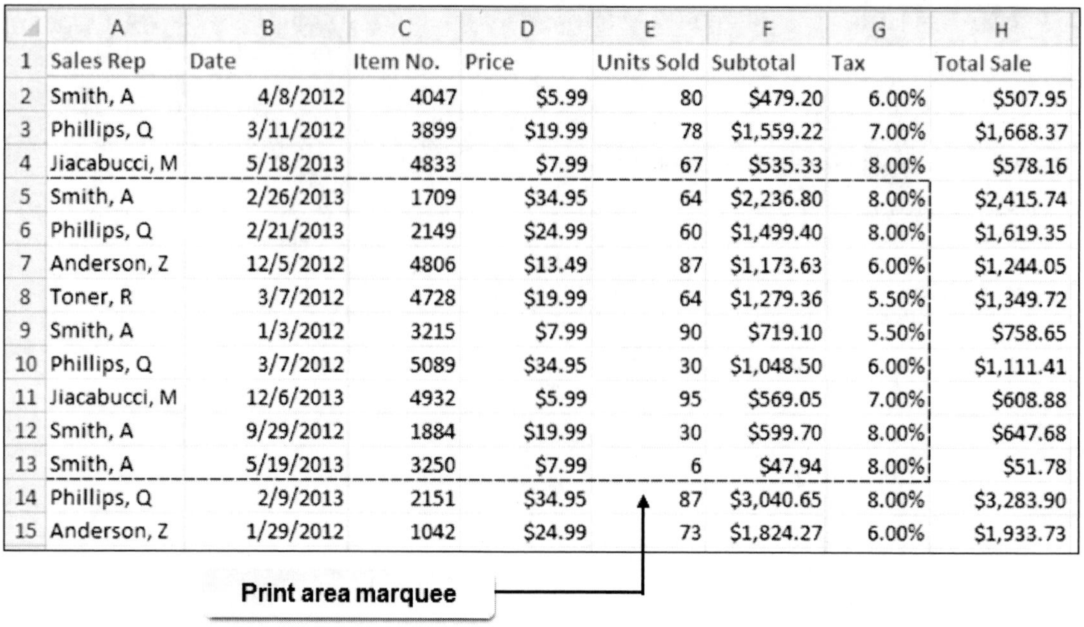

	A	B	C	D	E	F	G	H
1	Sales Rep	Date	Item No.	Price	Units Sold	Subtotal	Tax	Total Sale
2	Smith, A	4/8/2012	4047	$5.99	80	$479.20	6.00%	$507.95
3	Phillips, Q	3/11/2012	3899	$19.99	78	$1,559.22	7.00%	$1,668.37
4	Jiacabucci, M	5/18/2013	4833	$7.99	67	$535.33	8.00%	$578.16
5	Smith, A	2/26/2013	1709	$34.95	64	$2,236.80	8.00%	$2,415.74
6	Phillips, Q	2/21/2013	2149	$24.99	60	$1,499.40	8.00%	$1,619.35
7	Anderson, Z	12/5/2012	4806	$13.49	87	$1,173.63	6.00%	$1,244.05
8	Toner, R	3/7/2012	4728	$19.99	64	$1,279.36	5.50%	$1,349.72
9	Smith, A	1/3/2012	3215	$7.99	90	$719.10	5.50%	$758.65
10	Phillips, Q	3/7/2012	5089	$34.95	30	$1,048.50	6.00%	$1,111.41
11	Jiacabucci, M	12/6/2013	4932	$5.99	95	$569.05	7.00%	$608.88
12	Smith, A	9/29/2012	1884	$19.99	30	$599.70	8.00%	$647.68
13	Smith, A	5/19/2013	3250	$7.99	6	$47.94	8.00%	$51.78
14	Phillips, Q	2/9/2013	2151	$34.95	87	$3,040.65	8.00%	$3,283.90
15	Anderson, Z	1/29/2012	1042	$24.99	73	$1,824.27	6.00%	$1,933.73

Print area marquee

Figure 5-11: When you set a print area, Excel displays it surrounded by a dashed-line marquee.

The Ignore Print Area Option

Excel 2010 gives you the option of temporarily ignoring a defined print area if you wish to print content outside the print area. You can toggle this option on and off from the print selection settings on the **Print** tab in the Backstage view.

The Print Titles Command

Because Excel worksheets can contain thousands of columns and rows worth of data, it can be difficult for people to interpret printed worksheets if column and row labels don't print on all pages. Excel 2010 includes a feature that enables you to determine which rows and columns will print on every page: the **Print Titles** command. By using this feature, you can designate any number of rows, columns, or both to print on all pages of a printed workbook. In this way, worksheet viewers won't have to flip back to the first page to determine what particular data is in each row or column. Selecting **Page Layout→Page Setup→Print Titles** opens the **Page Setup** dialog box with the **Sheet** tab automatically selected. This is where you can enter row and column references to determine which cells are displayed on all printed pages.

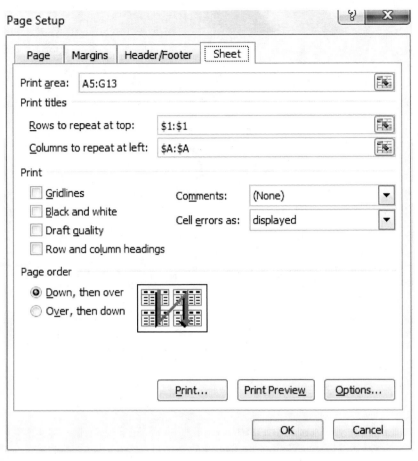

Figure 5-12: The Sheet tab on the Page Setup dialog box contains the fields you will use to determine which rows and columns print on all pages.

Page Breaks

Sometimes scaling your worksheets up or down to fit on the desired number of pages doesn't quite give you the results you're looking for in terms of what content prints on which page. In these cases, you may want to manually tell Excel where one printed page ends and another one begins. To do this, you can insert *page breaks*. Page breaks are, essentially, boundaries that divide worksheet pages for printing purposes only. Excel 2010 enables you to insert and delete specific page breaks and to remove all page breaks on a given worksheet. Page breaks are displayed as dashed lines on Excel worksheets. They are worksheet-specific, so you need to set them for each worksheet in a workbook individually. You can access the **Page Break** commands by selecting **Page Layout→Page Setup→Breaks**.

> **Note:** Excel 2010 also provides you with the ability to manually adjust page breaks. You can do this in the Page Break Preview view, which is covered in greater detail in the next lesson.

▲	A	B	C	D	E	F	G	H	I
1	Sales Rep	Date	Item No.	Price	Units Sold	Subtotal	Tax	Total Sale	
2	Smith, A	4/8/2012	4047	$5.99	80	$479.20	6.00%	$507.95	
3	Phillips, Q	3/11/2012	3899	$19.99	78	$1,559.22	7.00%	$1,668.37	
4	Jiacabucci, M	5/18/2013	4833	$7.99	67	$535.33	8.00%	$578.16	
5	Smith, A	2/26/2013	1709	$34.95	64	$2,236.80	8.00%	$2,415.74	
6	Phillips, Q	2/21/2013	2149	$24.99	60	$1,499.40	8.00%	$1,619.35	
7	Anderson, Z	12/5/2012	4806	$13.49	87	$1,173.63	6.00%	$1,244.05	
8	Toner, R	3/7/2012	4728	$19.99	64	$1,279.36	5.50%	$1,349.72	
9	Smith, A	1/3/2012	3215	$7.99	90	$719.10	5.50%	$758.65	
10	Phillips, Q	3/7/2012	5089	$34.95	30	$1,048.50	6.00%	$1,111.41	
11	Jiacabucci, M	12/6/2013	4932	$5.99	95	$569.05	7.00%	$608.88	
12	Smith, A	9/29/2012	1884	$19.99	30	$599.70	8.00%	$647.68	
13	Smith, A	5/19/2013	3250	$7.99	6	$47.94	8.00%	$51.78	
14	Phillips, Q	2/9/2013	2151	$34.95	87	$3,040.65	8.00%	$3,283.90	
15	Anderson, Z	1/29/2012	1042	$24.99	73	$1,824.27	6.00%	$1,933.73	
16	Toner, R	11/1/2013	2255	$13.49	29	$391.21	5.50%	$412.73	
17	Smith, A	5/19/2013	4291	$19.99	41	$819.59	8.00%	$885.16	
18	Phillips, Q	7/30/2012	2561	$7.99	59	$471.41	6.00%	$499.69	
19	Jiacabucci, M	9/30/2013	3265	$34.95	57	$1,992.15	5.50%	$2,101.72	
20	Smith, A	9/29/2013	4492	$24.99	55	$1,374.45	8.00%	$1,484.41	
21	Smith, A	4/8/2012	4047	$5.99	80	$479.20	6.00%	$507.95	
22	Phillips, Q	3/11/2012	3899	$19.99	78	$1,559.22	7.00%	$1,668.37	

Figure 5-13: Page breaks on an Excel worksheet.

Access the Checklist tile on your LogicalCHOICE course screen for reference information and job aids on How to Define the Page Layout.

ACTIVITY 5-2
Defining the Page Layout

Before You Begin
The my_sales_data_final.xlsx workbook file is open.

Scenario
Having previewed the sales data worksheet, you now have a better idea of the precise page layout you would like to define before printing the pages. You feel the printed sheets will work better in the landscape orientation, and you want to widen the page margins slightly. Additionally, you don't like the layout with all of the rows displayed on a single page, so you decide to change the scaling to fit all columns on a single page and make the column labels print on each page. You also decide to add headers and footers to the workbook to include the date of the sales meeting, a title for the workbook, and page numbers.

---

1. Change the orientation and widen the page margins.
   a) Select **Page Layout→Page Setup→Orientation→Landscape**.
   b) Select **Page Layout→Page Setup→Margins→Custom Margins**.
   c) In the **Page Setup** dialog box, ensure that the **Margins** tab is selected.
   d) Use the spin boxes to set the top and bottom margins to **1.25** and the left and right margins to **1.2**.
   e) Select **OK**.

2. Change the scaling so that all columns fit on a single page.
   a) Select **File→Print**.
   b) In the **Settings** section, change the scaling setting to **Fit All Columns on One Page**.
   c) Select the **Page Layout** tab to exit the Backstage view.

3. Set the column labels to print on each page.
   a) Select **Page Layout→Page Setup→Print Titles**.
   b) In the **Page Setup** dialog box, ensure that the **Sheet** tab is selected.
   c) In the **Print titles** section, to the right of the **Rows to repeat at top** field, select the **Collapse Dialog** button.
   d) Select rows **1:6** and press **Enter**.

4. Add headers and footers to the worksheet.
   a) Ensure that the **Page Setup** dialog box is still open, and then select the **Header/Footer** tab.
   b) Select **Custom Header**.
   c) In the **Header** dialog box, in the **Left section** field, type *My Footprint Sports*
   d) In the **Center section** field, type *US Sales*
   e) Select the **Right section** field, and then, above the text fields, select the **Insert Date** button.

   f) Select **OK**, and then select **Custom Footer**.
   g) In the **Footer** dialog box, select the **Right section** field.

---

h) Above the text fields, select the **Insert Page Number** button.

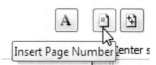

i) In the **Footer** dialog box, select **OK** and, in the **Page Setup** dialog box, select **OK**.

5. Preview the page layout.
   a) Select **File→Print**.
   b) Verify that all columns fit on the page.
   c) Navigate to page 2 and verify that the My Footprint Sports banner, the worksheet title, and the column headers all appear on the second page.

6. Move the summary information so it does not print on all pages.
   a) Exit the Backstage view, and then select the range **N2:O11**.
   b) Drag the range to the new range **N7:O16**.

7. Preview the page layout to verify that the summary data no longer appears on all printed pages.

8. Save and close the workbook.

Summary

In this lesson, you configured, previewed, and printed a workbook. You also defined the worksheet page layout to print only the desired content. Taking advantage of all of the print functionality available in Excel will allow to create hard copies of your workbook content for nearly any situation. By limiting what content you print to only what is necessary for any given need, you will save on paper, toner, and ink costs, support a healthier environment, and prevent your document viewers from having to sift through mounds of irrelevant or unimportant data.

Which page layout options do you expect to use most frequently? Why?

What do you see as being the main benefit of using the Print Area option?

> **Note:** Check your LogicalCHOICE Course screen for opportunities to interact with your classmates, peers, and the larger LogicalCHOICE online community about the topics covered in this course or other topics you are interested in. From the Course screen you can also access available resources for a more continuous learning experience.

6 | Managing Workbooks

Lesson Time: 1 hour

Lesson Objectives

In this lesson, you will manage workbooks. You will:

- Manage worksheets.

- Manage workbook and worksheet views.

- Manage workbook properties.

Lesson Introduction

So far, you have largely worked within workbooks and worksheets to enter, view, analyze, format, and present your organizational data. But there's more to being proficient in Excel than simply working within your workbooks. What if you need to add or remove worksheets from your workbooks? What if you want to preserve certain data, but not display it to colleagues or supervisors? Perhaps you need to work with multiple workbooks or multiple worksheets within a single workbook simultaneously. And, after a time, there's a good chance you'll have amassed a large number of workbook files that you'll need to reference later, perhaps even years down the road. These are but a few of the situations in which you'll need to know how to manage your Excel workbooks.

Managing the overall structure of your workbooks, manipulating how you view your workbooks, and knowing how to find the workbook you need when you need it are all critical tasks you'll need to perform from time to time. Understanding what functionality is available and knowing how to use it when you need it will ensure you're able to get the most out of the workbooks, worksheets, and data you've already worked so hard to create.

TOPIC A

Manage Worksheets

Workbooks with just a few worksheets are fairly easy to manage without much effort. What if you're developing a workbook with dozens of worksheets or more? You want to be able to clearly and easily recognize your worksheets, arrange them in the proper order, and, possibly, remove some from view to display or work with only particular worksheets at any given time. Fortunately, Excel 2010 provides you with an array of options when it comes to managing your worksheets. By taking control of your large workbooks, you'll save yourself the time, effort, and aggravation that can easily accompany attempts to muddle through an unwieldy, disorganized workbook.

Tab Formatting Options

By default, worksheet tabs in Excel 2010 are displayed with generic sheet names, such as Sheet1, Sheet2, Sheet3, and in the default blue user interface color scheme. As you add more and more worksheets to a workbook, it's easy to see how this could become difficult to navigate. You may wonder if your critical sales data is on Sheet11 or Sheet12 and, if you don't format your worksheet tabs, you'll have no visual cues to help you out. This is why Excel 2010 provides you with a number of options for formatting your worksheet tabs. The most basic of these are the options to rename your worksheets and to change the color of worksheet tabs. You can access the commands for doing either of these by right-clicking the desired worksheet tab.

31	Smith, A	9/29/2012	1884	$19.99	30	$599.70	8.00%
32	Smith, A	5/19/2013	3250	$7.99	6	$47.94	8.00%
33	Phillips, Q	2/9/2013	2151	$34.95	87	$3,040.65	8.00%
34	Anderson, Z	1/29/2012	1042	$24.99	73	$1,824.27	6.00%

Quarter 1 / Quarter 2 / **Quarter 3** / Quarter 4 / Annual Totals

Ready

Figure 6-1: Renamed worksheet tabs with color formatting.

 Access the Checklist tile on your LogicalCHOICE course screen for reference information and job aids on **How to Format Worksheet Tabs.**

Grouped Worksheets

In order to quickly apply the same formatting to multiple worksheet tabs, Excel 2010 allows you to temporarily group worksheets so you can format them simultaneously. Essentially, this is the same as selecting multiple cells on a worksheet to apply the same formatting to each cell. You can group contiguous worksheet tabs by selecting the first tab, pressing and holding down the **Shift** key, and then selecting the last tab. You can group non-contiguous worksheet tabs by pressing and holding down the **Ctrl** key and selecting the desired tabs. Although you can rename worksheet tabs one at a time only, you can move, hide, or apply color to a group of worksheets simultaneously.

You can also add and revise worksheet content on all grouped worksheets simultaneously. For example, if you group a series of worksheets and then add the value *100* to cell **A1** in the visible worksheet, you enter that value in cell **A1** on all worksheets in the group. This can be a handy way, for example, of setting up a number of worksheets with the same labels, sections, and so on. Whatever worksheet is visible at the time you group a set of worksheets remains the visible worksheet.

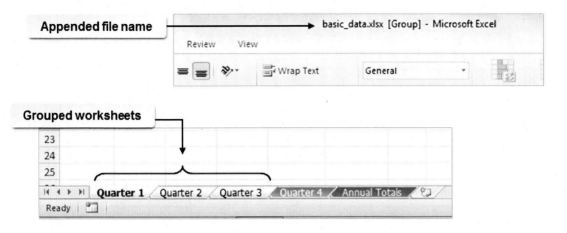

Figure 6–2: When you group worksheets in a workbook, Excel displays the workbook name appended with "[Group]" in the title bar.

Methods of Repositioning Worksheets

Excel 2010 provides you with two methods for repositioning your worksheets. The first method is to simply drag the desired worksheet tab or tabs to the desired new location. When you use this method, the tabs you're moving are displayed as small file icons and Excel displays a black location marker that indicates where the tabs will be located when you drop them in place. To move more than one worksheet simultaneously using this method, you must first group the worksheets. You can drag worksheets to a different location in the same workbook or into any other open Excel workbook. When you drag a worksheet tab into another workbook, the location marker will turn from black to white.

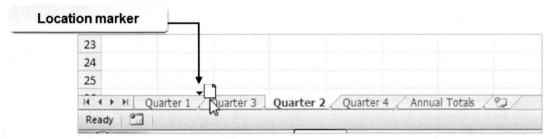

Figure 6–3: The location marker indicates where the worksheets will land when dropped.

The second method for repositioning worksheets is to use the **Move or Copy** dialog box. You can use the **Move or Copy** dialog box to reposition worksheets within the same workbook, move worksheets to another open workbook, or create a new workbook into which you can place existing worksheets. You also have the option of making a copy of a worksheet to paste to another location, an option not available when you drag worksheets into place. However, you can only move one worksheet at a time using the **Move or Copy** dialog box. You can access the **Move or Copy** dialog box either by right-clicking any worksheet tab and then selecting **Move or Copy**, or by selecting **Home→Cells→Format→Move or Copy Sheet**.

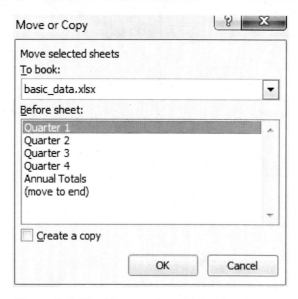

Figure 6-4: The Move or Copy dialog box.

The following table describes the various elements of the **Move or Copy** dialog box.

Move or Copy Dialog Box Element	Description
To book drop-down menu	Use this to select the workbook into which you wish to move or copy the selected worksheet. By default, this is set to the currently selected workbook. You can also choose to create a new workbook as the destination for the existing worksheets.
Before sheet list	Select the sheet you wish to move or copy from here.
Create a copy check box	Check this check box to copy and paste worksheets instead of moving them from one location to another.

Methods of Inserting and Deleting Worksheets

By default, new blank Excel 2010 workbooks contain three worksheets. But you can add up to as many worksheets as your system's RAM (memory) will support. Likewise, if you don't need all three default worksheets, you can delete any you aren't using. Although, there is no harm in leaving them in place. You can also change the default number of worksheets Excel will include in new, blank workbooks.

Excel 2010 provides you with three options for inserting worksheets in your workbooks, and two for deleting them.

Insert/Delete Option	Description
Selecting the **Insert Worksheet** button	This inserts a new worksheet after all existing worksheets. Alternately, you can use the **Shift+F11** keyboard shortcut.
Right-clicking any worksheet tab and then selecting **Insert**	This opens the **Insert** dialog box with **Worksheet** automatically selected. From there, you can simply select **OK** to insert a new worksheet immediately before the worksheet you right-clicked.
Using the **Insert** ribbon command	Select **Home→Cells→Insert down arrow→Insert Sheet** to insert a worksheet immediately before the currently selected worksheet.

Insert/Delete Option	Description
Right-clicking a worksheet tab, and then selecting **Delete**	This deletes the worksheet tab you right-clicked.
Using the **Delete** ribbon command	Select **Home→Cells→Delete down arrow→Delete Sheet** to delete the currently selected worksheet.

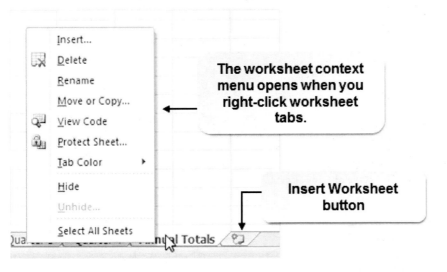

Figure 6-5: Some of the Insert and Delete commands for Excel 2010 worksheets.

The Hide and Unhide Worksheets Options

If you need to work with or display only some of the worksheets in your workbooks, you can choose to hide the worksheets you don't want to see. This can be especially helpful when working in workbooks that contain numerous worksheets or when you need to display a workbook that contains sensitive information not meant for all audiences. Like hidden columns and rows, hidden worksheets retain their data and formulas and functions can still reference their cells.

You can access the commands for hiding and unhiding Excel worksheets either by right-clicking the worksheet tabs or by selecting **Home→Cells→Format→Hide & Unhide**. Selecting the **Hide** command will hide all currently selected worksheets. Selecting the **Unhide** command opens the **Unhide** dialog box, which, much like the **Move or Copy** dialog box, enables you to unhide only one worksheet at a time.

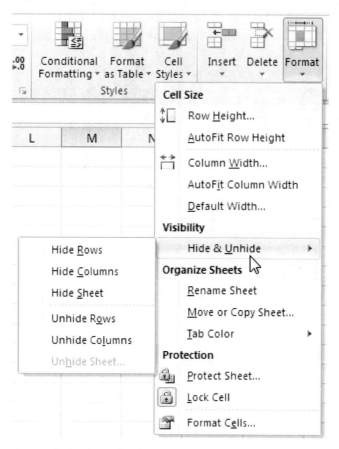

Figure 6-6: The Hide Sheet and Unhide Sheet ribbon commands. The Unhide sheet command is inactive until you hide a worksheet.

 Access the Checklist tile on your LogicalCHOICE course screen for reference information and job aids on How to Manage Worksheets.

ACTIVITY 6-1
Managing Worksheets

Data File

C:\091018Data\Managing Workbooks\sales_summary.xlsx

Before You Begin

Excel 2010 is open.

Scenario

My Footprint Sports' management is pleased with the report you gave at the sales meeting. Now they'd like you to present summary information about sales in several key global regions at several more meetings. You have already created a sales summary workbook with separate tabs for each of the regions. But it's difficult to navigate the workbook because the worksheet tabs still have the default names and there is no other formatting applied to them to help you tell them apart. You decide to rename and format the worksheet tabs to make the workbook easier to navigate.

Management has hinted that they'll be expecting more sales data from a number of other regions in the upcoming weeks. You decide proactively to add more worksheets to accommodate the additional data. You also feel it's a good idea to sequence the worksheets according to your needs and to hide the blank worksheets until you are able to populate them with data.

---

1. Open the **sales_summary.xlsx** workbook.

2. Rename the tabs to better reflect the data on each worksheet.
    a) Right-click the **Sheet1** tab and select **Rename**.
    b) Type *US* and press **Enter**.
    c) Double-click the **Sheet2** tab, type *Canada* and press **Enter**.
    d) Rename the **Sheet3** tab *Mexico*

3. Add color to the worksheet tabs to further help distinguish them from each other.
    a) Right-click the **US** tab and select **Tab Color**.
    b) In the **Standard Colors** section, select **Blue**.
    c) Select the **Canada** tab and select **Home→Cells→Format**.
    d) In the **Format** menu, in the **Organize Sheets** section, select **Tab Color**.
    e) In the **Standard Colors** section, select **Red**.
    f) Color the **Mexico** worksheet tab green.

4. Move the **Mexico** tab so that it is displayed between the **US** tab and the **Canada** tab.
    a) Drag the **Mexico** tab to the left until the black location marker points to the spot in between the **US** and the **Canada** tabs.
    b) Drop the tab in place.
    c) Verify that the **Mexico** tab appears between the **US** and **Canada** tabs.

5. Make a copy of the **Canada** worksheet to reuse for the European region.
    a) Right-click the **Canada** tab and select **Move or Copy**.
    b) In the **Move or Copy** dialog box, in the **To book** drop-down menu, ensure that **sales_summary.xlsx** appears.
    c) In the **Before sheet** list, select **(move to end)**.

      d) Check the **Create a copy** check box and select **OK**.

      e) Verify that the **Canada (2)** worksheet tab is displayed at the end of the other worksheet tabs.

6. Modify the new worksheet.

      a) Rename the **Canada (2)** tab *Europe*

      b) Change the color of the **Europe** tab to yellow.

      c) Select cell **D2**, type *European Sales Summary* and press **Enter**.

      d) Select the range **A5:H11** and press **Delete**.

7. Add a new worksheet you can use as a master employee list for all regions.

      a) To the right of the worksheet tabs, select the **Insert Worksheet** button.

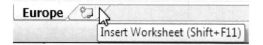

      b) Rename the new tab *Employee Summary*

8. Hide the newly added worksheet tabs.

      a) Group the **Europe** tab and the **Employee Summary** tab by selecting either tab, pressing and holding **Shift**, and selecting the other tab.

      b) Right-click either tab in the group, and then select **Hide**.

9. Save the workbook to the **C:\091018Data\Managing Workbooks** folder as *my_sales_summary.xlsx*

TOPIC B

Manage Workbook and Worksheet Views

You've likely already noticed that large worksheets can be difficult to read. You may have to scroll quite a bit vertically or horizontally to view cell data and when you do, you can't always see row and column labels. Also, let's say you want to compare data that exists in cells that are nowhere near each other or are entered into completely different workbooks. It's easy to see how fumbling around with scrolling and opening and closing workbooks can get confusing, become tedious, and lead to errors. What can you do if you need to view content from locations that are nowhere near each other? The answer: You change how you view your worksheets and workbooks.

Excel 2010 provides you with a wide array of options for configuring how you view Excel workbook files. By modifying the default view of your worksheets, you'll be able to easily review data from different sources simultaneously, copy and paste data to the correct location without risking error, and save yourself time and headaches by avoiding scrolling through endless rows and columns of data.

Workbook Views

You may not have even realized it, but you've probably been viewing your Excel workbooks in the Normal view, which is the default workbook view in Excel 2010. There are other preconfigured *workbook views* that display the Excel user interface and your worksheets in vastly different configurations. A workbook view is, simply, the way Excel displays an open workbook. Workbook views can affect the placement and layout of worksheets and the Excel user interface and can affect whether or not particular elements, such as headers and footers, appear. Workbook views are meant to configure the Excel environment to be easier to work with for a number of different tasks. Excel 2010 includes several preconfigured workbook views and it provides you with the ability to create custom workbook views. You can access the commands you will use to change your workbook views in the **Workbook Views** group on the **View** tab.

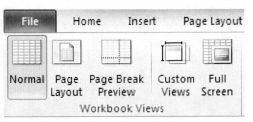

Figure 6-7: The commands in the Workbook Views group.

The Normal View

The Normal view is Excel 2010's default workbook view. This is designed to be the best all-around view for most workbook tasks.

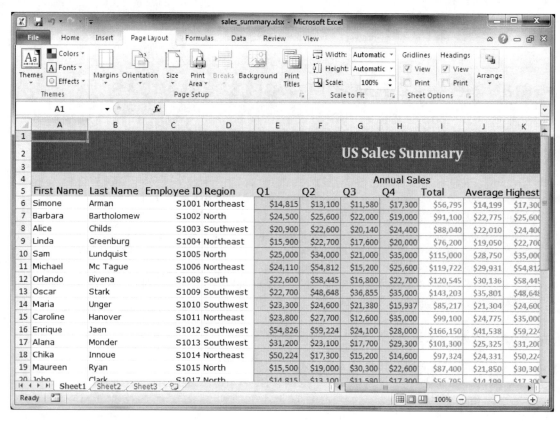

Figure 6–8: The Normal view.

The Page Layout View

The Page Layout view displays worksheets as they would print on separate pages based on the current print settings. When you select the Page Layout view, Excel also automatically displays rulers along the top and left sides of the user interface to assist with the placement of on-screen objects and it displays all header and footer placeholders, which allows you to graphically create, edit, and delete headers and footers. When you select a header or a footer placeholder while in the Page Layout view, Excel displays the **Header & Footer Tools** contextual tab, providing you with access to the various commands you can use to create and customize headers and footers.

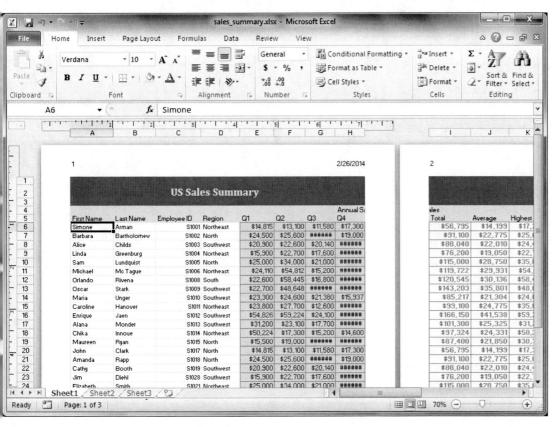

Figure 6-9: The Page Layout view assists with the placement of worksheet objects and enables you to graphically work with headers and footers.

The Page Break Preview View

The Page Break Preview view is ideal for inserting, deleting, and arranging page breaks on your Excel worksheets and for defining print areas. In this view, default page breaks appear as blue dashed lines, whereas manual page breaks appear as solid blue lines. To arrange page breaks when in this view, simply drag them to the desired location. Once you move a default page break, it becomes a manual page break.

When you set a print area in the Page Break Preview view, only cells within the print area will display. You can manually adjust the boundaries of print areas in this view just as you can manually adjust page breaks. When you right-click any cell in the Page Break Preview view, the context menu that is displayed contains commands for working with page breaks and print areas.

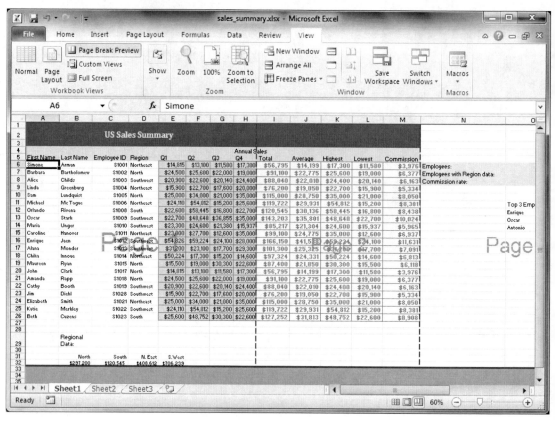

Figure 6-10: You can graphically arrange print areas and page breaks in the Page Break Preview view.

Full Screen View

The Full Screen view hides the display of the **title bar**, the **Quick Access Toolbar**, the **ribbon**, the **Formula Bar**, and the **status bar**. This view is ideal when you need additional space to view more cells in your worksheets, such as, for example, when you wish to display your data to an audience. It is important to note that the Full Screen view maintains whatever view you had previously selected with the exception of hiding the various user interface elements. So, for example, if you had previously selected the Page Break Preview view, and then you selected the Full Screen view, Excel will still display your worksheets in the Page Break Preview view, just without the application window elements.

First Name	Last Name	Employee ID	Region	Q1	Q2	Q3	Q4	Total	Average	Highest	Lowest	Commission
Simone	Arman	S1001	Northeast	$14,815	$13,100	$11,580	$17,300	$56,795	$14,199	$17,300	$11,580	$3,976
Barbara	Bartholomew	S1002	North	$24,500	$25,600	$22,000	$19,000	$91,100	$22,775	$25,600	$19,000	$6,377
Alice	Childs	S1003	Southwest	$20,900	$22,600	$20,140	$24,400	$88,040	$22,010	$24,400	$20,140	$6,163
Linda	Greenburg	S1004	Northeast	$15,900	$22,700	$17,600	$20,000	$76,200	$19,050	$22,700	$15,900	$5,334
Sam	Lundquist	S1005	North	$25,000	$34,000	$21,000	$35,000	$115,000	$28,750	$35,000	$21,000	$8,050
Michael	Mc Tague	S1006	Northeast	$24,110	$54,812	$15,200	$25,600	$119,722	$29,931	$54,812	$15,200	$8,381
Orlando	Rivena	S1008	South	$22,600	$58,445	$16,300	$22,700	$120,545	$30,136	$58,445	$16,300	$8,438
Oscar	Stark	S1009	Southwest	$22,700	$48,648	$36,855	$35,000	$143,203	$35,801	$48,648	$22,700	$10,024
Maria	Unger	S1010	Southwest	$23,300	$24,600	$21,380	$15,937	$85,217	$21,304	$24,600	$15,937	$5,065
Caroline	Hanover	S1011	Northeast	$23,800	$27,700	$12,200	$35,000	$99,100	$24,775	$35,000	$12,600	$6,937
Enrique	Jaen	S1012	Southwest	$54,826	$59,224	$24,100	$28,000	$166,150	$41,538	$59,224	$24,100	$11,631
Alana	Monder	S1013	Southwest	$31,200	$23,100	$17,700	$29,300	$101,300	$25,325	$31,200	$17,700	$7,091
Chika	Innoue	S1014	Northeast	$50,224	$17,300	$15,200	$14,600	$97,324	$24,331	$50,224	$14,600	$6,813
Maureen	Ryan	S1015	North	$15,500	$19,000	$30,300	$22,600	$87,400	$21,850	$30,300	$15,500	$6,118
John	Clark	S1017	North	$14,815	$13,100	$11,580	$17,300	$56,795	$14,199	$17,300	$11,580	$3,976
Amanda	Rapp	S1018	North	$24,500	$25,600	$22,000	$19,000	$91,100	$22,775	$25,600	$19,000	$6,377
Cathy	Booth	S1019	Southwest	$20,900	$22,600	$20,140	$24,400	$88,040	$22,010	$24,400	$20,140	$6,163
Jim	Diehl	S1028	Southwest	$15,900	$22,700	$17,600	$20,000	$76,200	$19,050	$22,700	$15,900	$5,334
Elizabeth	Smith	S1021	Northeast	$25,000	$34,000	$21,000	$35,000	$115,000	$28,750	$35,000	$21,000	$8,050
Katie	Merkley	S1022	Southwest	$24,110	$54,812	$15,200	$25,600	$119,722	$29,931	$54,812	$15,200	$8,381
Beth	Cuzens	S1023	South	$25,600	$48,752	$30,300	$22,600	$127,252	$31,813	$48,752	$22,600	$8,908

US Sales Summary — Annual Sales

Employees: 24
Employees with Region data: 21
Commission rate: 7

Top 3 Employees:
Enrique $41,537.50
Oscar $35,800.75
Antonio $31,813.00

Regional Data:

	North	South	N. East	S.West
	$297,200	$120,545	$408,612	$706,239

Figure 6-11: The Full Screen view is ideal for displaying your worksheets to an audience.

Custom Views

If none of the preconfigured Excel workbook views quite suit your needs, you can create a *custom view*. Custom views save all of your print settings along with any display settings you have currently applied to a worksheet. Custom views are worksheet specific, so you'll have to create them for each worksheet in a workbook. But, you can create multiple custom views for each worksheet. Custom views retain the following display and print settings: cell and column dimensions, hidden rows and columns, cell and range selections, page layout, print areas, margins, and headers and footers.

All custom views you have saved for a particular worksheet will be displayed in the **Custom Views** dialog box. From here, you can opt to create new custom views, delete existing custom views, or apply a custom view to the currently selected worksheet. You can access the **Custom Views** dialog box by selecting **View→Workbook Views→Custom Views**.

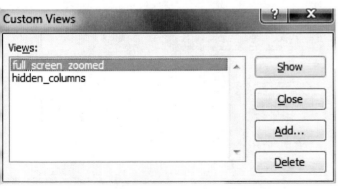

Figure 6-12: The Custom Views dialog box provides you with access to all of the custom views saved for the active worksheet.

The Add View Dialog Box

When you select the **Add** button in the **Custom Views** dialog box, Excel displays the **Add View** dialog box, which you can use to create and save new custom views. The **Add View** dialog box enables you to name your custom views and to decide whether or not to include print settings or hidden rows, columns, and filter settings in your custom views. Custom view names must begin with either a letter or an underscore, cannot contain spaces or special characters, and cannot conflict with the name of existing Excel elements or worksheets and worksheet objects.

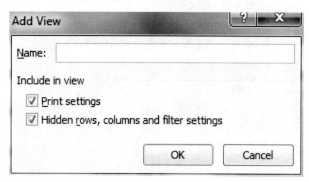

Figure 6-13: The Add View dialog box.

The Split Command

If you need to view various sections of the same worksheet simultaneously, you can use the **Split** command. The **Split** command divides your worksheet view into either two separate panes, vertically or horizontally, or into four separate panes to allow you to view up to four different places in a worksheet at the same time. Excel displays separate scroll bars on either side of the split bars that divide the view, so you can independently scroll to view any area of the worksheet in the various panes. You can also drag the split bars to adjust how much space is dedicated to each of the panes. You can access the **Split** command by selecting **View→Window→Split**.

Selecting either a column or a row header before selecting the **Split** command will split the view in half either vertically or horizontally. Selecting a cell before selecting the **Split** command will split the view into four panes above and to the left of the selected cell.

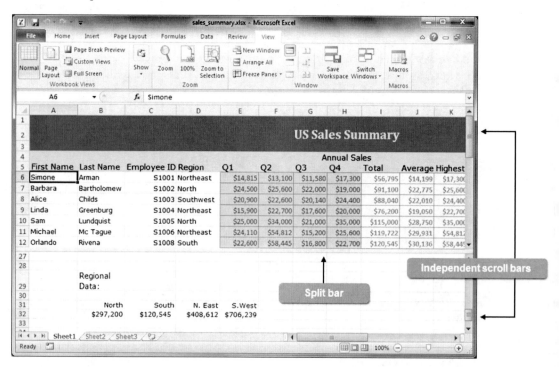

Figure 6-14: Use the Split command to view various sections of a worksheet simultaneously.

The Freeze Panes Options

You've already seen with the print settings how helpful it can be to ensure column and row labels print on each page. Well, it just makes sense, then, that the same would be helpful with how your column and row labels appear while you're working in Excel. Excel 2010 allows you to freeze particular cells so that they always appear on screen regardless of how far you scroll down or to the right. This way, you can always reference column and row labels so you can more clearly read and interpret your worksheets and enter and analyze data accurately.

You will use the **Freeze Panes** command to freeze the cells you wish to always have in view. The **Freeze Panes** command provides you with several options for freezing cells, enabling you to customize precisely how your worksheet cells scroll. You can access the **Freeze Panes** options by selecting **View→Window→Freeze Panes**. The **Freeze Panes** command is worksheet specific, so you can set different **Freeze Panes** options for each worksheet in your workbooks.

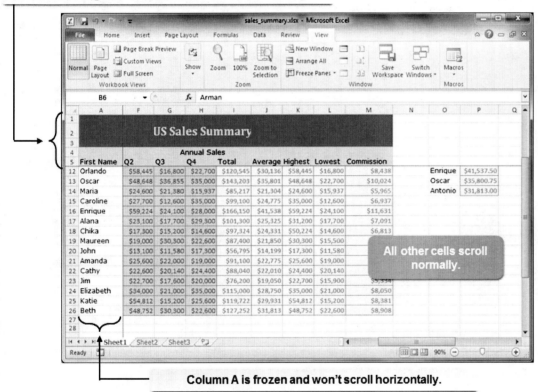

Figure 6-15: The Freeze Panes command enables you to control precisely how your worksheet columns and rows scroll.

The following table details what each of the **Freeze Panes** options will freeze.

Freeze Panes Option	Description
Freeze Panes	Freezes all rows above and all columns to the left of the currently selected cell. Use this option to keep both row and column labels in view at all times.
Freeze Top Row	Freezes the top row of the currently selected worksheet.
Freeze First Column	Freezes the first column of the currently selected worksheet.

Freeze Panes Option	Description
Unfreeze Panes	Unfreezes all cells on the currently selected worksheet. This option is displayed only once you've frozen panes on the worksheet.

The Arrange All Command

By default, you can view only a single workbook at a time in Excel 2010. But there are a number of reasons you may wish to view the contents of more than one workbook at a time. For example, you may need to compare data from one workbook to that of another, verify that data has been entered correctly, or even copy and paste data from one workbook to another. You can use the **Arrange All** command to perform any of these tasks. The **Arrange All** command displays all open workbook windows within the Excel application window simultaneously. You have a variety of view options to choose from depending on your particular needs.

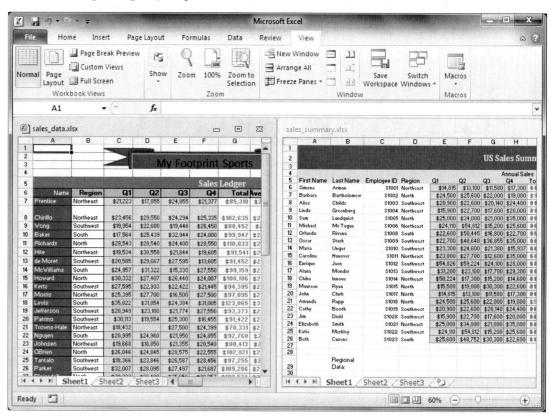

Figure 6-16: Multiple workbooks displayed within the Excel application window simultaneously.

The Arrange Windows Dialog Box

You can select the desired view option for the **Arrange All** command in the **Arrange Windows** dialog box. Selecting the **Arrange All** command automatically displays the **Arrange Windows** dialog box, which provides you with four display options.

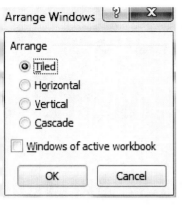

Figure 6-17: The Arrange All dialog box enables you to decide how to display your open workbooks.

The following table describes each of the display options for the **Arrange All** command.

Option	Displays Open Workbook Windows
Tiled	In rows and columns, with an even amount of space allotted to each workbook window, depending on the number of open workbooks.
Horizontal	One on top of the other, with each window taking up the full amount of horizontal space. Excel divides the vertical space evenly depending on the number of open workbooks.
Vertical	Side by side, with each window taking up the full amount of vertical space. Excel divides the horizontal space evenly, depending on the number of open workbooks.
Cascade	In an offset stack, with just enough of the title bar for each workbook window in view so you can select the workbook you'd like to bring to the front. In this view, the workbook windows do not automatically adjust when you select windows from the back. So, you may need to rearrange the windows manually to view subsequent workbooks.

The View Side by Side Command

The **View Side by Side** command is sort of a cross between the **Split** command and the **Arrange All** command. It enables you to view worksheets from two different workbooks side by side for easy comparison. By default, the **View Side by Side** command synchronizes the scrolling of both worksheets so you can review them simultaneously with ease. You have the option of toggling that functionality on or off by using the **Synchronous Scrolling** button. Whether synchronous scrolling is enabled or disabled, only the currently selected workbook displays scroll bars. Both the **View Side by Side** button and the **Synchronous Scrolling** button are available in the **Window** group on the **View** tab.

Note: If you have more than two workbooks open, Excel prompts you to select which workbook you want to compare to the actively selected workbook in the **Compare Side by Side** dialog box.

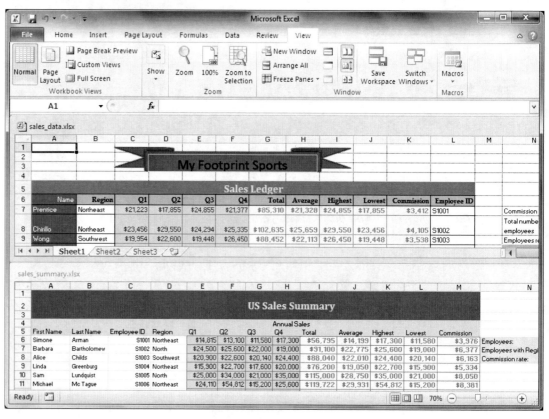

Figure 6-18: The View Side by Side command makes it easy to review two separate workbooks at once.

The Switch Windows Command

The **Switch Windows** command enables you to easily switch among multiple open workbooks. This way, you can change which open workbook you want to view without having to minimize or manually arrange your workbook windows. This feature can be helpful when you select the **Cascade** option in the **Arrange Windows** dialog box, but works with any Excel view. You can access the **Switch Windows** command in the **Window** group on the **View** tab.

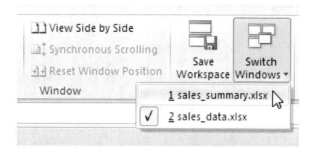

Figure 6-19: Use the Switch Windows command to select any open workbook.

The New Window Command

The **New Window** command enables you to open another instance of any workbook window so you can view and work in different parts of the same workbook simultaneously. You can use the **New Window** command in conjunction with the **Arrange All** or **View Side by Side** commands to arrange all instances of the workbook window to suit your needs. You can open multiple instances of the same workbook; Excel appends the workbook file name with a colon and a sequential number, indicating which copy of the workbook is contained in each workbook window. Changes made in any subsequent workbook windows affect all instances of the workbook window and become part of the original file when saved. You can access the **New Window** command in the **Window** group on the **View** tab.

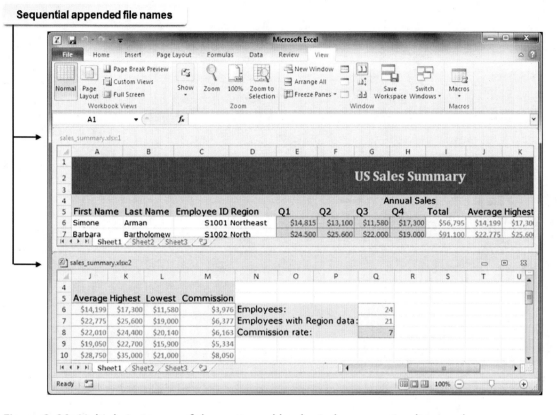

Figure 6–20: Multiple instances of the same workbook window open simultaneously.

Workspaces

If you frequently work with the same collection of multiple workbooks simultaneously, you may want to consider saving your workbook arrangement as a *workspace*. Workspaces allow you to save a particular configuration or arrangement of workbook windows as a workspace file. When you open a workspace file, Excel automatically opens all workbooks saved in the workspace and arranges the workbook windows exactly as you had them configured. This saves you the time and effort of opening multiple files and then rearranging them to be able to work as you need to. Workspaces can include multiple workbook files and they can contain multiple instances of the same workbook window opened by using the **New Window** command. The file type for Excel workspaces is the XLW file format. You can access the **Save Workspace** command in the **Window** group on the **View** tab.

Note: The XLW file format is not available from the **Save** or the **Save As** dialog boxes. You must save workspaces by using the ribbon command.

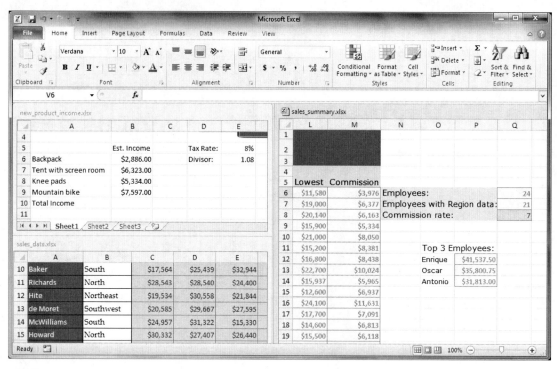

Figure 6-21: A workspace file opens in the precise arrangement you saved it in.

 Access the Checklist tile on your LogicalCHOICE course screen for reference information and job aids on **How to Manage Workbook and Worksheet Views.**

ACTIVITY 6-2
Managing Workbook and Worksheet Views

Data File

C:\091018Data\Managing Workbooks\sales_data.xlsx

Before You Begin

The my_sales_summary.xlsx workbook file is open.

Scenario

You'd like to verify that you have copied all of your sales data into the sales data and sales summary workbooks correctly, so you decide to open both workbooks at the same time and compare some of the entries. As the sales data worksheet has grown well beyond what can easily be viewed on one screen, and you need to review data from two different workbooks, you realize you will have to change your workbook views to be able to compare some of the data side by side.

1. Open the **sales_data.xlsx** workbook.

2. In the **sales_data.xlsx** workbook, split the workbook window to view different parts of the sales data worksheet simultaneously.
   a) Select all of row **16**.
   b) Select **View→Window→Split**.
   c) In the bottom pane, scroll to the bottom of the worksheet so you can compare the data in row 55 with the data in row **15**.
   d) Select **View→Window→Split** again to return to the Normal view.

3. Freeze panes so rows **1:6** don't scroll vertically and columns **A** and **B** don't scroll horizontally.
   a) Select cell **C7**.
   b) Select **View→Window→Freeze Panes→Freeze Panes**.
   c) Scroll vertically to verify that Excel froze the first six rows and scroll horizontally to verify that Excel froze the first two columns.

4. View the **my_sales_summary.xlsx** and the **sales_data.xlsx** workbooks side by side.
   a) Select **View→Window→View Side by Side**.
   b) Verify the two workbooks display one above the other, in two separate workbook windows, within the Excel application window.
   c) In the **my_sales_summary.xlsx** workbook window, ensure that the **US** worksheet tab is selected.
   d) Scroll down and up through either of the workbooks and verify both scroll simultaneously.
   e) Select **View→Window→Synchronous Scrolling** and verify the workbooks scroll independently of each other.

5. Close the **sales_data.xlsx** workbook without saving changes.

6. Verify the **my_sales_summary.xlsx** workbook file is now displayed fully maximized within the application window.

TOPIC C

Manage Workbook Properties

If you work for a large organization, it's likely that you and your colleagues generate a large number of Excel workbook files. Because many people often provide input or collaborate on the same projects, there are likely numerous versions of the same workbook files on your network shares and on people's computers. With all of these workbook files floating around, and with so many of them having similar titles and content, how can you find the exact file you're looking for? Consider also the possibility that someone will ask you to dig up and retrieve data from a workbook that hasn't been used in years. You may have to hunt through thousands of files to find what you're looking for, right? Maybe not.

Excel 2010 provides you with a way to include identifying information about your workbook files in your workbook files. This type of information can help you search through numerous workbook files to find precisely the one you need.

Workbook Properties

A workbook property is, quite simply, a bit of information about a workbook file. This kind of "data about your data" is also known as metadata. *Workbook properties* can help identify key pieces of information such as who created a particular file, when it was created, when it was last modified, and what its current status is. Workbook properties even enable you to include *tags* about a workbook file, similar to the tags web developers use to help people search for particular websites. Tags are short descriptions, or keywords, that help identify the kind of content you will find within a file. For example, a website for a professional baseball team might be tagged with the team's name, the city in which it plays, and terms such as baseball, sports, and fans. When a user searches for any of these terms, the team's site is more likely to show up in search results. The same is true when you search for a workbook file on a network or within a directory.

Excel generates some workbook properties automatically, such as the dates the file was created and last modified, the size of the file, and its current location. There are other workbook properties, such as tags and the workbook category, that are user specified. And Excel 2010 provides you with the ability to create custom properties to better suit your organization's particular needs.

Excel 2010 provides you with several options for adding properties to your workbook files and modifying existing ones. These properties can help you distinguish one particular instance or version of a file from among thousands.

Workbook Properties in the Backstage View

Perhaps the simplest and most direct way to view and modify your workbook properties is on the **Info** tab of the Backstage view. When you select the **Info** tab, some of the most common document properties are displayed in the right pane. Some of these are automatically created, saved, and updated by Excel and others can be modified. Properties that you can change here are displayed with a gold border around them when you place the mouse pointer over the text.

The **Show All Properties** link at the bottom of the right pane expands the view of workbook properties in the Backstage view so you can view and modify more of them. Once expanded, you can select the **Show Fewer Properties** link to collapse the view back to its default state.

Properties ▾

Size	21.0KB
Title	Add a title
Tags	Add a tag
Categories	Add a category

Related Dates

Last Modified	1/8/2014 1:23 PM
Created	8/16/2011 8:28 AM
Last Printed	7/2/2012 9:33 PM

Related People

Author	Student
	Add an author
Last Modified By	R Toner

Related Documents

Open File Location

Show All Properties

Figure 6–22: Workbook properties displayed on the Info tab in the Backstage view.

The Document Panel

If you want to be able to view and modify some of your workbook properties while working within your workbook, you can open the **Document Panel**. The **Document Panel** displays six of the most commonly used workbook properties and any comments users have included in the workbook's metadata. It appears above the workbook window and below the **Formula Bar** in the Excel user interface. You can modify workbook properties in the **Document Panel** simply by typing the desired information into the various text fields. You can open the **Document Panel** by selecting the **Properties** down arrow in the right pane on the **Info** tab in the Backstage view and selecting **Show Document Panel**. You can close it by selecting the **Close the Document Information Panel** button in the top-right corner of the **Document Panel**.

Document Panel

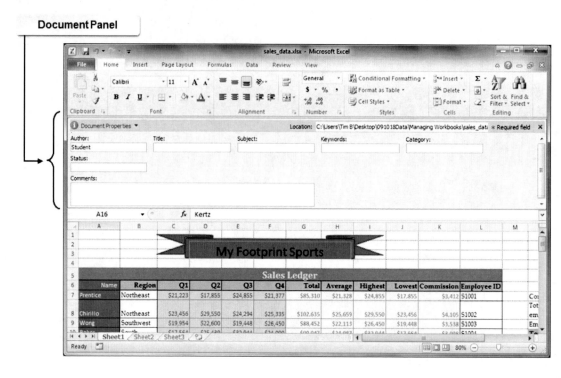

Figure 6-23: The Document Panel.

The Properties Dialog Box

If you want to view all of the document properties for your workbook or create custom document properties, you can open the **Properties** dialog box. The **Properties** dialog box is divided into five tabs that are displayed and allow you to work with all properties associated with the current workbook. You can open the **Properties** dialog box two ways:

- Select **File→Info**, select the **Properties** down arrow in the right pane, and select **Advanced Properties**.
- Display the **Document Panel**, select the **Document Properties** down arrow, and select **Advanced Properties**.

 Note: The **Properties** dialog box displays the file name of the currently selected workbook file before the word "Properties" in the title bar.

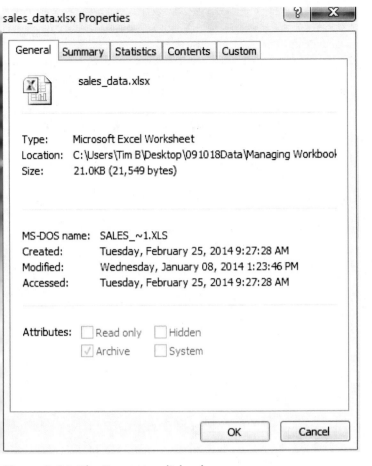

Figure 6-24: The Properties dialog box.

The following table identifies the workbook properties that are displayed on the various tabs in the **Properties** dialog box.

Properties Dialog Box Tab	Contains
General	General information about the workbook file, such as the file type, the file size, where the file is saved, and the dates when the file was created and last modified. Excel creates and updates these workbook properties automatically.
Summary	The default document properties that you can modify. Workbook properties on this tab include the document title, the author, keywords, and any included comments.
Statistics	System-level information about the workbook file, such as when it was created, last accessed, last modified, and last printed. Excel creates and updates these properties automatically.
Contents	The worksheet names for all worksheets in the document, and any named cell ranges. Excel creates and updates these properties automatically.
Custom	The commands you will use to create custom document properties.

Custom Workbook Properties

If you would like to create workbook properties that more specifically help you identify your files based on your organization's processes, departments, terminology, client list, or other standards, you can create *custom workbook properties*. These are user-defined workbook properties that can help you search for workbook files based on internal organizational conditions. Excel 2010 includes a number of preset categories of custom workbook properties, or you can create an entirely unique property. You can also restrict the values users can enter into custom property fields to ensure a large number of users will be able to successfully search for workbook files.

Figure 6-25: The Custom tab on the Properties dialog box.

The following table describes the various elements of the **Custom** tab.

Custom Tab Element	Description
Name field	If you select an existing name from the **Name** list, it will appear here. Or you can type a unique, new property name in this field.
Name list	Displays a list of the preset property categories. When you select a name from this list, it is displayed in the **Name** field.
Type drop-down menu	Allows you to select a content type to restrict what users can enter into your custom properties. You can select text, date, or number for values that can by typed into the property. Or you can select the **Yes or no** option to require users to select one of those two values. (This could be a useful option for properties such as "Approved" or "Review Complete.")
Value field	This is where you enter the value for the property.

Custom Tab Element	Description
Properties field	Displays all custom properties for the workbook.
Add button	Once you've configured a new custom property, the **Add** button adds it to the **Properties** field. When you select an existing custom property in the **Properties** field, the **Add** button becomes the **Modify** button, which allows you to save changes to existing custom properties.
Delete button	Deletes the selected custom property from the **Properties** field.

 Access the Checklist tile on your LogicalCHOICE course screen for reference information and job aids on How to Manage Workbook Properties.

ACTIVITY 6-3
Managing Workbook Properties

Before You Begin

The my_sales_summary.xlsx workbook file is open.

The C drive on your computer has been indexed.

Scenario

It has dawned on you that you will be creating a large number of workbook files that will contain similar types of data and have similar file names. So, you decide to include key information in your workbook file, in the form of workbook properties, to make it easier for you to search through your workbook files. You also want to add a custom property so document recipients can easily tell if a workbook file is the approved, final copy.

1. If necessary, select **File→Info**.

2. Add workbook properties to the file.

   a) In the right pane, below the **Properties** drop-down menu, next to **Title**, select **Add a title**.

Properties ▾	
Size	18.9KB
Title	Add a title
Tags	Add a tag
Categories	Add a category

   b) Type *Sales Summary*
   c) Next to **Tags**, select **Add a tag**.
   d) Type *sales data, regions, summary, US, Mexico, Canada, Europe, employee list*
   e) Next to **Categories**, select **Add a category**, and then type *Sales*

3. Create a custom workbook property.

   a) Select the **Properties** down arrow and then select **Advanced Properties**.
   b) In the **Properties** dialog box, ensure that the **Custom** tab is selected.
   c) In the **Name** field, type *Approved and Final*
   d) In the **Type** drop-down menu, select **Yes or no**.
   e) In the **Value** section, ensure the **Yes** radio button is selected.
   f) Select **Add**.
   g) Verify that the new custom workbook property appears in the **Properties** field and select **OK**.

4. Save and close the workbook and then close Excel 2010.

5. Search for the workbook by using the modified workbook properties.

   a) Open **Windows Explorer**.
   b) In the **Navigation** pane, select your computer's **C** drive.
   c) In the search field in the top-right corner of Windows Explorer, type *Europe*

d) Verify that the **C:\091018Data\Managing Workbooks\my_sales_summary.xlsx** workbook file is displayed in the search results.

e) Close **Windows Explorer**.

Summary

In this lesson, you managed worksheets, workbook and worksheet views, as well as workbook properties. By keeping your workbook files well-structured and organized, you'll save time, work more efficiently, and always know exactly where your critical data is. Adjusting workbook and worksheet views means you can make easy comparisons between data that is spread across large worksheets, more easily be able to reuse information and formulas, and have greater control over your print and display settings. And knowing how to find the precise file you need means you'll never have to waste your valuable time and effort combing over thousands of workbook files. As you develop and work with a greater number of workbook files, these skills will become invaluable resources that will help you maintain control over the information that is critical to your organizational success.

Which of the worksheet or workbook management options do you think you'll use most often?

Can you think of creative ways to use workbook properties to your advantage?

 Note: Check your LogicalCHOICE Course screen for opportunities to interact with your classmates, peers, and the larger LogicalCHOICE online community about the topics covered in this course or other topics you are interested in. From the Course screen you can also access available resources for a more continuous learning experience.

Course Follow-Up

Congratulations! You have completed the *Microsoft® Office Excel® 2010: Part 1 (Second Edition)* course. You have successfully created and developed Excel workbooks to enter, modify, analyze, and present critical organizational data.

Businesses, academic institutions, and other organizations generate massive amounts of important data on a continuous basis. As technology becomes faster, more powerful, and more pervasive, the amount of data these organizations create will grow to staggering levels. With that growth will come an increasing need for people like you to capture, organize, and make sense of that data. After all, data is useless unless someone can make sense of it, isolate issues, recognize opportunities, and communicate their findings to the people who make decisions. Strive to create well-structured, organized workbooks that you can quickly, easily, and efficiently work with. And, never stop trying to discover new ways to make Excel work for you. The more you can understand about your data, and the more insight you can glean from it, the better positioned your organizational leaders will be to make the decisions that will foster success.

What's Next?

Microsoft® Office Excel® 2010: Part 2 (Second Edition) is the next course in this series. In that course, you will build upon the skills you have acquired by customizing the Excel environment, creating advanced formulas, applying advanced conditional formatting, and using tables to organize and analyze your data by using tables. You will also perform some higher-level analysis by using PivotTables, slicers, and PivotCharts. You are also encouraged to explore Excel further by actively participating in any of the social media forums set up by your instructor or training administrator through the **Social Media** tile on the LogicalCHOICE Course screen.

A | Microsoft Office Excel 2010 Exam 77–882

Selected Logical Operations courseware addresses Microsoft Office Specialist certification skills for Microsoft Office 2010. The following table indicates where Excel 2010 skills that are tested in Exam 77-882 are covered in the Logical Operations Microsoft Office Excel 2010 series of courses.

Objective Domain	Covered In
1. Managing the Worksheet Environment	
1.1 Navigate through a worksheet	
1.1.1 Use hot keys	Part 1, Appendix C
1.1.2 Use the name box	Part 1, Topic 1-A; Part 2
1.2 Print a worksheet or workbook	
1.2.1 Print only selected worksheets	Part 1, Topic 5-A
1.2.2 Print an entire workbook	Part 1, Topic 5-A
1.2.3 Construct headers and footers	Part 1, Topic 5-B
1.2.4 Apply printing options	
1.2.4.1 Scale	Part 1, Topic 5-A, 5-B
1.2.4.2 Print titles	Part 1, Topic 5-B
1.2.4.3 Page setup	Part 1, Topic 5-B
1.2.4.4 Print area	Part 1, Topic 5-B
1.2.4.5 Gridlines	Part 1, Topic 5-B
1.3 Personalize the environment by using Backstage	
1.3.1 Manipulate the Quick Access Toolbar	Part 2
1.3.2 Customize the ribbon	
1.3.2.1 Tabs	Part 2
1.3.2.2 Groups	Part 2
1.3.3 Manipulate Excel default settings (Excel Options)	Part 2
1.3.4 Import data to Excel	Part 3
1.3.5 Import data from Excel	Part 3
1.3.6 Manipulate workbook properties	Part 1, Topic 6-C

Objective Domain	Covered In
1.3.7 Manipulate workbook files and folders	Part 1, Topic 1-C
1.3.8 Apply different name and file formats for different uses	Part 1, Topic 1-C
1.3.9 Using save and save as features	Part 1, Topic 1-C
2. Creating Cell Data	
2.1 Construct cell data	
2.1.1 Use paste special	
2.1.1.1 Formats	Part 1, Topic 2-C
2.1.1.2 Formulas	Part 1, Topic 2-C
2.1.1.3 Values	Part 1, Topic 2-C
2.1.1.4 Preview icons	Part 1, Topic 2-C
2.1.1.5 Transpose rows and columns	Part 1, Topic 2-C
2.1.1.6 Operations	Part 1, Topic 2-C
2.1.1.7 Comments	Part 1, Topic 2-C
2.1.1.8 Validation	Part 1, Topic 2-C
2.1.1.9 Paste as a link	Part 1, Topic 2-C
2.1.2 Cut, move, and select cell data	Part 1, Topic 1-D, 2-C
2.2 Apply AutoFill	
2.2.1 Copy data using AutoFill	Part 1, Topic 1-D
2.2.2 Fill series using AutoFill	Part 1, Topic 1-D
2.2.3 Copy or preserve cell format with AutoFill	Part 1, Topic 1-D
2.2.4 Select from drop-down list	Part 1, Topic 1-D
2.3 Apply and manipulate hyperlinks	
2.3.1 Create a hyperlink in a cell	Part 1, Topic 4-A
2.3.2 Modify hyperlinks	Part 1, Topic 4-A
2.3.3 Modify hyperlinked cell attributes	Part 1, Topic 4-A
2.3.4 Remove a hyperlink	Part 1, Topic 4-A
3. Formatting Cells and Worksheets	
3.1 Apply and modify cell formats	
3.1.1 Align cell content	Part 1, Topic 4-D
3.1.2 Apply a number format	Part 1, Topic 4-C
3.1.3 Wrap text in a cell	Part 1, Topic 4-D
3.1.4 Use Format Painter	Part 1, Topic 4-B
3.2 Merge or split cells	
3.2.1 Use Merge & Center	Part 1, Topic 4-D
3.2.2 Merge Across	Part 1, Topic 4-D
3.2.3 Merge cells	Part 1, Topic 4-D

Objective Domain	Covered In
3.2.4 Unmerge Cells	Part 1, Topic 4-D
3.3 Create row and column titles	
3.3.1 Print row and column headings	Part 1, Topic 5-B
3.3.2 Print rows to repeat with titles	Part 1, Topic 5-B
3.3.3 Print columns to repeat with titles	Part 1, Topic 5-B
3.3.4 Configure titles to print only on odd or even pages	Part 1, Topic 5-B
3.3.5 Configure titles to skip the first worksheet page	Part 1, Topic 5-B
3.4 Hide and unhide rows and columns	
3.4.1 Hide a column	Part 1, Topic 3-A
3.4.2 Unhide a column	Part 1, Topic 3-A
3.4.3 Hide a series of columns	Part 1, Topic 3-A
3.4.4 Hide a row	Part 1, Topic 3-A
3.4.5 Unhide a row	Part 1, Topic 3-A
3.4.6 Hide a series of rows	Part 1, Topic 3-A
3.5 Manipulate Page Setup options for worksheets	
3.5.1 Configure page orientation	Part 1, Topic 5-B
3.5.2 Manage page scaling	Part 1, Topics 5-A, 5-B
3.5.3 Configure page margins	Part 1, Topic 5-B
3.5.4 Change header and footer size	Part 1, Topic 5-B
3.6 Create and apply cell styles	
3.6.1 Apply cell styles	Part 1, Topic 4-E
3.6.2 Construct new cell styles	Part 1, Topic 4-E
4. Managing Worksheets and Workbooks	
4.1 Create and format worksheets	
4.1.1 Insert worksheets	Part 1, Topic 6-A
4.1.2 Delete worksheets	Part 1, Topic 6-A
4.1.3 Copy worksheets	Part 1, Topic 6-A
4.1.4 Reposition worksheets	Part 1, Topic 6-A
4.1.5 Copy and move worksheets	Part 1, Topic 6-A
4.1.6 Rename worksheets	Part 1, Topic 6-A
4.1.7 Group worksheets	Part 1, Topic 6-A
4.1.8 Apply coloring to worksheet tabs	Part 1, Topic 6-A
4.1.9 Hide worksheet tabs	Part 1, Topic 6-A
4.1.10 Unhide worksheet tabs	Part 1, Topic 6-A
4.2 Manipulate window views	
4.2.1 Split window views	Part 1, Topic 6-B

Objective Domain	Covered In
4.2.2 Arrange window views	Part 1, Topic 6-B
4.2.3 Open a new window with contents from the current worksheet	Part 1, Topic 6-B
4.3 Manipulate workbook views	
4.3.1 Use Normal, Page Layout, and Page Break workbook views	Part 1, Topic 5-B
4.3.2 Create custom views	Part 1, Topic 5-B
5. Applying Formulas and Functions	
5.1 Create formulas	
5.1.1 Use basic operators	Part 1, Topic 2-A
5.1.2 Revise formulas	Part 1, Topic 2-A
5.2 Enforce precedence	
5.2.1 Order of evaluation	Part 1, Topic 2-A
5.2.2 Precedence using parentheses	Part 1, Topic 2-A
5.2.3 Precedence of operators for percent vs. exponentiation	Part 1, Topic 2-A
5.3 Apply cell references in formulas	
5.3.1 Relative references	Part 1, Topic 2-C
5.3.2 Absolute references	Part 1, Topic 2-C
5.4 Apply conditional logic in a formula	
5.4.1 Create a formula with values that match your conditions	Part 3
5.4.2 Edit defined conditions in a formula	Part 3
5.4.3 Use a series of conditional logic values in a formula	Part 3
5.5 Apply named ranges in formulas	
5.5.1 Define, edit, and rename a named range	Part 2
5.6 Apply cell ranges in formulas	
5.6.1 Enter a cell range definition in the formula bar	Part 1, Topic 2-A
5.6.2 Define a cell range using the mouse	Part 1, Topic 2-A
5.6.3 Define a cell range using a keyboard shortcut	Part 1, Topic 2-A
6. Presenting Data Visually	
6.1 Create charts based on worksheet data	Part 2, Topic 5-A
6.2 Apply and manipulate illustrations	
6.2.1 Clip Art	Part 2
6.2.2 SmartArt	Part 2
6.2.3 Shapes	Part 2
6.2.4 Screenshots	Part 2

Objective Domain	Covered In
6.3 Create and modify images by using the Image Editor	
6.3.1 Making corrections to an image	
6.3.1.1 Sharpen or soften an image	Part 2
6.3.1.2 Changing brightness and contrast	Part 2
6.3.2 Use picture color tools	Part 2
6.3.3 Change artistic effects on an image	Part 2
6.4 Apply Sparklines	
6.4.1 Use Line, Column, and Win/Loss chart types	Part 3
6.4.2 Create a Sparkline chart	Part 3
6.4.3 Customize a Sparkline	Part 3
6.4.4 Format a Sparkline	Part 3
6.4.5 Show or hide data markers	Part 3
7. Sharing Worksheet Data with Other Users	
7.1 Share spreadsheets by using Backstage	
7.1.1 Send a worksheet via email or Skydrive	Part 3
7.1.2 Change the file type to a different version of Excel	Part 1, Topic 1-C
7.1.3 Save as PDF or XPS	Part 1, Topic 1-C; Part 3
7.2 Manage comments	
7.2.1 Inserting comments	Part 3
7.2.2 Viewing comments	Part 3
7.2.3 Editing comments	Part 3
7.2.4 Deleting comments	Part 3
8. Analyzing and Organizing Data	
8.1 Filter data	
8.1.1 Define filters	Part 2
8.1.2 Apply filters	Part 2
8.1.3 Remove filters	Part 2
8.1.4 Search filters	Part 2
8.1.5 Filter lists using AutoFilter	Part 2
8.2 Sort data	
8.2.1 Use sort options	
8.2.1.1 Values	Part 2
8.2.1.2 Font color	Part 2
8.2.1.3 Cell color	Part 2
8.3 Apply conditional formatting	
8.3.1 Apply conditional formatting to cells	Part 1, Topic 4-F; Part 2

Objective Domain	Covered In
8.3.2 Use the Rule Manager to apply conditional formats	Part 2
8.3.3 Use the IF function to apply conditional formatting	Part 2, Part 3
8.3.4 Icon sets	Part 2
8.3.5 Data bars	Part 2
8.3.6 Clear rules	Part 2

B | Microsoft Office Excel 2010 Expert Exam 77-888

Selected Logical Operations courseware addresses Microsoft Office Specialist certification skills for Microsoft Office 2010. The following table indicates where Excel 2010 skills that are tested in Exam 77-888 are covered in the Logical Operations Microsoft Office Excel 2010 series of courses.

Objective Domain	Covered In
1. Sharing and Maintaining Workbooks	
1.1. Apply workbook settings, properties, and data options	
1.1.1. Set advanced properties	Part 1, Topic 6-C
1.1.2. Save a workbook as a template	Part 1, Topic 4-G
1.1.3. Import and export XML data	Part 3
1.2. Apply protection and sharing properties to workbooks and worksheets	
1.2.1. Protect the current sheet	Part 3
1.2.2. Protect the workbook structure	Part 3
1.2.3. Restrict permissions	Part 3
1.2.4. Require a password to open a workbook	Part 3
1.3. Maintain shared workbooks	
1.3.1. Merge workbooks	Part 3
1.3.2. Set Track Changes options	Part 3
2. Applying Formulas and Functions	
2.1. Audit formulas	
2.1.1. Trace formula precedents, dependents, and errors	Part 3
2.1.2. Locate invalid data or formulas	Part 3
2.1.3 Correct errors in formulas	Part 3
2.2. Manipulate formula options	
2.2.1. Set iterative calculation options	Part 3

Objective Domain	Covered In
2.2.2. Enable or disabling automatic workbook calculation	Part 2
2.3. Perform data summary tasks	
2.3.1. Use an array formula	Part 2
2.3.2. Use a SUMIFS function	Part 2
2.4. Apply functions in formulas	
2.4.1. Find and correct errors in functions	Part 3
2.4.2. Apply arrays to functions	Part 2
2.4.3. Use functions	
2.4.3.1 Statistical	Part 1, Topic 2-B; Part 2
2.4.3.2 Date and Time	Part 2
2.4.3.4 Financial	Part 2
2.4.3.5 Text	Part 2
2.4.3.6 Cube	Part 3
3. Presenting Data Visually	
3.1. Apply advanced chart features	
3.1.1. Use Trend lines	Part 3
3.1.2. Use Dual axes	Part 3
3.1.3. Use chart templates	Part 3
3.1.4. Use Sparklines	Part 3
3.2. Apply data analysis	
3.2.1 Use automated analysis tools	Part 3
3.2.2 Perform What-If analysis	Part 3
3.3. Apply and manipulate PivotTables	
3.3.1 Manipulate PivotTable data	Part 2
3.3.2 Use the slicer to filter and segment your PivotTable data in multiple layers	Part 2
3.4. Apply and manipulate PivotCharts	
3.4.1. Create PivotChart data	Part 2
3.4.2. Manipulate PivotChart data	Part 2
3.4.3. Analyze PivotChart data	Part 2
3.5. Demonstrate how to use the slicer	
3.5.1. Choose data sets from external data connections	Part 2
4. Working with Macros and Forms	
4.1. Create and manipulate macros	
4.1.1. Run a macro	Part 3
4.1.2. Run a macro when a workbook is opened	Part 3
4.1.3. Run a macro when a button is clicked	Part 3

Objective Domain	Covered In
4.1.4. Record an action macro	Part 3
4.1.5. Assign a macro to a command button	Part 3
4.1.6. Create a custom macro button on the Quick Access Toolbar	Part 3
4.1.7. Apply modifications to a macro	Part 3
4.2. Insert and manipulate form controls	
4.2.1. Inserting form controls	Part 3
4.2.2. Set form properties	Part 3

C | Microsoft Excel 2010 Common Keyboard Shortcuts

The follow table lists common keyboard shortcuts you can use in Excel 2010.

Function	Shortcut
Switch between worksheet tabs, from left to right	Ctrl + PgDn
Switch between worksheet tabs, from right to left	Ctrl + PgUp
Select the region around the active cell (requires there to be content in the surrounding cells)	Ctrl + Shift + * or Ctrl + * (from the number pad)
Insert the current time	Ctrl + Shift + :
Insert the current date	Ctrl + ;
Display the **Insert** dialog box	Ctrl + Shift + +
Display the **Delete** dialog box	Ctrl + -
Display the **Format Cells** dialog box	Ctrl + 1
Select the entire worksheet	Ctrl + A
Apply or remove bold formatting	Ctrl + B
Apply or remove italic formatting	Ctrl + I
Copy the selected cells	Ctrl + C
Paste copied content	Ctrl + V
Display the **Find and Replace** dialog box	Ctrl + F
Display the **Insert Hyperlink** or **Edit Hyperlink** dialog box	Ctrl + K
Display the **Create Table** dialog box	Ctrl + T
Create a new workbook	Ctrl + N
Open a file	Ctrl + O
Print a file	Ctrl + P
Save the file	Ctrl + S

Function	Shortcut
Repeat the last command or action, if possible	Ctrl + Y or F4 (when the insertion point is not in the **Formula Bar**)
Undo the last command or action	Ctrl + Z
Redo the last undo	Ctrl + Y
Enter data in a cell while keeping it the active cell	Ctrl + Enter
Select all contiguously populated cells in a column from the selected cell to the end of the range	Ctrl + Shift + up-arrow or Ctrl + Shift + down arrow
Select all contiguously populated cells in a row from the selected cell to the end of the range	Ctrl + Shift + right-arrow or Ctrl + Shift + left-arrow
Toggle among relative, absolute, and mixed references when the insertion point is in or next to a cell reference in the **Formula Bar**	F4

Lesson Labs

Lesson labs are provided for certain lessons as additional learning resources for this course. Lesson labs are developed for selected lessons within a course in cases when they seem most instructionally useful as well as technically feasible. In general, labs are supplemental, optional unguided practice and may or may not be performed as part of the classroom activities. Your instructor will consider setup requirements, classroom timing, and instructional needs to determine which labs are appropriate for you to perform, and at what point during the class. If you do not perform the labs in class, your instructor can tell you if you can perform them independently as self-study, and if there are any special setup requirements.

Lesson Lab 1–1
Creating and Saving a Workbook

Activity Time: 10 minutes

Scenario

You're the sales manager for your organization and you've decided to create a workbook to track your sales reps by quarter. You want to determine who should be assigned to the most competitive regions and who should receive incentive rewards. As this year's first quarter sales figures are already in, you will add that data before saving the workbook.

Additionally, there are a few topics you're interested in learning more about regarding Excel. You decide to use Excel Help to review an article about one and a web-based resource on another.

1. Open Excel 2010 and create a new blank workbook.

2. Enter the following text labels and data on the **Sheet1** worksheet.

	A	B	C	D	E	F	
1	Sales Rep	Q1	Q2	Q3	Q4	Total	
2	Andy	32000					
3	Evan	47500					
4	Sara	53000					
5	Jose	28750					
6	Chan	37650					
7	Valerie	29995					
8	Kavitha	43275					
9	Raul	51200					
10	Daphne	48990					
11							

3. Use commands in the Backstage view to save the workbook to the **C:\091018Data \Getting Started with Microsoft Office Excel 2010** folder as *my_sales_tracker.xlsx*

4. Close the workbook, but leave Excel 2010 open.

5. Use Excel Help to search for and review an article on how to minimize the ribbon. Search only for articles saved on your computer.

6. Use Excel Help to search for and review a web-based resource about Excel file types.

7. Close your web browser and close the **Excel Help** window.

Lesson Lab 2-1
Creating and Reusing Formulas and Functions

Activity Time: 10 minutes

Data File

C:\091018Data\Performing Calculations\sales_tracker_02.xlsx

Before You Begin

Excel 2010 is open.

Scenario

You have just finished entering the past fiscal year's sales data into your sales tracker workbook. Now you wish to calculate the yearly total and the quarterly average sales for each of your reps, along with the overall total and average sales for your department. You decide to use Excel formulas and functions to do so. Additionally, you want to identify the highest and lowest quarterly sales figures out of all sales rep sales to get a sense of the range of sales your organization generates.

---

1. Open the **sales_tracker_02.xlsx** workbook file.

2. Enter a formula in cell **F2** that adds up the quarterly sales figures for Andy.

3. Enter a SUM function in cell **F3** to total the quarterly sales figures for Evan.

4. Use the AutoSum feature to total the quarterly sales figures for Sara in cell **F4**.

5. Copy the function in cell **F4** down the range **F5:F10**.

6. In cell **F12**, enter a function that calculates the overall sales total for the year.

7. Enter an AVERAGE function in cell **G2** to calculate the quarterly sales average for Andy.

8. Copy the function in cell **G2** down the range **G3:G10**.

9. In cell **G12**, enter a function to calculate the overall average quarterly sales for your entire team.

10. Enter a MAX function in cell **B12** that returns the greatest single quarterly sales figure for all of the sales reps.

11. Enter a MIN function in cell **B13** that returns the smallest single quarterly sales figure for all of the sales reps.

12. In cell **B14**, use a simple formula to calculate the difference between the greatest and the smallest quarterly sales figures.

13. Save the workbook to the **C:\091018Data\Performing Calculations** folder as *my_sales_tracker_02.xlsx* and close the workbook.

Lesson Lab 3-1
Modifying a Worksheet

Activity Time: 10 minutes

Data File

C:\091018Data\Modifying a Worksheet\employee_roster.xlsx

Before You Begin

Excel 2010 is open.

Scenario

You are in charge of maintaining the employee master list for your organization. Because the previous version of the employee master list was wiped out by a virus on the company network, you are rebuilding the document from scratch. You have already entered all of the raw information and are ready to adjust some of the column widths to accommodate the data. While looking over the worksheet, you realize there are several data entry errors that you need to correct. Some of the departmental entries for the Finance department are entered incorrectly, so you decide to use the **Replace** command to correct those as needed. You have also mistakenly entered ENF instead of ENG for all employees in the Engineering department. You realize you'll be able to correct those all at once. You also decide it would be a good idea to check the spelling of the entries for the employee position column to ensure there are no errors there.

In addition to these corrections, you also want to temporarily hide all rows containing employee information for the sales department. All other employees are eligible for an annual bonus (the sales reps are rewarded through commission payments), and you'd like to compile a list of only bonus-eligible employees to forward to the payroll department. Because you'd also like to track all employee bonuses, you decide to add a new column to the worksheet to accommodate that information.

1. Open the **employee_roster.xlsx** workbook file.

2. Adjust the width of all columns as needed to accommodate the employee information.

3. Use the **Find and Replace** dialog box to correct both instances of **FIM** to *FIN* in the **Department** column one at a time.

4. Correct all instances of **ENF** to *ENG* in the **Department** column simultaneously.

5. Check the spelling of entries in the **Position** column.

6. Hide rows **104:125**.

7. Insert a column between the **Pay Scale Code** column and the **Salary** column, and label it *Bonus*

8. Save the workbook to the **C:\091018Data\Modifying a Worksheet** folder as *my_employee_roster.xlsx* and close the workbook.

Lesson Lab 4–1
Formatting a Worksheet

Activity Time: 15 minutes

Data File

C:\091018Data\Formatting a Worksheet\employee_roster_04.xlsx

Before You Begin

Excel 2010 is open.

Scenario

You've built out your employee master list and have asked a colleague in the payroll department to include bonus information and a calculation of total compensation for all employees. When you get the workbook back, you realize that your colleague removed all of the number formatting you had already applied to the various columns. You realize you'll need to reapply the appropriate formatting to the columns. You'd also like to make the worksheet generally easier to read, so you decide to apply border and color formatting, format some of the text, apply cell styles to some of the cells, and realign some of the data.

You've also been asked to keep track of employee bonuses, specifically the largest ones, so you decide to conditionally format the cells in the **Bonus** column to highlight the top 20 percent of all bonuses paid. In addition, as you expect you'll likely need to create similar workbooks in the future, you decide to create a template from the workbook for future use.

---

1. Open the **employee_roster_04.xlsx** workbook file.

2. Reapply the number formatting your colleague removed.
    a) Apply the Short Date number format to the cells below the column label in the **Start Date** column.
    b) Format the cells below the column label in the **Years with Company** column to be displayed as numbers with only two decimal places showing.
    c) Apply the Currency number format to all cells below the column labels in the **Bonus**, **Salary**, and **Total Compensation** columns.

3. Apply other formatting to the worksheet to make it easier to read.
    a) Center the text in column I.
    b) Increase the font size to 12 and apply bold text formatting to the employee ID values.
    c) Add a light-blue background color to the cells containing employee IDs.
    d) Apply the **Heading 3** cell style to the column labels.
    e) Apply the **Input** cell style to the values in the **Bonus** and **Salary** columns.
    f) Apply the **Calculation** cell style to the values in the **Total Compensation** column.
    g) Add a right border to the cells in column **A**.
    h) Add a border between the **Bonus** and **Salary** columns.

4. Apply the **Thatch** theme to the workbook.

5. Conditionally format the cells in the **Bonus** column to highlight the top 20 percent of bonuses with a green fill and dark green text.

6. Save the workbook to the **C:\091018Data\Formatting a Worksheet** folder as *my_employee_roster_04.xlsx* and leave the workbook open.

7. Save the workbook as a template.
   a) Delete all data from columns **A:K**.
   b) Save the workbook to the **Templates** folder as a template file named *my_employee_roster_04.xltx* and then close the workbook.

8. Close the template file.

Lesson Lab 5-1
Printing Workbooks

Activity Time: 10 minutes

Data File

C:\091018Data\Printing Workbooks\employee_roster_05.xlsx

Before You Begin

Excel 2010 is open, and you have a printer driver installed.

Scenario

Your supervisor has asked you for printed copies of the employee master list to hand out to participants at an upcoming management meeting. You print a test copy and realize you will have to configure the print settings and define the page layout for the worksheet so document recipients can make sense of the data. Because the workbook will be presented to senior managers, you decide to add headers and footers to give it a more polished, official appearance.

---

1. Open the **employee_roster_05.xlsx** workbook file.

    Note: View the print preview for the workbook before configuring the print settings and defining the page layout to get a sense of what the printed document would look like if you didn't make the adjustments.

2. Configure the print settings for the worksheet.
   a) Ensure the print job is configured to collate the worksheet pages.
   b) Change the orientation from portrait to landscape.
   c) Scale the document so that all columns print on a single page.

3. Use the **Print Titles** command to ensure row **1** prints on every page.

4. Add custom headers and footers to the document.
   a) Create a custom header that prints the document title in the center of the first page only, and that prints the current date in the top right corner of all pages.
   b) Create a custom footer that prints the page number in the bottom right corner of each page.

5. Use page breaks to force Excel to print a relatively even amount of data on each printed page.
   a) Set the workbook view to the Page Break Preview view.
   b) Manually drag the first page break up so that it falls between rows **35** and **36**.
   c) Manually drag the second page break up so that it falls between rows **70** and **71**.

6. View the print preview.

7. If you are connected to a printer, print one copy of the document.

8. Save the workbook to the **C:\091018Data\Printing Workbooks** folder as **my_employee_roster_05.xlsx**, and then close the workbook.

Lesson Lab 6-1
Managing Workbooks

Activity Time: 10 minutes

Data Files

C:\091018Data\Managing Workbooks\sales_tacker_fy2012.xlsx

C:\091018Data\Managing Workbooks\sales_tacker_fy2013.xlsx

Before You Begin

Excel 2010 is open.

Scenario

You're looking over the net sales totals for you company for the past fiscal year. One of your staff members prepared the workbook for you, so you are reviewing the figures to give final approval. As you review the workbook, you notice the person who prepared it neglected to apply the proper worksheet tab formatting, has left the worksheets out of order, and has included two unnecessary worksheets. You decide to format the tabs and remove the unneeded worksheets. Because you have the worksheet open, you'd like to compare the annual figures to those from last year so you can begin preparing your annual report for senior managers. Also, because the workbook will be stored on a central network share and other users will likely need the data, you decide to configure the workbook's properties to ensure other users will be able to easily search for and find the document.

1. Open the **sales_tracker_fy2013.xlsx** workbook file.

2. Place the worksheets in sequential order by worksheet tab name.

3. Delete the **Sheet6** and **Sheet7** worksheets.

4. Rename the worksheet tabs.
   a) Change the name of worksheet **Sheet1** to *Q1*
   b) Change the name of worksheet **Sheet2** to *Q2*
   c) Change the name of worksheet **Sheet3** to *Q3*
   d) Change the name of worksheet **Sheet4** to *Q4*
   e) Change the name of worksheet **Sheet5** to *FY 2013 Totals*

5. Apply color formatting to the worksheet tabs.
   a) Group the following sheets together: **Q1**, **Q2**, **Q3**, and **Q4**.
   b) Apply a dark-blue background color to the grouped worksheet tabs.
   c) Apply a red background color to the **FY 2013 Totals** worksheet tab.

6. Save the workbook to the **C:\091018Data\Managing Workbooks** folder as *my_sales_tracker_fy2013.xlsx*

7. Compare the net sales figures for 2012 and 2013.
   a) Open the **sales_tracker_fy2012.xlsx** workbook file.
   b) Freeze the top row of the **Q1** worksheet in both workbooks.

   c) View both workbooks side by side to verify the first quarter sales for 2013 were better than those for 2012.

   d) View the fiscal year totals tabs for both workbooks side by side and verify that overall 2013 sales were better than 2012.

Save the current view of the two workbooks as a workspace in the **C:\091018Data\Managing Workbooks** folder as *my_sales_totals_workspace.xlw*.

 Note: When prompted, do not save the workbooks when creating the workspace if you do not want to overwrite the original data files.

Close all open workbooks and then re-open the workspace file to verify that Excel saved the view as expected.

0. Close all open workbooks without saving, and then close Excel.

Glossary

absolute references
Cell or range references that do not change when users move or copy a formula from one cell to another. Absolute references always refer to the same cell or range regardless of where formulas or functions are copied to.

active cell
The currently selected cell into which a user can directly input data.

application window
The outer-most element of the Excel 2010 user interface. The application window contains the commands used to develop and work with Excel workbooks and it displays particular information about workbook files.

arguments
Elements of Excel functions that define the values and references the function will use to perform a particular calculation.

AutoCorrect feature
Office 2010 feature that automatically corrects common misspellings as users enter them.

AutoFill feature
Excel 2010 feature that assists users with entering strings of sequential or patterned data.

Backstage view
Element of the Excel 2010 application window that is displayed when users select the **File** tab. The Backstage view provides users with access to file-level commands and settings.

cell
A singular object on an Excel worksheet that you can use to input, store, and manipulate data.

cell references
Alphanumeric values used to identify particular cells on an Excel worksheet. Cell references consist of a row header and a column header, which identify the cell at the intersection of the row and the column.

cell styles
Unique sets of formatting options that users can apply to cells and ranges.

column headers
Alphabetic labels that appear along the top of an Excel worksheet and are used to differentiate individual columns.

compatibility checker
Office 2010 feature that enables users to determine which elements of application files are not compatible with previous versions of the applications.

Compatibility mode
Feature of Office 2010 applications that allow users to open and work with files created in previous versions of the applications. Compatibility mode enables users to work with older file types in newer

versions of applications and then subsequently open the files in the older versions of the applications. Not all features of newer application versions are compatible with previous versions, though.

conditional formatting

Formatting that users can apply to worksheet cells or ranges based on particular criteria.

context menus

Small, floating menu windows that appear when users right-click particular worksheet or workbook objects. Context menus provide users with quick access to commonly used commands and options related to the selected object.

contextual tabs

Specialized, temporary ribbon tabs that display commands for working with a particular type of worksheet content.

convert option

Office 2010 feature that enables users to convert files created in previous versions of Office applications to the newer file types.

custom views

User-defined workbook views that are specific to a particular worksheet. Custom views include all of the print and display settings currently applied to a worksheet.

custom workbook properties

User-defined workbook properties that can help users search for workbook files based on internal organizational conditions.

dialog box launcher

Downward-facing arrow command button that appears in the bottom-right corner of some ribbon groups. These commands open dialog boxes that provide users with access to complete sets of commands and options related to the functionality of the particular group's commands.

Excel formulas

Equations that perform simple or complex mathematical computations in Excel worksheets.

fill

A type of worksheet formatting that enables users to add colors, patterns, and gradient shading to the background of a cell or a range.

fonts

Unique collections of alphanumeric and other characters.

footers

Small content placeholders that display additional information or images in certain Excel views and on printed pages. Footers appear along the bottom of the page.

Formula Bar

Element of the Excel user interface that enables users to enter and edit data and formulas, view cell contents, and quickly insert any of Excel's built-in formulas.

functions

Built-in, pre-existing formulas users can insert into Excel worksheets.

galleries

Type of Office application menu that displays commands and options as thumbnail previews or icons, which provide visual clues as to how the commands or options will affect an Office document.

headers

Small content placeholders that display additional information or images in certain Excel views and on printed pages. Headers appear along the top of the page.

hyperlinks

Links within a document that, when selected, perform a particular action, such as navigating to a different location within the document, opening another document, creating a new document, navigating to a Web page, or starting an email message.

key tips

An alternate method of executing Excel commands other than keyboard shortcuts and user interface commands. Key tips appear when the user presses the **Alt** key and, when active, provide the user with single key stroke actions that the can use to navigate the Excel user interface and execute commands.

live preview

Excel 2010 feature that enables users to view a temporary preview of particular formatting options before applying the formatting.

Microsoft Excel Help

Excel 2010 feature that provides users with access to information, in a variety of formats, on a number of Excel topics.

mini toolbar

Small, floating element of the Excel 2010 user interface that appears when users right-click certain worksheet objects. The mini toolbar provides users with quick access to commonly used commands related to the selected object.

mixed references

A cell or range reference that includes both relative and absolute references.

number formats

Formatting options that enable users to control the display of such values as currency figures, dates and times, fractions, decimal places, and negative numbers.

page breaks

Boundaries that divide worksheet pages for printing purposes only.

page margins

Invisible boundaries that define where particular content can be displayed on printed worksheets.

page orientation

In Excel, a page layout setting that determines the general, overall layout of each printed page. Pages can either print in the portrait orientation, where the page is taller than it is wide, or in the landscape orientation, where the page is wider than it is tall.

print area

Excel feature that allows users to select specific cells and ranges to print from workbooks.

Quick Access Toolbar

Component of the Excel 2010 user interface that, by default, is displayed above the left side of the ribbon. The Quick Access Toolbar proves users with easy access to commonly used commands.

range

A contiguous group of cells that typically contains related data.

range references

Alphanumeric values used to identify particular ranges of data in Excel worksheets. Range references consist of two cell references, separated by a colon, that represent cells at the top-left and bottom-right in the range.

reference operators

Single characters that define how Excel deals with particular cell and range references in calculations performed by formulas and functions.

region

A group of contiguous, populated cells.

relative references

Cell or a range references that change when users move or copy a formula from one cell to another. Excel uses relative references by default.

ribbon

Component of the Excel 2010 user interface that contains all of the most commonly used commands for creating, modifying, and working with Excel workbooks. The ribbon is divided into a series of tabs that contain functionally related groups of Excel commands.

row headers

Numeric labels that appear along the left side of an Excel worksheet and are used to differentiate individual rows.

screen tips

Small pop-up windows that appear when users place the mouse pointer over commands and some other elements of the Excel user interface. Screen tips provide information such as a command's name, a description of what the command or screen element does, and the keyboard shortcut that performs the same function.

spreadsheet

A paper or an electronic document, arranged in tabular form, that is used to store, manipulate, and analyze data.

syntax

The structure necessary to properly express Excel functions and to define their arguments

tags

Short descriptions, or keywords, that help identify the kind of content users will find within a particular file.

themes

Collections of formatting options that users can apply to an entire workbook, as opposed to a particular cell or range.

workbook

An Excel file that serves as a container to store related Excel worksheets.

workbook properties

Individual elements of information about workbook files that helps users search for and identify particular workbook files. Workbook properties can provide information such as who created a file, when a file was created or last modified, and whether or not a file has been reviewed and approved.

workbook views

Specific configurations that affect the way Excel displays an open workbook. Workbook views can affect the placement and layout of worksheets and the Excel user interface, and can affect whether or not particular elements, such as headers and footers, appear. Workbook views are meant to configure the Excel environment to be easier to work with for a number of different tasks.

workbook window

The inner-most element of the Excel 2010 user interface. The workbook window displays worksheets and their data, and provides users with access to common navigation features.

worksheet

An electronic spreadsheet that is used for entering, storing, and analyzing data in Excel.

workspace

Excel file that saves a particular configuration of how multiple open workbooks are displayed. The file extension for workspaces is .xlw.

Index

091018S rev 1.01
ISBN-13 978-1-4246-2248-1
ISBN-10 1-4246-2248-6

9 781424 622481